Michael P. Wellman
AI Technology Office
Wright-Patterson AFB, OH

Formulation of Tradeoffs in Planning Under Uncertainty

Pitman, London

Morgan Kaufmann Publishers, Inc., San Mateo, California

PITMAN PUBLISHING
128 Long Acre, London WC2E 9AN

A Division of Longman Group UK Limited

© Michael P. Wellman 1990

First published 1990

Available in the Western Hemisphere from
MORGAN KAUFMANN PUBLISHERS, INC.,
2929 Campus Drive, San Mateo, California 94402

ISSN 0268-7526

British Library Cataloguing in Publication Data

Wellman, Michael P.
  Formulation of tradeoffs in planning under uncertainty.
  1. Management. Planning. Management planning. Decision
making. Influence. Uncertainty
  I. Title
  658.403

  ISBN 0 273 08824 6

Library of Congress Cataloging in Publication Data

Wellman, Michael P.
    Formulation of tradeoffs in planning under uncertainty / Michael
P. Wellman.
    p.   cm.—(Research notes in artificial intelligence,
ISSN 0268-7526)
    Includes bibliographical references.
    ISBN 1-55860-132-5
    1. Artificial intelligence.   2. Uncertainty (Information theory)
I. Title.   II. Series: Research notes in artificial intelligence
(London, England)
    Q335.W43   1990
    006.3—dc20

All rights reserved; no part of this publication may be reproduced,
stored in a retrieval system, or transmitted in any form or by any
means, electronic, mechanical, photocopying, recording or
otherwise, without either the prior written permission of the publishers
or a licence permitting restricted copying issued by the Copyright
Licencing Agency Ltd, 33–34 Alfred Place, London WC1E 7DP.
This book may not be lent, resold, hired out or otherwise disposed of
by way of trade in any form of binding or cover other than that in
which it is published, without the prior consent of the publishers.

Reproduced and printed by photolithography
in Great Britain by Biddles Ltd, Guildford

Contents

List of Figures

List of Tables

Preface

Whether we like it or not, decision making is increasingly becoming the province of machines. As we entrust more responsibility to computers, the need for principles of decision engineering and standards of automaton accountability grows acute. This concern has led me to adopt a decision-theoretic approach to automated planning, with the aim of establishing a normative relation between an agent's plans and its beliefs and desires. The normativity of the relationship guarantees a form of coherence in the agent's behavior. Even more appealing is the prospect for knowledge-level engineering, where designers can achieve desired behaviors in autonomous agents by imposing beliefs and preferences on them.

Medical therapy is a good testbed for decision-theoretic planning because the classical predicate representation of goals is patently inadequate in this domain. Health outcomes always meet the objectives to some degree, never absolutely; and the effects of therapeutic actions can be highly uncertain. Problems of this sort are prime candidates for *decision analysis*, the methodology of applied decision theory developed by operations researchers over the last few decades.

I am fortunate to have had the opportunity to observe and work with a leading group of medical decision analysts at the Division of Clinical Decision Making of the Tufts-New England Medical Center (TNEMC). The decision consultants, led by Stephen Pauker, routinely construct and analyze decision models for specific patient cases arising throughout the hospital. My charge on beginning this collaboration in early 1983 was to investigate the possibility of automating all or part of the decision consultant's task.

Having no medical training, I originally found the case discussion meetings quite baffling. It was immediately apparent that a large part of the modeler's expertise depended on a broad and deep knowledge of the medical domain surrounding the patient's problem. Years later, I am still baffled about the medical content of the decision problems tackled by the TNEMC analysts. Nevertheless, I discovered early on that I could follow the analyses and even contribute to the discussions given only a structural understanding of the problem in terms of some generic concepts.

Unfamiliarity with medical terminology need not be a fundamental barrier to substantive understanding. The essential feature of a foobarectomy is that it is a surgical procedure for cutting out a foobar—how the foobar is removed or where the foobar is in the body usually does not affect the qualitative structure of the problem. Similarly, a gross categorization of unknown medical nouns into drugs, body parts, diseases, diagnostic tests, test results, symptoms, etc. was often sufficient to determine their role in the case under discussion. The relations among these generic objects constitute the qualitative structure of the decision problem.

The qualitative structure determines where the "real decisions" are in a problem. Even without the more detailed understanding required to justify a recommendation, one can readily explain in structural terms the nature of the tradeoff faced in the patient's choice among therapeutic options. An appreciation of the centrality of qualitative structure (and the example of other AI work in qualitative reasoning) led me to attempt to formalize in decision-theoretic terms the features of these relations that make them qualitatively significant. The result is the Qualitative Probabilistic Network (QPN) formalism described in this book.

QPNs serve as the target modeling language for SUDO-PLANNER, an implemented program that formulates tradeoffs by proving that broad classes of plans are dominated on purely qualitative grounds. Tradeoff formulation is the "commonsense" stage of planning, where the planner identifies the space of admissible plans deserving serious consideration. This commonsense part of the problem seems a logical prerequisite to a more comprehensive automomous decision-making capacity. The ability to separate tradeoffs from obvious choices defines a lower bound on competence for decision-making agents.

The current state-of-the-art provides considerable cause to doubt the wisdom of routinely trusting our important decisions to machines. I like to think that the work described here is a step toward more accountable and more reliable autonomous decision makers. We obviously have a long way to go on the path; its exploration is sure to provide interesting challenges in the years ahead.

Michael P. Wellman

Dayton, Ohio
December 1989

Acknowledgments

This book is a revised version of my dissertation, completed in July 1988 at the Massachusetts Institute of Technology. Financial support was provided by the National Institutes of Health under Grant No. R01 LM04493 from the National Library of Medicine. I am grateful to my current organization, the Air Force AI Technology Office, for supporting my continued work in this area.

My thesis committee members played an enabling and inspiring role in this work. Peter Szolovits has provided guidance and informed encouragement from day one, when I wandered into his office in search of a Bachelor's thesis project. His solid thinking helped keep me on course even during times of reduced visibility. Steve Pauker opened to me the world of medical decision problems, and served as the paragon of decision-analytic thinking. Discussions (bull sessions) with Ramesh Patil were the source and sustenance of many ideas that formed my thinking about AI and medical decision making.

The Clinical Decision Making Group at MIT has been a source of friendship as well as colleagueship. Research environments are everything; thanks to all those who made it such a pleasurable and productive one. You know who you are. I am specifically thankful for the heroic draft-reading efforts and substantive suggestions of Elisha Sacks and Jon Doyle. It has been a happy outcome that we have been able to continue to work together at distances greater than a hallway length.

I learned a great deal from five years of Fellows at the New England Medical Center's Division of Clinical Decision Making. Collaborations with Jim Hollenberg, Alan Moskowitz, Mark Eckman, Frank Sonnenberg, and Craig Fleming were especially profitable.

This research has also benefited from discussions with Jack Breese, Tony Cox, Al Drake, Max Henrion, Ron Rivest, Ross Shachter, and the Stanford Medical probabilists: Greg Cooper, David Heckerman, Eric Horvitz, and Curt Langlotz. This is not an exhaustive list.

Finally, thanks to family and friends, and to Kate for being both.

1 Introduction

1.1 Tradeoff Formulation

A typical decision whether to perform surgery on a patient involves a tradeoff. The operation might alleviate the patient's disease, but it also carries a risk of death or other undesirable outcomes. Before resolving this dilemma, we might perform a diagnostic test to assess the surgery's potential effectiveness. In contrast to the original decision, determining how the result of the test should influence our surgical policy presents no tradeoff. It is obvious that our willingness to operate should increase as the test indicates surgery is more likely to be effective.

Most of the choice problems we recognize as "decisions" are tradeoff situations. Strategies such as "operate only if the test suggests surgery will be ineffective" never occur to us because they violate common sense. Unfortunately, we cannot rely on decision-making computer programs to limit themselves automatically to only the sensible options. Given a rich enough set of actions and limited only by syntax, a planning program is free to assemble strategies that are arbitrarily ridiculous.

The task of *tradeoff formulation* is to separate the "real decisions" from the trivial choices. Plans that can be ruled out on simple, uncontroversial grounds are called *inadmissible* and are unworthy of serious consideration. Tradeoffs indicate potential controversy, therefore plans involved in a tradeoff should be considered admissible pending further investigation.

Once the tradeoffs are identified, other decision-making mechanisms must be employed to *resolve* them. Even when powerful decision methods are available, however, there are several reasons to accord tradeoff formulation special status in the planning architecture.

Abstraction. The situation above is described in terms of highly general concepts like surgical mortality and effectiveness. In contrast, to resolve the tradeoff we would need to specify the particular disease and surgery under consideration. For tradeoff formulation, it is possible to reason at abstract levels because the conclusions are valid in general situations.

Robustness. Decision making generally requires precise assessments of such magnitudes as the relative desirability of living with the disease compared to death. The qualitative assertions needed for tradeoff formulation, for example, "more severe disease is less desirable," typically hold with much greater confidence.

Modularity. Qualitative assertions hold in a wide variety of contexts—diseases are bad for patients of all ages, sizes, and shapes. The magnitude assessments, in contrast, often depend on these and other known patient features. The context-insensitivity of qualitative properties translates to significant modularity advantages in representing tradeoff formulation knowledge.

Explanation. The strength of a justification varies directly with the weakness of its premises. A decision-making program's explanation of a non-tradeoff, therefore, should avoid reference to the stronger assertions employed for tradeoff resolution. In addition to being more controversial, an argument in terms of an overly powerful mechanism fails to reflect the salient issues in a decision. Ruling out the strategy "operate only if surgery will be ineffective" on the basis of a low evaluation score overlooks the commonsense reason for rejecting this policy.

Efficiency. In a large knowledge-based decision system, recognizing classes of inadmissible plans at a high level before applying general decision methods may improve performance. The advantages of precompiling the admissible plan space can be great when a large fraction of the syntactically valid plans are nonsensical.

This book is an account of an implemented tradeoff formulator, called SUDO-PLANNER, and the role of tradeoff formulation in a general architecture for planning. SUDO-PLANNER (the Synergy-driven, Utilitarian, Dominance-Oriented Planner) employs decision-theoretic principles to formulate tradeoffs in domains characterized by partially satisfiable goals and actions with uncertain effects.

1.2 An Example

A patient with a known history of coronary artery disease (CAD) and cerebrovascular disease (CVD) presents with a large abdominal aortic aneurysm (AAA).[1] The aneurysm is a dilatation of the arterial wall of the aorta, of concern because it could rupture causing death. There is a surgical procedure to repair the AAA, but surgery carries the risk of operative mortality or disability. The operation is especially risky for this patient because the CAD increases the likelihood of a heart attack (MI, for *myocardial infarction*) during AAA surgery, and the CVD enhances the probability of a stroke.

Other available actions include tests and treatments to gauge and alleviate the CAD and CVD. Table 1.1 provides simple descriptions of the major events and actions discussed in this example. For reference, the associations among events and actions are summarized in Table 1.2.

The tradeoff formulation task for this case is simply to characterize the space of reasonable therapy strategies. Although we cannot tell from the given information whether AAA repair is recommended, we can determine that our willingness to perform the surgery should increase with the aneurysm's size, because larger aneurysms are more likely to rupture. On the other hand, indications from the diagnostic tests that the underlying diseases are worse would argue against fixing the aneurysm. Thus we can conclude, for example, that the strategy "perform AAA repair if and only if catheterization reveals severe CAD"

---

[1]This case is taken from the files of clinical decision consultations of the Division of Clinical Decision Making at the New England Medical Center [33]. In previous work, I have used the manual formulation of this decision problem to illustrate mechanisms for reasoning about preferences [171].

AAA	*Abdominal aortic aneurysm.* A dilatation of the wall of the aorta, a major abdominal artery.
arteriography	Short for *carotid arteriography*, a radiographic test to assess the degree of cerebrovascular disease.
CABG	*Coronary artery bypass graft.* A surgical operation to circumvent diseased coronary vessels by splicing in healthy vessels from another part of the body.
CAD	*Coronary artery disease.* Disease of the vessels supplying blood to the heart.
catheterization	Short for *cardiac catheterization*, a diagnostic test to assess the extent of coronary artery disease.
CVD	*Cerebrovascular disease.* Disease of the carotid artery, the major neck vessel supplying the brain.
endarterectomy	Short for *carotid endarterectomy*, a surgical procedure to remove blood clots from the carotid artery.
MI	*Myocardial infarction.* Destruction of heart tissue due to interruption of blood flow ("a heart attack").

Table 1.1: A brief glossary of medical terminology as used in the example.

Disease	Test	Assoc. Event	Treatment
AAA	—	rupture	AAA repair
CAD	catheterization	MI	CABG
CVD	arteriography	stroke	endarterectomy

Table 1.2: Events and actions associated with each disease in the example case.

is inadmissible.

Some strategies include treatment of one or both of the underlying diseases before proceeding with the AAA surgery. A coronary artery bypass graft (CABG), for example, could be performed to treat the CAD and therefore reduce the risk of MI during AAA repair. To alleviate the risk of stroke, the patient's CVD might be treated with carotid endarterectomy, a procedure to clean out vessels leading to the brain.

Our willingness to perform these treatments is positively influenced by the severity of the underlying diseases as indicated by the test results. Therefore, there is some threshold value (CAD_1 in Figure 1.1a) for CAD extent as measured by catheterization beyond which CABG is recommended.[2] Because CAD extent is an argument against AAA repair, the CAD threshold policy for this procedure is reversed. As shown in Figure 1.1b, the repair should be performed if catheterization indicates CAD less than CAD_2, but not otherwise.

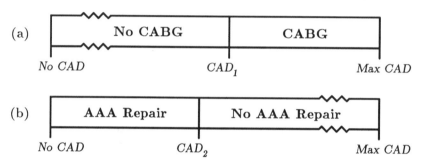

Figure 1.1: Threshold policies: (a) Perform CABG if CAD is greater than CAD_1. (b) Perform AAA repair if CAD is less than CAD_2. The accordion lines indicate that the box widths convey no scale information.

Finally, the tradeoff formulator must take into account interactions among the actions. The CAD threshold for an action is really a function of the other actions performed and other observations. In this case, because CABG alleviates the CAD, the threshold (in terms of *original* CAD extent) for AAA repair given CABG must be at least as high as the threshold given No CABG. In other words, $CAD_2(CABG) \geq CAD_2(No\ CABG)$—performing CABG shifts the threshold to the right. Thus, if aneurysm repair is recommended for three-vessel disease (CAD extending to three coronary vessels) without CABG, it must also be recommended after a triple-bypass is performed.

1.3   Barriers to Tradeoff Formulation

Most research on decision formulation is oriented toward aiding human decision makers. The research on autonomous decision-making that takes formulation seriously also tends to treat this phase as necessarily heuristic, domain-dependent, and separate from the task of

---

[2]To ensure that the threshold is well-defined, we assume there exists an ordered scale for CAD extent. The analysis also assumes that the CAD is not so extensive as to be untreatable.

to treat this phase as necessarily heuristic, domain-dependent, and separate from the task of choosing among alternatives. The common view of the formulation task is as generator in a generate-and-test planning architecture.

The approach described here departs from the common view by treating the formulation task as a formal decision problem no different from choice within a more refined set of options. Because of this uniformity, plans are constructed according to the same set of principles used to compare them. Nevertheless, we can exploit the advantages mentioned above by recognizing the decisions that do not require the precise, context-sensitive knowledge needed for tradeoff resolution.

The next three sections discuss central problems in automating the reasoning behind the tradeoff formulation behavior illustrated above. The solutions incorporated in SUDO-PLANNER represent the primary technical contributions of this work. The problems are not specific to formulation; they arise in the broader task of planning under uncertainty for partially satisfiable goals. I present the problems in their full generality, even though the "SUDO solutions" that follow do not always match them in scope. Nevertheless, while SUDO-PLANNER only plans "up to tradeoffs," some of the mechanisms developed to deal with these problems are applicable to the broader planning problem as well.

1.4 Uncertainty and Partial Goal Satisfaction

Classical AI robot planners solve problems by searching for a plan of action guaranteed to transform the initial situation into one that satisfies some goal predicate. Robots taking this approach in the real world are likely to be defeated because the classical paradigm has nothing to say when a guaranteed plan cannot be found, or when one does not exist. Such situations are typical for two reasons:

1. Knowledge of the world is imperfect; in practice it is not possible to guarantee much about the result of performing actions in a given situation.

2. Predicates on world states cannot express reasonable goals for real-world agents.

1.4.1 Problem: Uncertain Effects of Actions

The classical planning paradigm is categorical. Although there may be uncertainty implicit in the incompleteness of the planner's theory, there is no provision for expressing anything about the degree to which an event is likely and its relationship to other uncertain events.

Categorical planners have the luxury of deductive inference. While it is impossible to derive everything true about the result of applying an action in a situation, many logical consequences of pre- and post-conditions can be determined. When the logical properties of a plan provably entail the goal, the planner succeeds. Figure 1.2 diagrams this planning paradigm.

Because the effects of actions in the world are uncertain—at least from any robot's perspective—it is rarely possible to establish with certainty that a given plan will en-

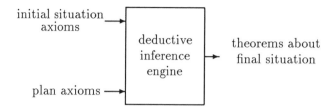

Figure 1.2: Categorical planning. Situations and actions are described by axioms. The task is to find a plan that achieves the goal predicate G in the final situation.

sure that its goal G holds in the final situation. Failing this, a robot must consider the probability of achieving the goal with the various courses of action open to it.[4]

It would appear that taking this notion seriously alters our basic planning picture dramatically. The robot must keep track of the various possible situations resulting from executing a plan and their probabilities. One way to do this, illustrated in Figure 1.3, is to relate a given plan to the likelihood that the goal is satisfied after its execution via a *probabilistic model.*

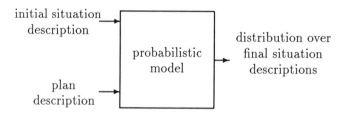

Figure 1.3: Planning under uncertainty. A probabilistic model relates plans to outcomes. The task is to find the plan with the greatest probability of achieving G.

A major problem with this approach is the difficulty of representing knowledge required to generate probabilistic predictions. While research on categorical planning has produced modular representations that associate all knowledge with individual actions, such encodings are more difficult to create for the uncertain case. I return to this issue in Section 1.5.

Given a probabilistic model, the task presented by Figure 1.3 may still be computationally less attractive than that of Figure 1.2. In categorical planning, search can be terminated as soon as a plan guaranteed to achieve the aspiration level G is found. In

---

[4]McCarthy and Hayes, in the classic paper on classical planning [98, page 490], recognize that "the formalism will eventually have to allow statements about the probabilities of events." More often recalled from that discussion is their declaration that numerical probabilities are "epistemologically inadequate." This latter statement, however, was an objection to the proposal that the basic knowledge representation should attach probabilities to all sentences, an objection strongly endorsed in Section 1.5.1 below. It is unfortunate that subsequent work in AI planning has proceeded virtually as if likelihood did not matter.

general, optimizing is harder than satisficing [148] because it is rarely possible to determine locally that a given probability of goal achievement is in fact the maximum.

We can avoid this problem by satisficing on the probability of goal satisfaction. This approach retains the predicate representation of goals (here the predicate contains statements about likelihood), but it is ultimately unsatisfactory for the reasons presented below.

1.4.2   Problem: Goals are not Predicates

Even if the difficulties related to uncertainty could be overcome, serious obstacles to planning within the classic framework would remain. Rarely will the robot limit its cares to the probability of a particular goal predicate being satisfied in the plan result state. Instead, the degree to which a goal is satisfied may vary, or several objectives may be achieved in partial measure. Achieving a goal with probability less than unity is one important kind of partial satisfiability, but there are others as well.

The inadequacy of a predicate representation is apparent as soon as we attempt to express the goals relevant to our medical example. Broadly speaking, our objectives are to maximize lifespan and achieve the best quality of life by minimizing disabilities and other health problems. Predicates on world situations can only divide them into situations in which the objectives are satisfied and situations in which they are not. This binary classification cannot capture even the basic preference for longer lifespans. Even when it is heuristically advantageous to plan according to aspiration levels, an agent should also have access to some representation of its actual preferences.

While it may have appeared possible to salvage much of the basic planning paradigm while admitting uncertainty, the deficiency of goal predicates undermines the fundamental structure of the methodology. Some actual planners have tried to patch this hole in the framework by including heuristic rules to handle anticipated planning decisions. McDermott's NASL [99], for example, uses *choice rules* to arbitrate among alternative task reduction paths that arise in planning. As McDermott recognizes, such an approach is vulnerable to harmful interactions with other eventualities in the planning environment, as is any scheme that associates actions directly with situations. The only way to cope with unanticipated choice contexts is to consider explicitly the predicted effects of actions and select among the alternatives according to a more general decision criterion.

1.4.3   Problem: Decision Theory and Planning

At this point we might reconsider whether it makes sense to adopt the planning paradigm at all. Indeed, it may seem that I have been setting up a straw man all along; it should have been obvious from the start that traditional planning methods are not up to the general task of planning under uncertainty with multiple objectives.

A decision criterion of the generality required is provided by Bayesian decision theory [136]. Decision theory replaces the goal predicate with a utility function mapping *outcomes* to real numbers (called *utilities*), and prescribes maximization of expected utility for decision making. The general picture is the same as Figure 1.3, augmented with a utility model for evaluating the final-situation descriptions.

With or without uncertainty, planning with decision theory inherits the computational problems of the optimization task mentioned above. In practice, decision-theoretic applications (using the methodology of *decision analysis* [124]) have been possible only because the set of alternatives is manually restricted to a small collection of strategies. This is precisely the formulation task we are trying to automate.

The space of alternatives available to an AI planner is usually specified indirectly as those generable from a given collection of primitive actions within the syntax of a plan language. This is typically an enormous combinatorial space, with nonsensical plans forming a large fraction of the syntactically allowed strategies. AI planning research has concentrated on techniques to construct complex strategies from primitive actions by searching this space.

Charniak and McDermott [18, page 523] say the following about the relationship between decision theory and planning:

> One might think that an elegant theory of this kind would have been assimilated into robot planners, but this has so far not been the case. The issues addressed by the two approaches are complementary. Planning research has focused on how plans are *constructed*; decision theory has focused on how they are *evaluated*.

Combining the two methodologies is difficult because in the ideal integration they are mutually dependent. Conventional application of decision theory requires a restricted plan set, but supplying one is precisely the formulation problem we are trying to solve. Principled plan construction calls for a decision criterion with the generality of expected utility maximization, even at the earliest formulation stages.

Previous attempts to apply decision theory to planning have avoided this apparent paradox in one of two ways. The first approach employs heuristic methods to generate a restricted plan set without reference to decision-theoretic criteria [68]. For example, the generate-and-test architecture of ONYX [86] completely separates the decision-theoretic evaluation module from the candidate generator. This separation is ultimately unsatisfactory because the heuristic generator cannot justify its decisions with respect to the agent's objectives.

The second approach adds restrictions on the form of probability and utility models to fit particular planning algorithms. For example, Feldman and Sproull [37] present some techniques that inherently take the utility of a plan to be additive in its steps. Prerequisites of this strength are rarely satisfied by planning problems, and therefore cannot serve as the basis for domain-independent planning architectures.

1.4.4 SUDO Solution: A Dominance-Proving Architecture for Planning with Partially Satisfiable Goals

The key to resolving the paradox above is to change the perspective of the planner from evaluating the results of individual plans to reasoning about the admissibility, or reasonableness, of plan classes. Rather than viewing probability and utility models as pieces of a static *absolute* evaluator, the SUDO-PLANNER architecture uses decision theory to establish the *relative* value of plans.

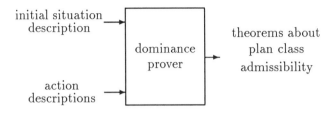

initial situation description → dominance prover → theorems about plan class admissibility

action descriptions →

Figure 1.4: SUDO planning. The task is to characterize the space of admissible plans.

As illustrated in Figure 1.4, SUDO-PLANNER applies a dominance prover to characterize the space of admissible plans. The dominance prover uses knowledge about the effects of actions and the relative desirability of outcomes to derive facts about the preferred plan. In our AAA case, for example, among the plans that include CABG conditional on the result of catheterization, the dominance prover determines that the condition must call for CABG to be performed whenever the indicated CAD is more extensive than some threshold value. Nonsensical plans that include CABG for mild CAD but not for severe CAD (all else being equal) are therefore deemed inadmissible.

In order to express results of this sort, we need a representation for classes of plans. The dominance result above refers to the classes "plans with catheterization" and "plans with CABG conditional on catheterization result," among others. SUDO-PLANNER encodes these classes by the series of constraints that distinguish them from other plan classes. A partial plan produced by a conventional constraint-posting planner can be viewed as an abstract representation of the set of all plans generated by its potential completions.

The class of plans with "CABG if catheterization result is above threshold" is a subclass of those that include catheterization with no further restrictions. SUDO-PLANNER maintains a *plan graph* that partially orders the plan classes by generality. This data structure, annotated with results derived by the dominance prover, represents the space of admissible plans.

The concept of plan class dominance is founded on the basic decision-theoretic notion of a preference relation. A preference order on prospective outcomes provides the flexibility (notably absent from situation predicates) required to express the partial satisfiability of goals. By appropriately constraining the preference order, we can specify, for example, that longer lifetimes are preferred to shorter ones, and that disabilities are undesirable.

To prove dominance, the planner needs to relate some feature of plans to the preference order on prospective outcomes, and hence to expected utility. Once identified, this relation can be incorporated into the plan graph by recording the dominance condition on the appropriate plan classes. Using the fact that dominance is inherited in the plan graph (as well as other properties of the formal definition of dominance, presented in Section 2.3),

9

the implications of this result are propagated to other related plan classes.

In tradeoff formulation, the dominance prover's task is to detect inadmissible plan classes by applying the planner's qualitative knowledge of the effects of actions. Ideally, at the end of tradeoff formulation the plan graph includes dominance conditions ruling out these strategies. Figure 1.5 shows a piece of the plan graph derived by SUDO-PLANNER for the AAA/CAD/CVD example of Section 1.2.

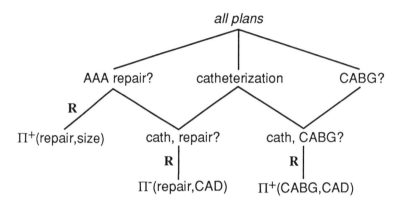

Figure 1.5: A plan graph fragment for tradeoff formulation in the AAA/CAD/CVD example.

Because I have not yet defined the plan and constraint languages, the plan classes in Figure 1.5 are informally described. The graph is a partial order on its classes, with the most general on top. Thus, the class of plans where AAA repair is under consideration ("AAA repair?") is a subclass of the universal plan class and a superclass of those in which the repair policy is a monotonically increasing function of the aneurysm size. The **R** annotation on the specialization link indicates that the dominance prover has derived a *restriction* relation (defined in Section 2.3), which implies that the planner can limit its attention to policies of the specialized form.

A complete discussion of the dominance-proving architecture, including formal definitions of the various relations mentioned here, appears in Chapter 2. The particular representations for plan classes employed by SUDO-PLANNER are introduced in Chapter 3.

1.5 Representations for Uncertain Knowledge

The dominance-proving architecture provides a framework for planning under uncertainty with partially satisfiable goals. However, the performance of the dominance prover depends critically on effective representations for the effects of actions and the desirability of outcomes. We have already seen that representations from classical planning are inapplicable to reasoning about uncertain events. In this section, I argue that traditional decision-analytic models are also insufficient for knowledge representation, and sketch the ideas behind the qualitative probabilistic networks that support tradeoff formulation in SUDO-PLANNER.

1.5.1 Problem: Decision Models are not Knowledge Bases

For purposes of decision making, a complete knowledge base (KB) specifies the joint probability distribution of all relevant actions and events. A *probabilistic model* is a representation from which joint distributions can be computed in a reasonably direct manner. Researchers in decision analysis have developed representations called *decision models*, essentially probabilistic models augmented with a specification of preferences for the joint events.

Decision models are the obvious candidate for a knowledge representation to support planning under uncertainty. Recent advances in mechanisms for encoding and evaluating probabilistic and decision models, particularly the *belief networks* of Pearl [112, 114], have led to increasing interest in them within the AI research community.[4] From a knowledge engineering perspective, however, the idea of a decision model as a knowledge base has serious drawbacks.

The main problem is scalability. It appears feasible to build decision models of modest size, perhaps approaching the scope of today's expert systems [2, 60]. Knowledge bases in this range constrain the problem solver to a narrow decision context applicable only to a restricted set of selected cases. The more ambitious goal of building planners that operate with near autonomy over a broad range of decision environments calls for significantly larger knowledge bases. For example, to avoid the manual pre-selection of cases currently required by medical expert systems, a therapy planner would need at least the knowledge of a general practitioner to determine which specialized domain knowledge is relevant and applicable for a given patient. More general autonomous reasoners require a huge body of commonsense and world knowledge, perhaps on the order of Lenat's CYC KB [89].

There are several reasons to expect that decision models will not be viable knowledge representations for robot planners expected to work over a broad range of decision contexts. I discuss two of them as subproblems below and describe how these issues have influenced the design of SUDO-PLANNER.

1.5.2 Subproblem: Pre-Enumeration of Relevant Variables

Figure 1.6 depicts a belief network fragment presented by Kim and Pearl [78] to illustrate their representation. In the problem under consideration, an agent named Mr. Holmes gets a phone call from his neighbor reporting that his burglar alarm has sounded. He also hears a radio announcement of an earthquake in the vicinity, suggesting a possible cause of the alarm. The belief network models the relationships among the proposition that the Holmes home has been burglarized and the other factors in this situation.

Though it may be a perfectly suitable representation for this particular problem, it is unreasonable to expect that this model fragment would be available as a piece of some giant belief network KB supporting Mr. Holmes's generally intelligent behavior. Such a

---

[4]Although a variety of other modeling formalisms exist, belief networks and the related *influence diagram* representation [68, 136] are sufficiently representative that little generality is lost by devoting exclusive attention to them in the following arguments.

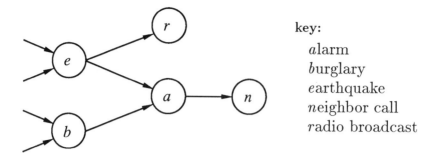

key:

*a*larm
*b*urglary
*e*arthquake
*n*eighbor call
*r*adio broadcast

Figure 1.6: Fragment of a belief network for the burglar alarm problem.

knowledge base commits the reasoner to a pre-enumerated set of parameters describing the relevant actions and events, and therefore could only apply to a narrow set of anticipated situations.

Imagine a KB designed to support general problem-solving about burglar alarms and earthquakes. We would expect that a reasoner able to handle the problem described above should also behave reasonably when, for instance, some other neighbor makes the call, the situation takes place at night rather than day, Mr. Holmes is at some other location, or an earthquake or burglary occurred the previous day.[6] While it is certainly possible to identify variables and relationships to encode each of these problem features, including all conceivably useful parameters in a static network KB would be infeasible.

Formally, the issue is analogous to the limitations of propositional as compared to first-order logic. If one could pre-enumerate a finite set of relevant atomic formulas, first-order quantification constructs would be superfluous. The ability to express facts about abstract situations without reference to complete detail, however, has proven to be essential in knowledge representation. Instantiation mechanisms to apply knowledge in this form to particular situations are part of every automated reasoning program.

A small increment of generality can be obtained through the use of template models. Templating supports a rigid form of instantiation where the parameter replacement paths are in effect hard-wired in advance. The set of parameters provided is restricted, and the topology of relationships is fixed.

Mr. Holmes could not be easily realized by a template. To handle the range of natural problem variants mentioned above, he would be best served by a large general body of knowledge about communication acts, news reporting, and alarm mechanisms. The ultimate pattern of instantiation from this general knowledge to concrete parameters for a given problem cannot be predicted.

1.5.3 SUDO Solution: Customized Model Construction

We can solve the pre-enumeration problem without dismissing decision models altogether by dynamically constructing models in response to the problem at hand. In this approach,

---

[6]See Breese [14] for an elaboration of this example and discussion of its implications for customized model construction.

the decision model is viewed as a target representation, not as a language for the KB itself.

Aside from the basic feasibility issue, customized decision models offer important advantages over monolithic decision-model knowledge bases. A model covering more than a narrow body of decision contexts would be inappropriate for any *particular* planning problem because the extraneous features entail an unnecessary computational burden and obscure explanations of the result. General models cannot take advantage of simplifying features that—while present in any given decision problem—vary from case to case.

The task of building customized models raises a wide range of issues, discussed in Section 1.6 below.

1.5.4 Subproblem: Non-Modularity of Probabilistic Assertions

A second major difficulty with decision models as KBs is the fundamental non-modularity of probabilistic assertions [58]. Unlike logical implications, statements of conditional probability cannot be combined without further information or assumptions about interactions among the conditions. Whereas in pure logical inference the derivation path leading to a fact is irrelevant to further conclusions,[6] under uncertainty the source of belief in a proposition may strongly affect its relation to other statements [113].

A consequence of this observation is that probabilistic assertions are highly sensitive to context. The association between a symptom and a disease generally depends on the patient's age, sex, and a host of other features. To support reasoning about the broad mix of patients naturally arising in practice, knowledge relating the symptom and disease must take these features into account. Unless the interactions among them take some regular form (or the number of interactions is bounded), the probabilistic model requires a size exponential in the number of patient features [67, 158].

Expert systems and decision-analytic models cope with this problem by adopting narrow scopes. Problems are described by a relatively small number of parameters describing the important factors in the program's specialized domain. Other features are considered irrelevant or are implicitly taken into account as "background knowledge." The latter approach is reasonable as long as the population of cases fed to the program is homogeneous with respect to the background features. Builders of probabilistic systems for medical diagnosis have found that models validated for the population of a particular community cannot be reliably transported to medical centers with demographic differences [149].

1.5.5 SUDO Solution: A Qualitative Representation for Uncertainty

Another way to cope with non-modularity is to isolate some relatively context-insensitive components of probabilistic assertions and reason with these as far as possible before resorting to knowledge encoded in less convenient representations. This approach is especially

---

[6]The inadequacy of standard logical formalisms for representing real-world planning knowledge has led AI researchers to develop *nonmonotonic* logics that do not have this locality property and therefore share the modularity problems of probabilistic representations.

attractive for the task considered here because, as suggested in Section 1.1, knowledge required for tradeoff formulation is considerably more modular than that necessary for complete decision-making.

The *Qualitative Probabilistic Network* (QPN) formalism is designed to support precisely the knowledge required for tradeoff formulation. QPNs are abstractions of numeric probabilistic networks that encode only qualitative constraints on the joint probability distribution over the variables. Although these constraints do not determine probabilities uniquely, they support *relative* likelihood conclusions that are sufficient for the dominance results SUDO-PLANNER uses to characterize plan class admissibility.

QPNs contain two basic kinds of *qualitative relationship*. *Qualitative influences* describe the direction of the relationship between two variables. *Qualitative synergies* describe interactions among influences. The qualitative nature of these relationships affords robustness through context-insensitivity. While the precise numeric magnitude of the relationship between a symptom and a disease tends to vary with other factors, the *direction* of the relationship is often unaffected. For example, assessing the implications of a cardiac stress test on the probability of CAD requires consideration of the patient's age and smoking habits, among many other factors. On the other hand, the direction of the relation between test parameters and coronary disease is context-independent: for any given age and smoking behavior, CAD tends to decrease a patient's exercise tolerance.

An example of qualitative synergy is the interaction between AAA repair and CAD in their effect on MI. Both variables have a positive influence on MI: CAD increases the likelihood of a heart attack in any situation, and AAA repair increases MI risk for any given patient. The positive qualitative synergy, depicted in Figure 1.7 as a boxed plus sign connecting the two nodes to MI, holds because these influences are mutually reinforcing. That is, the *increase* in MI risk due to surgery for the aneurysm is greater for patients with more severe CAD. In other words, the expected joint effect on MI of increasing both CAD and AAA repair is greater than the sum of the two effects taken independently.

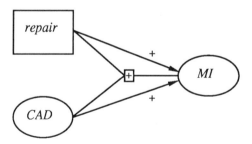

Figure 1.7: AAA repair and CAD are positively synergistic on MI. The rectangular node *repair* is a decision variable and the circular nodes are event variables beyond the planner's direct control.

Qualitative relations of this sort provide the basis for tradeoff formulation in SUDO-PLANNER. Because of their comparative modularity, a KB comprised of these constructs is more easily scaled up than one based on precise probabilistic assertions. Extending

14

the KB to cover other cardiac disorders, for example, would not require modification of the CAD/stress-test relation, nor would a relocation of the reasoning system to a demographically dissimilar environment. This phenomenon is not merely an artifact of applying less precision; arbitrary weakenings of the assertions would offer meager modularity gains. Robustness depends on the extent to which qualitative relations capture causal structure in the domain. For example, suppose someone invents a new stress test based on entirely different measurement technology. As long as the new test is faithfully correlated with the underlying concept of *stress*, we would expect the qualitative relation to remain valid. Other forms of incomplete information about the relationship—such as conditional probability intervals—would only transfer by coincidence.

Figure 1.8 illustrates a QPN for part of our AAA example. The network consists of four variables and the relationships among them. The decision variable *repair* represents the proposition that surgery to fix the aneurysm is performed. *Repair* has a negative influence on *rupt*, because surgery decreases the probability of aneurysm rupture. The *size* of the aneurysm, on the other hand, has a positive relation to *rupt*. The undesirability of ruptures is captured in the network by the negative link from *rupt* to the special *value* variable *v* (the hexagonal node in QPN diagrams, sometimes drawn without the *v*). The negative influence from *repair* to *v* indicates that, aside from its known beneficial influence on ruptures, the effects of AAA surgery are undesirable.

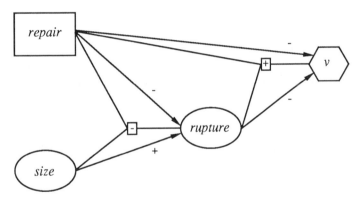

Figure 1.8: Qualitative probabilistic network for part of the AAA example.

The network also includes two qualitative synergies. First, *repair* and *size* are negatively synergistic on *rupt*. This statement means that the larger the aneurysm, the larger the *negative* influence of *repair* on rupture probability. A symmetric perspective is that performing the *repair* lessens the positive influence of *size* on *rupt*. Second, *repair* and *rupt* are positively synergistic on *v* because the negative effects of surgery are less important when ruptures occur.

Formal probabilistic definitions of these qualitative relations, along with a description of the QPN inference mechanisms, appear in Chapter 4. Inference in QPNs consists primarily of reduction rules for combining influences and synergies to derive the relations among indirectly related variables. For this network, reducing *rupt* reveals that *repair* and *size* are positively synergistic on v, which implies that the optimal repair policy is an increasing function of size. This simple conclusion is the dominance result derived by SUDO-PLANNER and posted on the leftmost path down the plan graph of Figure 1.5.

1.6   Constructing Decision Models

Part of our solution to the unsuitability of decision models as knowledge bases calls for dynamically constructing models from more reasonable knowledge representations. Previous attempts to automate the model generation task (reviewed in Section 6.5), however, have uncovered some serious obstacles to the goal.

1.6.1   Problem: Avoid Exhaustive Model Construction

Perhaps the greatest obstacle to automated model construction is the difficulty of avoiding exhaustive inclusion in the model of every factor in the KB. Because a model is effectively a closed world (that is, reasoners or evaluators apply a closed-world assumption when operating on the model), failure to include a factor is only justified when that factor is irrelevant to the task. However, it is typically difficult to establish that a given factor is irrelevant. In medicine, for example, it seems that any event can be related to any other by some conceivable path of associations. It would be surprising to find a large medical KB with significant disconnected components.

Reasoning with decision models—whether qualitative or numerically precise—cannot commence until the model is completed, or "closed." An exhaustivity constraint, therefore, delays the production of any results whatsoever from the planner. Worse, the KB could easily specify an infinite number of potentially relevant factors for inclusion in the model.

Paradoxically, this suggests that tractable models will only be generated by programs with small knowledge bases. In contrast, human decision analysts and knowledge engineers are capable of producing models and expert systems for customized tasks despite their knowledge of neighboring domains not included in their systems. To achieve similarly selective behavior, an automatic model builder requires a winnowing strategy, ideally based on sound decision-theoretic principles.

1.6.2   SUDO Solution: Model Construction at Multiple Levels of Abstraction

One powerful technique for selective model construction is abstraction. A valid abstraction is a license to ignore detail. Even detail that is relevant to the planning task as a whole need not be considered for every subtask. A planner can derive useful dominance results at high levels of abstraction before considering more detailed problem features.

For example, the direct negative link from *repair* to v in Figure 1.8 is based on knowledge found at the upper abstraction levels. Potentially undesirable consequences are associated with all treatments; *AAA repair* inherits the qualitative influence by virtue of its place in the action taxonomy. The more detailed description of the undesirable consequences of this treatment—possible surgical mortality, MI, or stroke—is inessential to SUDO-PLANNER's derivation of the threshold policy for aneurysm size, discussed above.

Explicit consideration of these specific events, however, is required to solve other pieces of this planning problem. For example, the relevance of CAD to the AAA-repair decision becomes apparent only when we introduce the variable *MI* as an event along the path from *repair* to *v*, shown in Figure 1.9.[8] Based on the derived implications of CAD, SUDO-PLANNER determines whether to pursue the possibility of performing CABG to decrease the risk of MI during AAA repair.

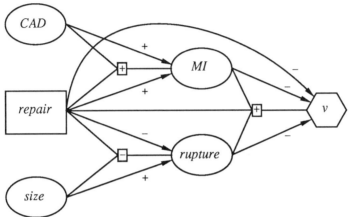

Figure 1.9: Explicit consideration of MI and CAD in the model.

A planner capable of model-building at multiple levels of abstraction can tailor a separate model for each distinct issue it faces in designing a plan. This permits the reasoner to avoid simultaneous consideration of all the factors potentially relevant to the planning problem.

SUDO-PLANNER traverses its multilevel KB to generate a series of QPN models for analysis. Search is driven by the goal of deriving useful qualitative synergies. SUDO-PLANNER does not employ any sophisticated control strategies to optimize the path of model generation. Although attention to this issue will undoubtedly be important as the KB grows, reliance on an optimized model generation procedure for a problem of the size demonstrated here would indicate excessive fragility. Rather, the aim is to show that even a relatively uncontrolled procedure can generate decision models of some value to a planner.

As illustrated by the example, abstraction is central to SUDO-PLANNER's ability to derive useful dominance results early in the planning process. Without this feature, planning from decision models would be infeasible for large knowledge bases.

---

[8]The QPNs of Figures 1.8 and 1.9 are simplified for expository purposes from the networks directly constructed by SUDO-PLANNER. They are equivalent, however, to intermediate models produced by dominance-proving operations on the actual QPNs. The full account of SUDO-PLANNER's behavior on this example is presented in Chapter 8.

For a complete description of the model construction algorithm, see Chapter 6. Although the current methods are sufficient to demonstrate some interesting multilevel behavior, the model construction component of SUDO-PLANNER is not the final word in decision model generation. Experience with this task has suggested a set of desiderata for multilevel reasoning (presented in Section 6.1) that offer perspective on the competence of SUDO-PLANNER, the status of other AI work on abstraction, and promising topics for further research in this area.

1.7 SUDO-Planner Overview

1.7.1 Basic Architecture

Figure 1.10 illustrates the input/output behavior of SUDO-PLANNER. Planning problems are described in terms of changes. Assuming that current strategy is optimal given current knowledge,[8] any plan modifications must be grounded in situation changes.

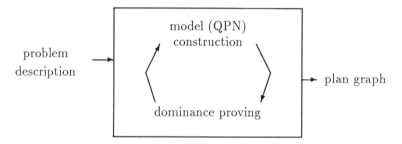

Figure 1.10: High-level behavior of SUDO-PLANNER.

SUDO-PLANNER's reasoning process consists of a repeating cycle of model construction and dominance proving. The dominance prover posts its conclusions on the plan graph as they are derived. The undominated fringe of the plan graph represents the space of admissible plans, which is the output of the tradeoff formulation process. This process does not necessarily terminate at some natural point; SUDO-PLANNER will continue to generate QPNs as long as there are potentially relevant variables in the KB.

1.7.2 SUDO-Planner on the Running Example

For the example case, SUDO-PLANNER is told only that the variable $AAA\ size$ has changed. The initial model generated is the trivial QPN shown in Figure 1.11, which says only that aneurysm growth is bad.

As it evolves the model, SUDO-PLANNER derives facts about plan class dominance, including, for example, that the AAA repair strategy should be a threshold policy on

---

[8]The application of this assumption is discussed in Section 6.4.

Figure 1.11: Initial qualitative probabilistic network for the example.

aneurysm size. Along the way, the program encounters some subtle tradeoffs, not resolvable by qualitative information alone. Given resolutions for these (discussed further in Section 7.4), SUDO-PLANNER proceeds to generate further dominance results. The QPN for this problem eventually reaches the complexity of Figure 1.12. The final plan graph incorporates all of the conclusions mentioned informally in Section 1.2, including the restriction relations shown in Figure 1.5.

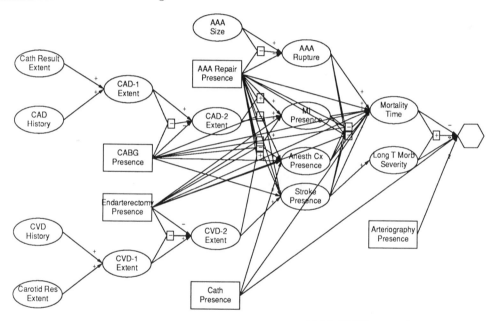

Figure 1.12: Exhaustive QPN for the AAA/CAD/CVD example.

1.7.3 Contributions of SUDO-Planner

The contributions of this research are the "SUDO solutions" presented in Sections 1.4 through 1.6. The main technical developments are in the dominance-proving planning architecture (Chapter 2) and the qualitative probabilistic network formalism (Chapter 4). Less tangible products of this work include:

- Identification of the tradeoff formulation task and its role in planning.

19

- Design and analysis of knowledge representations for plan classes, actions, and the effects of actions.

- Exploration of issues in the automatic construction of decision models.

- Demonstration of representations and reasoning strategies that effectively exploit knowledge at multiple levels of abstraction.

1.8 Preview

This introductory chapter has provided a broad perspective on the tradeoff formulation task, problems with current technology, and the solution approaches offered by SUDO-PLANNER. The remainder of the monograph provides the details.

Chapter 2 introduces a dominance-proving framework for planning with partially satisfiable goals. Although illustrated primarily with examples from SUDO-PLANNER, the dominance-proving architecture is presented more generally, allowing for application to tasks other than tradeoff formulation. The chapter includes a generic specification for the architecture components, which is instantiated for the particular SUDO-PLANNER mechanisms in subsequent chapters.

Chapter 3 describes the representations for plans, plan classes, and actions in SUDO-PLANNER. Discussion of the design decisions involved emphasizes the implications on computational complexity within the dominance-proving architecture of Chapter 2.

The qualitative probabilistic network formalism is motivated, rigorously defined, and illustrated in Chapter 4. The probabilistic semantics of qualitative influences and synergies justify efficient, powerful QPN inference procedures, as well as decision-theoretic results derived by SUDO-PLANNER's dominance prover. Like Chapter 2, this chapter is presented in a self-contained fashion because the results are applicable outside the scope of SUDO-PLANNER.

Some of the most difficult knowledge representation issues arise in specifying the effects of actions, the subject of Chapter 5. The chapter includes detailed descriptions of constructs for asserting effects in the SUDO-PLANNER KB, as well as discussion of the broader epistemological issues surrounding their design.

SUDO-PLANNER's techniques for automatic model construction at multiple levels of abstraction are presented in Chapter 6. To evaluate the performance of these methods, I consider properties of an ideal multilevel reasoning system and compare SUDO-PLANNER to other AI work in this area.

Chapter 7 focuses on the dominance-proving component of SUDO-PLANNER. Some subtle tradeoffs encountered in the running medical example are presented and analyzed. The example demonstrates how SUDO-PLANNER can proceed from these apparent dead ends by incorporating externally supplied tradeoff resolutions.

Chapter 8 presents SUDO-PLANNER's complete analysis of the running example.

Chapter 9 concludes the work with a summary, a discussion of limitations, and some speculation about further developments and the outlook for SUDO-PLANNER.

2 A Dominance-Proving Architecture for Planning

I have argued above (Section 1.4) that the classical planning framework is inadequate because goal predicates are not expressive enough for choice in the face of partially satisfiable goals. Decision theory, in contrast, offers a sufficiently general plan selection criterion, but says nothing about constructing plans from descriptions of the effects of component actions. In this chapter, I present a framework for applying the flexible decision-theoretic criterion in a constructive context by integrating a dominance prover into the planning process.

Dominance-proving planners reason about possible courses of action by establishing preference properties of classes of plans. The basic dominance-proving architecture represents a general approach to planning for partially satisfiable goals. The particular knowledge representations and dominance proving techniques employed by SUDO-PLANNER, developed in subsequent chapters, apply specifically to tradeoff formulation. In this chapter, I characterize the architecture abstractly, independent of this or any other specialized planning task. The architecture is illustrated with a brief discussion of SUDO-PLANNER's components. The final sections of the chapter discuss general planning issues within this framework.

2.1   The Plan Graph

Let Ω be the set of all syntactically valid plans, called the *universal plan class*. For example, if $A = \{a_1, \ldots, a_n\}$ is an alphabet of primitive actions, then $\Omega = A^*$ is the class of linear plans. The class of nonlinear plans is similar, extended by a partial order on plan steps. A *plan class* is any set of plans, $\Pi \subseteq \Omega$. We sometimes call Π a *partial plan*, to emphasize its representation as a collection of constraints incompletely specifying the plan of interest.

We can view the planning process as one of reasoning about properties of partial plans formed by adding constraints to candidate plan classes. The partial plans generated during the planning process can be organized in a specialization graph according to the subset relation. An example of a plan specialization graph appears in Figure 2.1. The node in the graph marked "$A^*a_1A^*$" denotes the set of all plans with at least one instance of action a_1. The set of plans *starting* with a_1 forms a subclass, as does the set of plans with an a_1 followed by an a_2.

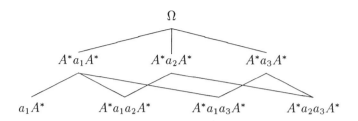

Figure 2.1: A plan specialization graph.

2.2   Constraint-Posting Planning

The plan graph representation of a search space supports a *constraint-posting* approach to planning. A constraint-posting planner—illustrated best by Stefik's MOLGEN [151]—refines the plan graph incrementally until some problem is solved regarding the plan to be executed. With the traditional representation of goals as predicates, the problem is to identify a satisfying plan. With partially satisfiable goals, the problem is to find the best plan. But except for some special cases where convenient optimization techniques are applicable, it is not possible to determine whether a given plan is optimal by examining it in isolation. It may be more reasonable to answer questions about the optimal plan, without necessarily constructing a complete description. I consider the issue of reasoning objectives for a planner further in the description of the dominance-proving architecture in Section 2.4.1.

A constraint-posting planner can be more efficient than a planner that only evaluates complete plans because eliminating a partial plan prunes an entire region of the search space. However, this advantage depends on having some justification for the constraints based on properties of the partial plan. For example, MOLGEN knows that for a **screen** operation to be useful, it must select the appropriate bacteria. Thus, when adding a **screen** step to a plan, MOLGEN is justified in posting a constraint of the form (**resists** *antibiotic-1 bacterium-4*). Constraining the antibiotic to a particular chemical agent would be unjustifiably specific at this stage.

By adding only the constraints that have the best justifications, a planner implements a *least commitment* strategy. An extreme form of least commitment propagates only provable properties of admissible plans. In practice, however, planners have to make guesses when no provable constraints are available. The least commitment heuristic tends to minimize both the likelihood of wrong guesses and the extent of backtracking required to recover from such mistakes. A policy of working on plan classes at upper tiers of the plan graph is a form of least commitment strategy because the partial plans there are minimally constrained.

2.3 Dominance in the Plan Graph

A *dominance-proving* planner is a constraint-posting planner that justifies constraints by determining that the plan classes they define dominate other plan classes of interest. To speak meaningfully of dominance among plan classes, we need to introduce a *preference relation*, $\succ$, over plans. In categorical planning, for example, one plan is preferred to another if it achieves the goal and the other does not. To state this in terms of the *situation calculus* [97], we write:

$$\pi_1 \succ \pi_2 \Leftrightarrow G(result(robot, \pi_1, s_i)) \wedge \neg G(result(robot, \pi_2, s_i)) \qquad (2.1)$$

G is the goal predicate, defined on situations resulting from the robot performing a plan π in a given situation. Here s_i denotes the initial situation. Two plans that both achieve or both do not achieve the goal are equally preferred, or *indifferent*, denoted by $\sim$. The expression $\pi_1 \succeq \pi_2$ means that π_1 is preferred or indifferent to π_2. Indifference is an equivalence relation, and $\pi_1 \succ \pi_2 \equiv \pi_1 \succeq \pi_2 \wedge \pi_1 \not\sim \pi_2$.

The preference relation characterizes the choice criterion employed by the planner. A planner based on expected utility takes

$$\pi_1 \succ \pi_2 \Leftrightarrow E\left[u(\pi_1)\right] > E\left[u(\pi_2)\right]. \qquad (2.2)$$

The discussion of dominance that follows does not depend on any particular criterion for plan choice. We do need to assume, however, that the non-strict preference relation, $\succeq$, is a total order on plans.[1] Effective dominance proving may require further regularities in the preference relation.

A class of plans *dominates* another if for any plan in the second class, there is some plan in the first that is preferred or indifferent. Formally, the dominance relation is given by the following.

Definition 2.1 (D) Π_1 *dominates* Π_2, *written* $D(\Pi_1, \Pi_2)$, *iff*

$$\forall \pi_2 \in \Pi_2 \, \exists \pi_1 \in \Pi_1 \, \pi_1 \succeq \pi_2 \qquad (2.3)$$

This definition leaves open the possibility that two plan classes be mutually dominating. Also, it should be emphasized that it is possible to prove dominance without identifying the particular superior plan π_1 corresponding to each π_2.

The strict version of dominance, D', is defined similarly, except that a particular plan in the first class is preferred to any in the second.[2]

---

[1] The architecture does *not* require that the planner be given a complete specification of the preference relation. Indeed, for our purposes $\succ$ is merely a formal device for defining plan class dominance.

[2] This difference is required by the possibility of infinite plan classes with no maximal elements. If (2.4) were exactly a strict version of (2.3), then such a class would strictly dominate itself. For the same reason, a definition of weak dominance which merely substituted $\succeq$ for $\succ$ in (2.4) would not entail the reflexive property. Assuming that every plan class has a maximal plan is unreasonable, even if it is appropriate to require that the universal class Ω does.

Definition 2.2 (D') Π_1 *strictly dominates* Π_2, $D'(\Pi_1, \Pi_2)$, *iff*

$$\exists \pi_1 \in \Pi_1 \; \forall \pi_2 \in \Pi_2 \; \pi_1 \succ \pi_2 \tag{2.4}$$

Strict dominance implies dominance. In addition, the properties below follow directly from the definitions:

$$D \text{ is reflexive, transitive, and complete.} \tag{2.5}$$

$$D' \text{ is anti-reflexive and transitive (and therefore anti-symmetric).} \tag{2.6}$$

$$D(\Pi_1, \Pi_2) \Leftrightarrow \neg D'(\Pi_2, \Pi_1) \tag{2.7}$$

$$\Pi_2 \subseteq \Pi_1 \Rightarrow D(\Pi_1, \Pi_2) \tag{2.8}$$

$$D(\Pi_1, \Pi_2) \wedge D(\Pi_3, \Pi_4) \Rightarrow D(\Pi_1 \cup \Pi_3, \Pi_2 \cup \Pi_4) \tag{2.9}$$

$$D(\Pi_1, \Pi_3) \vee D(\Pi_2, \Pi_3) \Leftrightarrow D(\Pi_1 \cup \Pi_2, \Pi_3) \tag{2.10}$$

$$D'(\Pi_1, \Pi_2) \wedge D(\Pi_2, \Pi_3) \Rightarrow D'(\Pi_1, \Pi_3) \tag{2.11}$$

These properties serve as dominance propagation rules within the plan graph. Plan classes trivially dominate their subclasses (2.8) because adding plans to a class can only improve its optimum. By (2.8) and the transitivity of D, dominance by a particular class is inherited in the plan graph. Strict dominance is also inherited, by (2.8) and (2.11). Thus, markers or links indicating dominance relations need be stored only at the upper envelope of classes to which they apply. Application of the union properties (2.9 and 2.10), which also hold for D', propagate dominance upwards in the graph

A plan class is *restricted* by asserting that it is weakly dominated by one of its subsets. In the MOLGEN example given above, if Π_1 is the class of plans that include the **screen** operation, and Π_2 is the subclass defined by posting the constraint (**resists** *antibiotic-1 bacterium-4*), then $D(\Pi_2, \Pi_1)$ asserts that Π_2 restricts Π_1. The new dominance assertion represents progress because it lets us focus our attention on a smaller set of plans. Deriving these restrictions is an important task of the dominance prover.

Constraints might be posted to explore the search space even though the dominance relation does not provably hold. Often, such constraints are justified by identifiable *assumptions* that imply dominance. We can express this case by asserting the *conditional dominance relation*, D_S, for S an assumption proposition.

Definition 2.3 (Conditional Dominance) $D_S(\Pi_1, \Pi_2) \equiv S \Rightarrow D(\Pi_1, \Pi_2)$.

Normal dominance is just $D_{\mathbf{true}}$. As an example of conditional dominance, suppose that we are uncertain about the identity of the organism of interest: it could be *bacterium-2* or *bacterium-3*. For $i = 2$ and 3, let S_i be the proposition "Bacterium-i is the organism of interest" and Π_i the plan class that restricts Π_1 to those plans in which the **resists** relation holds between *antibiotic-1* and *bacterium-i*. Then we have $D_{S_2}(\Pi_2, \Pi_1)$, $D_{S_3}(\Pi_3, \Pi_1)$, and $S_2 \vee S_3$. Applying Definition 2.3, we get $D(\Pi_2, \Pi_1) \vee D(\Pi_3, \Pi_1)$. Property 2.10 yields the result $D(\Pi_2 \cup \Pi_3, \Pi_1)$.

Of particular value are conditional dominance relations where S itself contains dominance assertions. For example, if $S_1 \equiv D(\Pi_1, \Omega)$, then $D_{S_1}(\Pi_2, \Pi_1)$ asserts that if we know the optimal plan is in Π_1, we can further confine attention to Π_2.[3] Reasoning of this form can be useful for deriving restriction relations. Indeed, conditional dominance provides an interpretation for the strategies employed by Pednault [118] and Chapman [15] to limit the search space of their planners, discussed further in Section 2.8.2 below.

A dominance-based reasoner can be extended straightforwardly to handle conditional dominance by inserting a truth-maintenance layer between conditions (which correspond to assumptions or justifications) and their dominance implications [23, 95]. The interesting task for the dominance prover is to come up with meaningful conditions that imply useful dominance relations.

2.4 Dominance-Proving Planning

2.4.1 The Dominance-Proving Architecture

The schematic architecture of Figure 2.2 illustrates the roles of the plan graph and dominance relation in a dominance-proving planner.

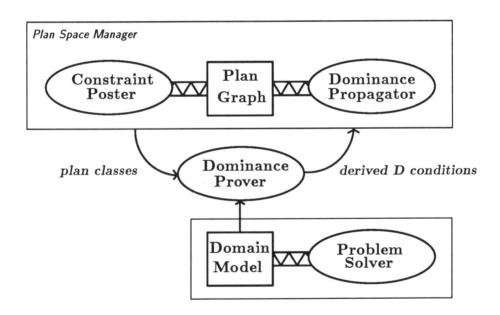

Figure 2.2: The basic dominance-proving architecture.

The active modules of the planner operate on the plan graph and domain model (KB) in the following ways:

---

[3]In categorical planning, D_{S_1} is the same as D (that is, $D_{S_1}(\Pi_1, \Pi_2) \Leftrightarrow D(\Pi_1, \Pi_2)$) due to the binary nature of the preference relation (2.1).

- The *problem solver* reasons about the relations among actions and events in the domain model.

- The *constraint poster* generates new plan classes by adding constraints to undominated classes in the plan graph.

- The *dominance prover* applies knowledge from the domain model to derive dominance conditions (including restrictions and conditional dominance) among the plan classes of interest.

- The *dominance propagator* updates the plan graph to reflect the dominance relation D according to its properties presented in Section 2.3.

Together, the plan graph and the modules that operate on it constitute the *plan space manager*.

In this architecture, planning is not a search for a single plan to execute, but an exploration of properties of admissible plans. A planner performs useful work by refining the plan graph, even if it never reduces the lowest-level classes to singleton sets. Narrowing the admissible plans to a set that contains 10^{400} or even an uncountable infinity of plans may seem like little progress. But if we can determine that all of them contain, for instance, an appendectomy, we solve a significant problem. In general, cardinality is not an accurate measure of the refinement of a plan class. If the plan language includes real-valued parameters, then all but the tightest constraints still leave an uncountable set of candidate plans. The plan class "Administer a dose of drug X within the next minute" includes individual plans where the time the drug is given is any point in the 60-second interval.

The prevailing view of planning as the construction of a completely specified course of action is never totally accurate. Planners devote their resources to isolated questions, such as whether to perform an appendectomy or what to do *next*, without specifying all other features of the plan. A plan to obtain some bananas, for example, is complete only with respect to a *have-bananas* goal; in the larger context of satisfying all physical and emotional needs forever, the agent never stops planning. Figuring out how to get the bananas is a small act of refinement on THE GRAND PLAN.

The classic concept of a *decision* can be understood in terms of the dominance-proving architecture as a choice among exclusive and exhaustive plan classes. Decisions to eat a banana or to join the Air Force are commitments to a class of plans having a particular property, at the expense of those lacking that property. The decision-making agent remains uncommitted to the innumerable other plan class properties under its control.

The decision-theoretic formulation of decision-making as choice among basic plans (called "acts" in that literature) is a gross idealization, made explicit by Savage in his discussion of "small worlds" and "grand worlds" [134]. The plan graph representation lets us dispense with this idealization, as far as plans are concerned.[4] A dominance-proving

---

[4] That is, the plan classes refer to grand-world acts. But we cannot remove the idealization completely; the domain models remain small worlds, after all. For further discussion of small worlds, see Section 6.6.3.

planner can proceed as if it were working on THE GRAND PLAN because it needs never approach an explicit encoding of individual acts.

2.4.2 Instantiating the Architecture

The framework presented so far is an abstract model of planning for partially satisfiable objectives. It generalizes the case of goal predicates and applies to uncertain situations. Rather than prove that a plan necessarily achieves a goal, as in traditional AI planning, the planner tries to prove properties of the optimal plan. These properties define the class of admissible plans.

To instantiate the abstract model to a particular planning mechanism, one needs to specify each of the modules of Figure 2.2 and their interfaces. In particular, realization of a dominance-proving planner requires design of:

- A universal plan class, Ω.

- A constraint language, or representation for partial plans. The set of plan classes expressible in the constraint language is $\mathcal{P} \subseteq 2^{\Omega}$.

- A domain modeling language, including a way to describe the effects of actions and a representation for the preference relation, $\succ$.

The structures described earlier—the plan graph and dominance relations—serve mainly as theoretical machinery for analysis of this class of planners. Specifying the languages and modules is the real work in designing a planner.

As a simple illustration, consider mathematical optimization techniques as planners from this perspective. Optimization is a special case of dominance proving where the program tries to find a singleton dominator, often in one step. For example, if our plan language is $\Re^n$ and the domain model consists of a linear objective function and a set of linear constraints among the elements of the vector, then our dominance prover should be a linear programming algorithm. In this case there are no partial plans. Branch-and-bound integer programming is an example of an optimization procedure that does make use of partial plans and explicit dominance proving.[5]

For the example presented in Figure 2.1, the universal plan class is A^*: strings of actions in the action alphabet A. The constraint language consists of the *regular expressions* [66] over A.[6]

In the development of the planning model to this point, I have not addressed the issue of efficiency. The computational viability of a planner depends on a judicious choice of the languages and algorithms that define it. Although it is difficult to characterize performance at the present level of generality, we can identify a few high-level issues

---

[5]In fact, Ibaraki's characterization of the general branch-and-bound procedure [73] makes use of a dominance relation essentially equivalent to D. The main difference is that his D refers to an explicitly computed relation on partial solutions rather than the abstract condition induced by $\succ$, which may be only partially characterized.

[6]The term A^* in partial plan expressions is syntactic sugar for $(a_1 + \cdots + a_n)^*$.

critical to efficiency. First, the addition of constraints during graph refinement cannot be arbitrary. The planner must generate constraints that relate to the problem at hand and are meaningful to the dominance prover. Unless the prover can establish dominance relations on the graph, refinement is irrelevant. Second, it is important to consolidate the plan graph to avoid redundancy and further the propagation of dominance relations. I examine this topic further in Sections 2.6 and 2.7 below.

2.5   The SUDO-Planner Architecture in Brief

The design of languages and reasoning modules for SUDO-PLANNER illustrates one instantiation of the dominance-proving architecture. I present brief descriptions of SUDO-PLANNER's components below; subsequent chapters specify its design in detail.

A *plan* is a function from observations (events the agent can test in the world) to actions (controllable events). Any set of such functions is a *plan class*, but the plan graph may contain only those classes $\Pi \in \mathcal{P}$ expressible in SUDO-PLANNER's constraint language. The *universal plan class* is the partial plan with no constraints (Ω). A partial plan is specified by posting a series of constraints on Ω. Constraints fall in three basic categories:

- *Action.* Restricts the plan to include an action of the given type. For example, we can form the plan class "plans with CABG" by posting an action constraint of type CABG[7] on the universal plan class.

- *Action policy.* Restricts the plan's policy for the given action to have some regular (monotonic, for example) relationship to the given observable event. An action policy constraint of type "monotonic increasing" specifies the class of plans where CABG is an increasing function of CAD. This plan class, appearing in the plan graph of Figure 1.5 under the notation $\Pi^+(\text{CABG}, \text{CAD})$, corresponds to the threshold policy of Figure 1.1a. For binary actions, a monotonic policy implies the existence of a threshold on the observed variable.

- *Conditional action or action policy.* As above, in effect only under a given condition on observable events. To generate the class "CABG if three-vessel disease," we would post a conditional action constraint with action CABG and condition specifying that the observed CAD (from catheterization) is three-vessel disease.

The plan constraint language is defined formally in Section 3.4.

The domain modeling language for SUDO-PLANNER is based on qualitative probabilistic networks (QPNs). Qualitative relations serve to represent the effects of actions, the connections among events, and preferences. Some QPN fragments for the AAA example appear in Figures 1.7 through 1.9.

---

[7]The actual type specification looks more like "CABG, presence = **true**," due to the particular representation of actions in SUDO-PLANNER, described in Section 3.2. For expository reasons, in this chapter I present only the simplified versions.

Given these representations, the next step is to specify the modules in the architecture schematic of Figure 2.2. SUDO-PLANNER's constraint poster is a passive module, generating plan classes opportunistically. That is, a new class is introduced to the plan graph only when the dominance prover derives a potentially useful result concerning that class. In contrast, a planner under heuristic control would apply an active constraint poster to direct the search for dominance results.

SUDO-PLANNER's problem solver generates QPNs from the KB (summarized in Section 1.6.2, discussed in depth in Chapter 6). There are two parts of the domain model at any given time: the KB as a whole and a dynamically constructed QPN. The problem solver uses facts from the KB to progressively modify the QPN throughout the process of tradeoff formulation.

The dominance prover operates on QPNs rather than directly on the KB. Dominance proving in SUDO-PLANNER consists of manipulating QPNs to derive qualitative relations with implications for plan class dominance. The central basis for deriving dominance in QPNs is qualitative synergy between an action and an event on the value node. Such synergies dictate action policy constraints on plan classes, as explained in Section 4.7.3.

For example, based on a QPN generated by the problem-solver, SUDO-PLANNER determines that CABG and CAD are positively synergistic on *value*. This relationship directly implies that the optimal CABG policy is increasing in CAD severity. Let "cath, CABG?" denote the class of plans that include catheterization and make some commitment about whether to perform CABG. Any plan in this class that is not a threshold policy must be inferior to some plan in $\Pi^+(\text{CABG}, \text{CAD})$. The situation satisfies the condition for plan class dominance (2.3), yielding

$$D(\Pi^+(\text{CABG}, \text{CAD}), \text{"cath, CABG?"}).$$

Because $\Pi^+(\text{CABG}, \text{CAD})$ is a subclass of "cath, CABG?" the dominance relation is a restriction, as posted on the plan graph of Figure 1.5.

The dominance propagator records these results on the plan graph and derives their consequences for dominance among other plan classes. For instance, adding a new plan class intermediate between these two would modify the restrictions recorded on the plan graph, shown in Figure 2.3.

Figure 2.3: Dominance propagation upon insertion of an intermediate plan class.

The overall behavior of SUDO-PLANNER is best described by a superposition of the architecture schematics of Figures 1.10 and 2.2. The product of the process is the plan graph reflecting dominance results SUDO-PLANNER derives from the sequence of QPNs produced by its problem solver.

2.6 Searching the Plan Space

Different designs for the plan constraint language, knowledge representations, and processing modules can lead to dominance-proving planners with disparate behaviors. Nevertheless, the common architectural skeleton provides a basis for a general discussion of some computational issues for this family of planners.

One important generic issue is management of the search space. In the dominance-proving architecture, the search space is represented by the plan graph, and the dominance relation supplies the criterion for pruning the space.

Search in constraint-posting planners proceeds to refine the plan graph by adding constraints to partial plans. The straightforward application of this procedure, however, can lead to considerable redundancy in search. For example, Figure 2.4a shows a refinement to the left side of the plan graph of Figure 2.1. The new partial plan is obtained by posting a constraint on $a_1 A^*$ that the second action be an a_2.

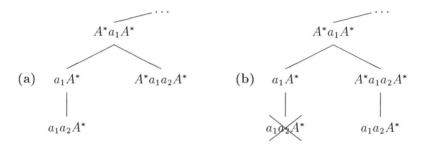

Figure 2.4: Redundancy in plan graph search. (a) Posting a constraint on $a_1 A^*$ yields $a_1 a_2 A^*$. (b) The same plan class is obtained by posting a constraint on $A^* a_1 a_2 A^*$.

Suppose that after further reasoning the planner decides to prune away the new plan class based on dominance or some other criterion. The same class may be re-introduced on refinement of the next branch of the plan graph. As illustrated in Figure 2.4b, constraining the first A^* to be empty in $A^* a_1 a_2 A^*$ defines a partial plan identical to that already pruned. A planner that did not recognize such coincidences would duplicate much of its dominance proving and other reasoning efforts.

The *chronological backtracking* strategy described above is inefficient because it cannot transfer reasoning results between contexts. *Dependency-directed backtracking* [150] avoids considerable redundancy by determining the most general reasons for a failure and pruning a larger region of the search space. In our example, however, the redundancy problem emerges on separate branches of the search space. More flexible dependency-directed reasoning mechanisms, such as truth maintenance systems (TMSs) [28, 95], are required to transfer results across arbitrary contexts.

2.6.1 Classification

The redundancy of Figure 2.4b went unrecognized because the plan graph at the first stage (Figure 2.4a) failed to reflect all specialization relations. This suggests that we add to the plan space manager a third module operating directly on the plan graph, as shown in Figure 2.5. When the constraint poster generates partial plans, the *classifier* situates them in the plan graph by computing their greatest lower and least upper bounds. This classification operation is identical to that performed by terminological knowledge representation languages like KL-ONE [11, 135].

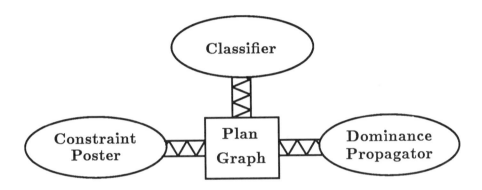

Figure 2.5: The plan space manager augmented with a classifier to consolidate the plan graph.

The correct classification for $a_1a_2A^*$ in the plan graph of Figure 2.4 places this class under both a_1A^* and $A^*a_1a_2A^*$. Consolidating the plan graph in this way avoids redundancy in plan space search. The additional specialization links enhance pruning and provide more pathways for propagation of dominance results throughout the plan graph.

2.6.2 Dependency Mechanisms

In the context of plan space search, classification can be viewed as a kind of dependency mechanism for minimizing duplication in reasoning. Comparison of classification to other techniques is difficult because a precise characterization of the avoidable redundancies is often lacking in descriptions of dependency-directed problem solvers.

From the perspective of dependency maintenance, the dominance relation serves to define so-called *nogood* contexts. Planners without a notion of dominance can consider plan classes nogood only if they are inconsistent or provably cannot achieve the goal. Other pruning criteria must be built into the control mechanism. The availability of nogoods based on dominance can dramatically reduce the search space.

Following the terminology used by de Kleer in describing his *assumption-based* truth maintenance system (ATMS) [23], each plan class is an *assumption context* represented in terms of the constraint language. The plan specialization graph corresponds to the context graph of the ATMS with context subset replaced by plan specialization. Indeed, an implementation using an ATMS would be equivalent to the classification scheme presented here *provided that* we could construct a propositional interface [24] describing the content of partial plans. In general, however, this may not be the most convenient representation of plan classes.[8] As shown in Section 2.7, a mapping of the constraint language to sets of propositions may necessitate an unacceptable growth in the size of partial plan descriptions.

Like the assumption-based approach, the plan graph structure facilitates the exploration of multiple consistent contexts simultaneously. But contrary to the ATMS view, we are not necessarily interested in finding all solutions (the class of all admissible plans). Rather, the planner may focus on an isolated decision defined by a particular distinction in the plan graph. Therefore, we can restrict the domain of assumption sets that need to be considered to those explicitly created as plan classes by the constraint poster.

2.6.3 Plan Graph Queries

Another application of classification is to answer dominance questions about plan classes not explicitly appearing in the plan graph. At any point in the planning process, the plan graph represents the current view of the admissible plan space. To find out whether a given plan class is admissible, we merely classify the class in the plan graph and propagate dominance as usual. Queries about the classes dominating or dominated by this new class can then be answered by local inspection of its position in the plan graph.

2.6.4 Plan Space Search: Summary

Redundancy in searching the plan space is avoided in the dominance-proving architecture by classifying plans in the plan graph as they are generated. The plan graph thus serves a dual role as representation of the admissible plan space and as the main structure for dependency maintenance.

The scheme presented here offers two benefits with respect to plan search efficiency. First, the dominance relation provides a major new class of nogoods, which may potentially shrink the search space. Second, classification of partial plans takes advantage of dependencies that might be obscured by an interface with a propositional TMS.

---

[8]The design of SCHEMER [183, 184]—a dependency-directed interpreter for a non-deterministic LISP—illustrates some issues in constructing a propositional interface for arbitrary dependencies.

2.7 The Complexity of Subsumption

In terminological knowledge representation languages, the key operation for concept classification is the computation of *subsumption* relations [10, 105]. The same applies to classification of partial plans; the appropriate position of a plan class in the plan graph is determined by its subsumption relations to other classes. One plan class *subsumes* another if the latter must be a specialization purely by virtue of its description. We saw above that classifying plans as they are generated minimizes the search space.[9] Conversely, an optimal dependency mechanism (one that minimizes search) in effect computes these subsumptions.

The centrality of subsumption to classification suggests that the complexity of this operation has a large impact on the computational performance of this planning architecture. Consequently, analyses of dominance-proving planners should emphasize the complexity of subsumption in the chosen constraint language.

As an example, consider the plan graphs of Figures 2.1 and 2.4, where regular expressions describe the partial plans. In general, computing subsumption of regular expressions is intractable.[10] By restricting the constraint language to expressions that use disjunctions and Kleene stars exclusively in A^* terms, however, subsumption can be performed in linear time (the problem is essentially string matching with wildcards). All of the plan classes included in the figures above satisfy this restriction.

We can also analyze some more common partial plan representations in terms of subsumption complexity. *Nonlinear plans* [131] are partially ordered sets of actions, used as a basic representation by numerous constraint-posting planners [15]. A nonlinear plan is actually a plan class, comprising all possible linearizations of the partial order [25]. (A planner with a parallel execution capability (for example, a multi-agent planner) could truly have nonlinear plan individuals. The constraint language for such a planner would be more complex.) Unfortunately, partial order—and hence nonlinear plan—subsumption is NP-complete.[11] The exponential potential of the computation lies in the combinatorial number of possible mappings between the steps of the two plan classes. If, however, we can specify the correspondences between steps (for example, which *put-on* in Π_1 corresponds to which in Π_2) then subsumption is at worst quadratic. In practice we will not generally have complete correspondences, but typically the possible mappings between steps will be constrained by one or more of the following factors.

- Actions may only map to others of the same type.

---

[9]For true optimality we must also determine the most general plan class that is dominated. Complete dominance-proving corresponds to extracting the minimal nogood assumption set, which is not generally tractable or even decidable. Note also that minimality is only with respect to a particular constraint language; slight changes may have dramatic effects on the dominance prover's ability to derive nogood sets at high levels of generality.

[10]Hunt et al. [72] show that the equivalence problem for regular expressions is PSPACE-hard. Equivalence can be trivially reduced to two (non-strict) subsumption operations.

[11]The proof, by reduction from EXACT COVER BY 3-SETS, was provided by Ronald L. Rivest, personal communication.

- Compatibility among constraints on the arguments to actions.

- The planner may supply explicit identifications among steps when introducing them in several partial plans at once.

It is an empirical question whether these constraints will render subsumption feasible in practice.

The intractability of nonlinear plan subsumption illustrates the potential difficulty of specifying a propositional interface to generic dependency reasoning mechanisms like the ATMS. In the ATMS, contexts are represented by sets of propositions, and context subsumption is simply the subset operation. Determining whether one context specializes another can therefore be accomplished in time at worst quadratic in the size of the proposition sets. Given that nonlinear plan subsumption is NP-complete, the worst-case size of the propositional representation for the plan classes must be exponential in the partial order encoding, unless $P = NP$.

One should consider the effect on subsumption complexity of any proposed extension to the constraint language. For example, we could allow actions themselves to be expressed at multiple levels of abstraction (as in the sequence *low-dose steroid therapy* is-a *steroid therapy* is-a *drug therapy*) without significant cost in complexity, as long as action subsumption itself is not expensive.[12] I analyze the tradeoff between expressiveness and subsumption tractability for SUDO-PLANNER's constraint language in Section 3.5.

2.8 Miscellaneous Topics

The following sections discuss some implications of the dominance-proving architecture for three issues in knowledge-based planning.

2.8.1 Anytime Planning

The dominance-proving architecture possesses some of the desirable features of *anytime algorithms* [26] that support real-time decision making performance. The plan space manager continually maintains the plan graph, which can be produced at any time the process may be interrupted. Because dominance-proving is monotonic, the class of admissible plans shrinks with time. In other words, the plan space is refined further as more computational time is available.

The difficulty with performing an anytime analysis is that the dominance-proving architecture defines only part of the complete planning and execution system. In this framework, the output of the planner is a class of plans, and the utility of this output depends on how the execution module uses this plan class to select an actual behavior (see Section 3.1).

---

[12]Given a static action graph, action subsumption takes linear time in the worst case. If actions are described more flexibly—perhaps as dynamically generated KL-ONE concepts—then subsumption is more complex [10].

34

This is further complicated by the fact that the dominance-prover may be working on aspects of the plan covering any period of time, while the executor needs only to select actions for the immediate situation. Anytime analysis would be simplified if we could separate the planner's attention to different facets of the plan (for example, responses to distinct events), then combine them via a process of *deliberation scheduling* [26].

Overall, we should expect—under reasonable assumptions—that utility will increase as the plan class gets more specific. However, making this argument in particular cases requires attention to the specifics of the planning and execution interface.

2.8.2   Dominance-Based Knowledge Level Analysis

In his description of the *knowledge level*, Newell proposes that programs can be characterized in terms of the content as opposed to the form of their knowledge by analyzing their behavior with respect to principles of rationality [108]. The dominance relation can a be useful tool for such analyses, whether or not the planner resembles the dominance-proving architecture at the *symbol level*. By admitting partially satisfiable goals, the preference order on plans provides a more comprehensive and flexible rationality principle than one based entirely on goal predicate satisfaction. Note that a program may still be nondeterministic at the knowledge level because we may have an incompletely specified preference order.

Even though the categorical preference relation does not exercise its flexibility, the dominance relation can shed some light on classical planners. In a previous description of this work [173], I illustrated the dominance-proving architecture by recasting TWEAK [15] in its framework. Because TWEAK encapsulates the results of much of the state-of-the-art in nonlinear planning, an account of this planner embodies considerable generality.

The product of this exercise was an interpretation for TWEAK's central principle— the "modal truth criterion" [15, page 340]—in terms of dominance in the plan graph. TWEAK searches the plan space by posting constraints on partial plans until it finds one that achieves its goals. The search is not exhaustive, yet TWEAK is guaranteed to terminate with a solution if one exists. The source of its power lies in the modal truth criterion, which justifies TWEAK's selectivity in exploring the search space. Briefly, the criterion specifies that if a plan class contains a successful plan, then search can be further limited to the subclasses obtained by posting particular sequences of constraints. In our dominance-proving terminology, this is an instance of a *conditional restriction* as described in Section 2.3. For a formal statement of the dominance condition, see the previous paper [173]. Although the details have not been worked out, I expect that a similar interpretation could be developed for Pednault's results for a more expressive constraint language [118].

The utility of the dominance relation as an analytical device is potentially more significant in applications to planners that consider partially satisfiable goals. A variety of AI programs perform resource-allocation tasks, where goal satisfaction is always a matter of degree. In general, the programs employ domain-dependent search heuristics and ad hoc representations, so it is difficult to assess and compare alternative techniques.

One well-known AI resource planner is ISIS, a program that schedules production orders in a job shop [45]. ISIS constructs schedules through a heuristic constraint relaxation process. The program is difficult to evaluate empirically because of its large number of parameters and the lack of a performance standard for its scheduling task. Theoretical analysis also presents a challenge because interactions among the constraints in the program's domain are not well understood.

Recasting ISIS in terms of the dominance-proving architecture may lead to insights about its performance. The framework of this chapter enforces a strong distinction between the non-relaxable constraints and those that are relaxable, called "organizational goals" or "preference constraints" in ISIS terminology. The relaxable constraints serve to define the preference relation on schedules, while the non-relaxable are part of the domain modeling language. The partial schedules ISIS constructs during search correspond to partial plans, as do the abstract schedule classes defined by sets of relaxable constraints. Preferences among various relaxations induce a dominance relation on the plan graph.

The discussion of ISIS here is meant only to illustrate a potential application of dominance concepts to existing constraint-posting planners. The sketchiness of this description implies that any claims for the practical value of analyses of this sort are purely speculative at this time. Theoretically, however, the dominance relation provides a normative criterion for determining the soundness of ISIS's relaxation procedure, and classification in the plan graph is a standard for evaluating the redundancy of the program's search for optimal production schedules.

2.8.3 On Meta-Planning

The idea of *meta-planning* [29, 152, 179] is to apply the machinery of a planner to decisions about the planning process itself. Because planning algorithms are often complicated and opaque, a declarative encoding of the goals and operators at higher levels should lead to more understandable and modifiable planners.

It is important to distinguish two types of higher-level decisions that meta-planners address:

1. allocation of the planner's computational resources, and

2. choice among competing plans or plan fragments.

Most of Wilensky's "meta-themes" and "meta-goals" [179, Section 2.2] relate to the second type of decision.

Choice among competing plans is appropriately considered a "higher-level" issue if the object-level planner lacks the basis for making this decision. This is typically the case for traditional planners because the predicate representation of goals offers only a crude binary distinction. Designers of planners have historically dealt with this inadequacy by developing elaborate conflict resolution mechanisms. Wilensky's meta-planning enterprise was an attempt to demystify these schemes.

A flexible representation for plan choice via the preference relation, however, obviates the need for meta-level decision mechanisms. The meta-theme "don't waste resources"

36

is more accurately expressed as a dominance condition on plans that use more resources, other things being equal. The dominance condition offers a precise semantics for such a statement; interpretation of the meta-theme, in contrast, is not so clear.

The first type of high-level decision—allocation of computational resources—remains a legitimate activity for meta-planning in the dominance-proving framework.

2.9 Summary

In this chapter I have presented and discussed a dominance-proving architecture for planning for partially satisfiable goals. The architecture takes a constraint-posting approach to planning, representing the search space by a plan graph that encodes the specialization relations among the partial plans generated. Goals are defined by a preference order over plans, which induces a dominance relation defined over plan classes. I motivated these concepts with simple examples from MOLGEN and a more detailed account of SUDO-PLANNER.

Redundancy in searching the plan space is minimized by classifying the partial plans in the graph as they are generated and pruning based on dominance. Recognizing the centrality of subsumption computation in classification suggests a novel approach to analyzing the complexity implications of plan constraint languages.

The dominance-proving architecture avoids the pitfalls of goals as predicates by adopting a more general representation for the planner's objectives. Exploiting this flexibility in a computationally feasible manner requires careful design of the component modules and representations that compose the dominance-proving architecture.

3 Representations for Plans and Actions

In this chapter I specify the representations SUDO-PLANNER employs for expressing plan classes and actions. Section 3.1 characterizes the plan space abstractly as a formal basis for defining the semantics of plan class constraints. The next two sections describe the action and event representations employed by SUDO-PLANNER for both domain modeling and expressing plan classes. These specifications fulfill part of the requirements, outlined in Section 2.4.2, for instantiating the dominance-proving architecture in SUDO-PLANNER. The chapter concludes with an analysis of the computational complexity of subsumption for SUDO-PLANNER's plan constraint language.

3.1 Plans

A *plan* is a specification for a course of action, directly executable by an agent. SUDO-PLANNER does not manipulate plans directly; the dominance-proving architecture prescribes computations on plan classes only. Therefore, we can design this type of planner without specifying an encoding for individual plans, as long as the interpretation for plan class constraints is clear. Of course, an integrated planning and execution system would require a complete plan language specification.

3.1.1 Planning and Execution

Abstractly, plans are functions from observations to actions. Formally, given

$\mathcal{O}$ — the set of possible patterns of observation over time, and

Ω_{exe} — the set of executable courses of action,

the universal plan class Ω consists of all functions $\pi : \mathcal{O} \to \Omega_{exe}$. Ω_{exe} defines the scope of pure activity the agent is capable of performing. Plans map situations, distinguished by their observation patterns, into activities. Intuitively, a course of action $\omega \in \Omega_{exe}$ specifies a set of primitive end-effector commands unconditional on any explicitly planned observations.

Figure 3.1 illustrates the relationship between the planning and execution modules in a complete agent. The plan to be executed, $\omega_{obs} = \pi(obs)$, specifies all planned activity, including any sensing operations that enable the agent to observe *obs*.

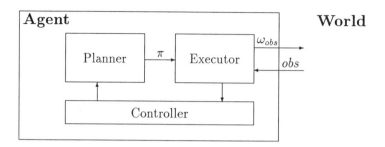

Figure 3.1: An integrated planning and execution system.

Time is handled implicitly in this functional notation. All temporal information must be encoded in the descriptions for observations and courses of action. This treatment is unsatisfactory because it cannot enforce fundamental temporal constraints, such as the prohibition on conditioning current activity on future events.[1] The permissiveness of this syntax implies that ultimately we must decide the legality of plans on semantic grounds. The class of legal plans, Ω_0, is given informally by

$$\Omega_0 = \{\pi \in \Omega \mid \pi \text{ satisfies semantic constraints}\}. \tag{3.1}$$

A more restricted plan language syntax, perhaps incorporating some of these temporal and other legality constraints, would be provided for any particular integrated planning and execution system. The context also dictates computability constraints on π, perhaps requiring real-time performance. REX, a language designed for situated planning [127], is an example of the kind of representation suitable for the plans passed to the executor in the framework of Figure 3.1.

3.1.2 Cascaded Planners

We can generalize this framework by decomposing the planning module into a series of submodules, each of which is itself a planner. As shown in Figure 3.2, the output of each module is a plan class, which serves as the root of the plan graph for the next planner in the sequence. Each planner has its own constraint language, determining the plan classes $\mathcal{P}_i \subseteq 2^\Omega$ expressible in its plan graph. The $\mathcal{P}_i$ also constrain inter-module communication: planner-j must output a plan class $\Pi_{j+1} \in \mathcal{P}_{j+1}$.

A variety of cascaded planning architectures can be defined by specifying conventions regarding the plan constraint languages. For example, the condition $\mathcal{P}_i \subseteq \mathcal{P}_{i+1}$, $1 \leq i \leq n-1$ entails a successive refinement of the plan spaces for the cascaded planners. On the other hand, if $\mathcal{P}_i \supseteq \mathcal{P}_{i+1}$ for that range, successive planners possess cruder distinguishing abilities. Such an architecture might be appropriate for a system in which high-level planners pass on partial results to lower-level control algorithms. In general, however, the $\mathcal{P}_i$ will overlap, reflecting divisions of labor according to expertise or other resources.

---

[1]For further discussion of SUDO-PLANNER's atemporality, see Section 9.2.2.

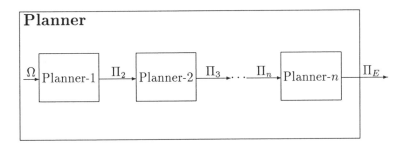

Figure 3.2: Cascaded planners. Planner-i maintains a plan graph with plan classes expressible in its constraint language, $\mathcal{P}_i$. The output of the system, Π_E, is the plan class passed to the executor.

The final planner in the chain, planner-n, produces a plan class Π_E for the executor. The framework of Figure 3.1 implicitly assumes that the constraint language for the executor admits only singleton plan classes.

$$\mathcal{P}_E = \{\{\pi\} \mid \pi \in \Omega_0\}.$$

This restriction on $\mathcal{P}_E$ is in no way essential to the view of planning and execution presented here.

In the cascaded planning framework, SUDO-PLANNER plays the role of planner-1. The constraint language described in Section 3.4 defines the expressible plan classes, $\mathcal{P}_1$. I assume planner-2's constraint language to be sufficiently expressive so that $\mathcal{P}_2$ includes the admissible plan spaces output by SUDO-PLANNER.

3.2   Action Representation

In contrast to the abstract plan language discussion above, this section describes concrete representations for actions as they appear in the SUDO-PLANNER knowledge base. Actions play a part in defining two components of SUDO-PLANNER:

1. Constraint language. Actions are the building blocks of plans. Plan classes are described by constraints on the actions making up their constituent plans.

2. Domain modeling language. The effects of plans are determined by the effects of their component actions.

This section presents the basic action representation, with an emphasis on features necessary for the constraint language. Issues in representing the effects of actions are the subject of Chapter 5.

3.2.1 Action Taxonomies

The knowledge base of actions is implemented in NIKL [74, 165], a terminological knowledge representation language based on KL-ONE [11]. Action types are represented by NIKL *concepts*, frame-like specifications of classes of individuals. Concepts are defined by their position in the concept lattice and restrictions on their *roles*, or associated features.[2] Roles are also taxonomized, according to the generality of their domains (concepts for which the feature is relevant) and ranges (possible values of the feature). The *extension* of an action type a, denoted $\mathcal{X}(a)$ is the set of actions satisfying its specification.

The NIKL taxonomy of action concepts specifies a multilevel description of actions that plans may include. Let **action** be the root of the taxonomy, a superconcept of every other action concept a_i. $\mathcal{A} = \mathcal{X}(\textbf{action})$ is the set of all actions. One way to specialize partial plans in the plan graph is to specialize individual action types included in that plan class. If Π_1 includes action $a_1 = \textbf{drug-therapy}$, the class of plans Π_{1D} that replace a_1 with $a_D = \textbf{drug-therapy}(D)$ is a specialization of Π_1.

The dimension of specialization in the example above corresponds to the **drug** role of action a_1. The concept **drug-therapy**(D) is defined by a *value restriction* [11] on that role, limiting its range to D.[3] Additional specializations might restrict the drug further (perhaps D is a family of drugs) or may include other information, such as dosage or method of administration.[4] In realistic knowledge bases the axes of specialization are quite numerous.

Action-type abstraction is used in MOLGEN [151] and other hierarchical planners [104, 160]. Although MOLGEN lab operators constitute a simple two-level hierarchy of actions, in combination with the hierarchy of lab objects in their domain they form a rich, multiply hierarchical action structure. From this perspective the lab objects are merely further axes for specializing the lab operators.

As Tenenberg points out [159], this specialization form of abstraction is orthogonal to the step-components type of abstraction hierarchy used in NOAH [131]. In NOAH actions may be decomposed into sequences of lower-level actions, effectively viewing each action as a sub-plan. A decomposition hierarchy associates actions by a "part-of" rather than an "is-a" relation. SUDO-PLANNER does not explicitly support this sort of abstraction.

Another distinct kind of abstraction is the precondition hierarchy of plan spaces Sacerdoti introduced in ABSTRIPS [130]. Abstract actions are defined implicitly by temporarily ignoring preconditions. Note that preconditions refer to the implications of including an action in a plan, rather than to features intrinsic to the action. Ordering the preconditions imposes structure on the search space rather than on the actions themselves.

Basing the knowledge representation on a terminological reasoner like NIKL has the

---

[2] For an alternate action representation implemented in NIKL, see Swartout and Neches [156]. In their scheme, plans as well as actions are represented as NIKL concepts.

[3] I adopt the notation $a_i(\textit{value-restriction})$ for convenience whenever the role involved is obvious in context.

[4] As in planning, this specialization process never ends. Actions exist in the knowledge base only as types; the action individuals specifying an actual plan π are required only if the planner is integrated with an execution capability as in Section 3.1.1.

important advantage of dynamic flexibility. New action types may be created at planning time by adding constraints to, specifying new features of, or combining existing action concepts. These new action types can often be automatically classified [135]; that is, NIKL can determine the location of the new type in the existing taxonomy. This is important because

1. an action type's place in the taxonomy determines the properties it inherits from and supplies to other types, and

2. action subsumption is employed by the constraint language subsumption algorithm of Section 3.5 to classify plan classes.

Some simple examples of dynamic action creation in SUDO-PLANNER during dominance proving are described in Section 7.2.

3.2.2 Action Variables

As described in Section 3.4 below, the plan constraint language uses action types to restrict a plan class to plans including actions with certain features. It is sometimes convenient to refer to properties of action features directly, for example, in relating the dosage of a drug to other characteristics of events or plans. The SUDO-PLANNER objects denoting such features are called *action variables*.

Action variables are represented by pairs of NIKL concepts and roles. Drug dosage, for example, is the combination of the action **drug-therapy** with its role **dosage**. Other variables are constructed by pairing the concept with other roles, such as **duration** and **method** (whether the drug is given as a pill, intravenously, or in some other form). The notation $av \equiv role\langle a_i \rangle$ makes the components of an action variable type av explicit. The *domain* of the action variable is the value restriction on its role component.

Like actions, SUDO-PLANNER action variables are types, not individuals. A taxonomy of action variables can be defined in terms of the concept and role taxonomies. One action variable specializes another if and only if both the action concept and role of the first specialize the corresponding components of the second.

For each action variable *instance AV*, there is a function $AV(\omega)$ that returns AV's value in the course of action $\omega \in \Omega_{exe}$. If ω does not commit to a value for AV, the function is undefined.

3.2.3 SUDO-Planner Actions

Figure 3.3 illustrates the form of action definitions in NIKL. The definition of **surgery** declares that it is a subconcept of **action** (the NIKL concept for SUDO-PLANNER's universal action class $\mathcal{A}$) and that it has a role named **route** with the value restriction **invasive-path-into-body**. The action **open-lung-biopsy** is defined similarly.

SUDO-PLANNER uses NIKL for two types of inference: classification and inheritance. Given that **biopsy** is a subconcept of **action**, and that **open-lung-path** is a kind of

A **surgery** is an **action**
    with one **route** which is an **invasive-path-into-body**.

An **open-lung-biopsy** is a **biopsy**
    with one **route** which is an **open-lung-path**.

Figure 3.3: Stylized NIKL definitions for the actions **surgery** and **open-lung-biopsy**.

invasive-path-into-body, NIKL's classifier can determine that an **open-lung-biopsy** is a kind of **surgery**. Facts about surgical actions—that they require anesthesia, for example—are automatically inherited by **open-lung-biopsy** and other specializations of **surgery**.

The SUDO-PLANNER action knowledge base includes all of the actions for the running AAA example. A portion of this taxonomy appears in Figure 3.4.

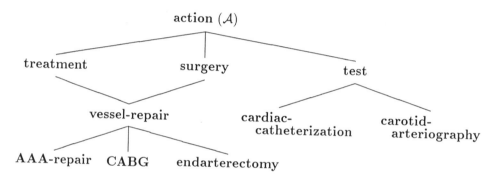

Figure 3.4: A fragment of SUDO-PLANNER's action taxonomy.

3.3 Events

The representational structures denoting events in the knowledge base are very much like those for actions. In fact, actions in SUDO-PLANNER are a special type of event, distinguished because they are controllable by the planner. That is, the root of the event taxonomy, **event** ($\mathcal{E}$), is a superconcept of **action** ($\mathcal{A}$). The primary role of events in the knowledge base is in the representation for the effects of actions (Chapter 5). Events also serve to describe observed conditions in plan class constraints.

The *event variables* representation is identical to that for action variables, described in Section 3.2.2. The extension of an event variable, $\mathcal{X}(ev)$, is equivalent to the cross product of the extensions of its concept and role. The function $EV(obs)$ returns the value taken by an observable event variable instance EV in the observation *obs*. If EV is unobservable, the function is undefined. By convention, action variables are accessible to the agent

44

without explicit observation. That is why the *AV* functions are defined in terms of π rather than *obs* even though action variables are a special case of event variables.

The event variable **value⟨agent⟩** corresponds to the special value node v in QPNs.

3.4 Constraint Language

The unconstrained plan class object denotes Ω, the universal plan class. Partial plans are constructed by adding constraints to Ω or to other existing plan classes. Representations and interpretations for the three types of SUDO-PLANNER constraints (action constraints, action policy constraints, and conditional constraints, introduced in Section 2.5) are presented in sequence below.

3.4.1 Action Constraints

An action constraint on a plan class asserts that an action of a specific type is in its plans. Action types are simply the NIKL concepts appearing in SUDO-PLANNER's action taxonomy. The constraint poster records a sequence of action constraints in an *in-list* describing the action types included in the partial plan.

An in-list consisting only of a collection of types can be ambiguous, however, due to the hierarchical nature of action types. For example, suppose the in-list is [**surgery**,**CABG**]. Because **CABG** is a subconcept of **surgery**, any plan that includes an instance of **CABG** automatically satisfies both constraints. Under this interpretation, we need some other way to express the constraint that a plan include a **CABG** *plus* some other unidentified surgical procedure.

The solution is to associate each separate action constraint with a unique identifier. An in-list of the form $[(a_1, id_1), \ldots, (a_n, id_n)]$ indicates that the plan must include actions of types $a_1, \ldots, a_n$ and that no single action can account for both a_i and a_j unless $id_i = id_j$. If $id_i = id_j$, then there must be a single action that is both an a_i and an a_j. When there is a known type a_k corresponding to the conjunction of a_i and a_j, the two in-list entries can be merged into one for a_k. For example, $[(\mathbf{surgery}, 1), (\mathbf{CABG}, 1)]$ is equivalent to $[(\mathbf{CABG}, 1)]$, but $[(\mathbf{surgery}, 1), (\mathbf{CABG}, 2)]$ cannot be simplified. Because NIKL can express conjoined concepts, we need not consider in-lists with more than one action type having the same identifier.[5]

Some action types offer little real constraint on a plan class. For example, asserting that an action of type **drug-therapy** is in the plan isn't saying much because the **dosage** could be zero. By this standard, all plans, medical or otherwise, include a **drug-therapy**. In fact, they also include **surgery**, which (like all SUDO-PLANNER actions) has a boolean **presence** role specifying whether the action is actually performed. Any action constraint

---

[5]In fact, this property renders identifiers superfluous for plan classes defined exclusively by action constraints. The *ids* are retained, however, because they are indispensable for representing conditional constraints (Section 3.4.3).

whose type has the null action as an instance does not meaningfully restrict the executable plans.

In the cascaded planning architecture of Section 3.1.2, however, such action constraints can make a difference. In general, a plan class produced by the planner need not commit to a policy for every available action. An action constraint restricts that freedom, dictating that the plan class passed to the next module make some commitment about the action. For example, if **drug-therapy** appears on a class's in-list, any subclass passed on to the next module must specify something further about the value of the therapy variable. In this situation, we say that **drug-therapy** is "under consideration" in the plan class.

For example, in the plan graph of Figure 1.5, the partial plan "CABG?" refers to the class of plans where **CABG** is under consideration. It is formed by posting an action constraint on Ω. If our semantics did not supply any force to this constraint, the classifier should have merged the class with Ω and with any other class with such weak action constraints.

To assert that **CABG** should actually be performed, we must post an action constraint for the type **CABG(true)**, the subconcept of **CABG** where the **presence** role is value-restricted to **true**. An action constraint for **CABG(false)** asserts that **CABG** is not performed in the plan.

3.4.2 Action Policy Constraints

An action policy constraint specifies an action variable, an event variable, and a relationship that must hold between them. For the constraint to be operational, the event variable must be observable at execution time. This condition is satisfied automatically when the event variable is also an action variable because the agent knows what actions it has performed.

The monotonicity conditions mentioned in previous chapters are the only action policy constraints employed by SUDO-PLANNER. A monotonicity constraint is written (δ, av, ev), with δ the direction of the relationship and av and ev the action and event variables, respectively. Adding such a constraint to a plan class Π yields the subclass Π', where

$$\Pi' = \{\pi \in \Pi \mid \forall o_1, o_2 \in \mathcal{O}, \forall EV \in \mathcal{X}(ev).$$
$$EV(o_1) \geq EV(o_2) \Rightarrow \forall AV \in \mathcal{X}(av). \ AV(\pi(o_1)) \ R_\delta \ AV(\pi(o_2))\}, \quad (3.2)$$

with $x \ R_+ \ y$ defined to hold if either $x \geq y$ or one of the arguments is undefined. R_- is the inverse of R_+, and R_0 the conjunction of R_+ and R_-. In words, a plan π satisfies the constraint if for every action variable AV of type av, the policy for AV is monotonic (of the appropriate polarity) in every event variable of type ev.

Policy constraints where both variables refer to actions are split into two constraints, with av and ev taking on reversed roles. Because the event component of ev is an action, the first inequality in condition (3.2) is replaced by

$$EV(\pi(o_1)) \geq EV(\pi(o_2)).$$

A monotonicity constraint is ill-defined unless the action for av is under consideration in Π.

For example, the action policy constraint

$$(+, \mathbf{presence}\langle \mathbf{CABG} \rangle, \mathbf{extent}\langle \mathbf{cardiac\text{-}cath\text{-}result} \rangle) \qquad (3.3)$$

asserts that the CABG policy is an increasing function of the CAD extent as revealed by cardiac catheterization.[6] Because $\mathbf{presence}\langle \mathbf{CABG} \rangle$ is a boolean variable, this implies that the plan is a threshold policy.

3.4.3 Conditional Constraints

Conditional constraints are action or policy constraints that have effect only under some observed condition. For example, we could assert that **CABG** should be performed if **catheterization** reveals three-vessel disease (**3vd**) by posting such a constraint. Although SUDO-PLANNER's dominance prover never directly derives results about plan classes defined by conditional constraints, such constraints could be generated if the inputs were conditioned externally.

Syntactically, constraints are conditioned by including an associated event type e_i. Unconditional constraints are implicitly associated with the universal event **event**. Let $e_i : \Pi$ denote a constraint that the plan must be in Π under condition e_i. The semantics of a conditional constraint can be defined in terms of the semantics for the corresponding unconditional constraint.

Let $\pi[e_i] : \mathcal{O} \to \Omega_{exe}$ be the partial function defined by

$$\pi[e_i](o) \equiv \begin{cases} \pi(o) & \text{if } o \in \mathcal{X}(e_i) \\ \text{undefined} & \text{otherwise,} \end{cases}$$

and let

$$\Pi[e_i] \equiv \{\pi[e_i] \mid \pi \in \Pi\}.$$

Note that $\pi[\mathbf{event}] = \pi$ and $\Pi[\mathbf{event}] = \Pi$.

If Π_1 is the plan class we obtain by posting a constraint on Π, then the class obtained by posting a conditional version of that constraint on Π is

$$\{\pi \in \Pi \mid \pi[e_i] \in \Pi_1[e_i]\}.$$

The SUDO-PLANNER event taxonomy induces a relationship among conditional constraints. If e_i subsumes e_j, constraints conditional on e_i are also in effect under e_j. As in Section 3.4.1, identifiers on the in-lists disambiguate the meaning of separate appearances of compatible actions. For example, the plan class

$$e_i : [(\mathbf{surgery}, id_1)]; \quad e_j : [(\mathbf{CABG}, id_2)]$$

must have a **surgery** *in addition* to a **CABG** in event e_j, unless $id_1 = id_2$.

---

[6]The variable $\mathbf{extent}\langle \mathbf{CAD\text{-}event} \rangle$ is not directly observable. Its value would be identical to $\mathbf{extent}\langle \mathbf{cardiac\text{-}cath\text{-}result} \rangle$ if catheterization were a perfect test.

3.5 Computing Subsumption

This section presents the subsumption algorithm in three stages, extending the constraint language to include each type of constraint in turn. The version of Section 3.5.2, accounting for action and policy constraints, is sufficient for expressing all of the plan classes about which SUDO-PLANNER can derive dominance results.

3.5.1 Subsumption with Action Constraints

With only the first type of constraint, a partial plan consists of an in-list of action types. Because each identifier is unique in an in-list (see Section 3.4.1), we can ignore them in this part of the subsumption algorithm.

In general, one plan class subsumes another iff the constraints on the second are at least as strong as those on the first. Because individual action constraints restrict the role of exactly one action in the plan, we can test this subsumption condition action-by-action. However, we cannot tell immediately which actions constrained in the second partial plan correspond to each mentioned in the first. Instead, we must determine whether there is any mapping between the two in-lists such that each action type in the first is matched with a distinct action type in the second that is at least as specific.

For example, suppose the action taxonomy consists of action types $a_1, \ldots, a_6$ such that a_i subsumes a_j iff $i \leq j$. Let $\Pi_1 = [a_1, a_2, a_5]$ and $\Pi_2 = [a_3, a_4, a_6]$. Figure 3.5a illustrates these two classes, with a link between each pair such that the upper action type subsumes the lower. From this diagram, we can tell that Π_1 subsumes Π_2 because for each action in the former it is possible to select a distinct one in the latter connected to it.

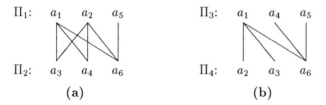

Figure 3.5: Plan class subsumption by bipartite matching. Links indicate that the upper action subsumes the lower. (a) Π_1 subsumes Π_2, but (b) Π_3 does not subsume Π_4.

On the other hand, Figure 3.5b demonstrates that $\Pi_3 = [a_1, a_4, a_5]$ does not subsume $\Pi_4 = [a_2, a_3, a_6]$, because there is no such one-to-one mapping. Action a_6 can be paired with at most one of a_4 and a_5, leaving the other unaccounted for.

To compute subsumption among plan classes Π_1 and Π_2 (represented by their in-lists), we first construct a graph of the sort illustrated in Figure 3.5. An action type in Π_1's in-list is linked to every type in Π_2's that it subsumes. Construction of this graph requires $O(n^2)$ action subsumption computations. This graph is *bipartite* because the vertices are partitioned into two groups such that all edges connect vertices in different groups. A *matching* on a bipartite graph is a collection of unconnected edges. Given a bipartite graph, Π_1 subsumes Π_2 iff there is a matching that uses all of the actions in Π_1's in-list.

We can compute a maximum matching in a bipartite graph in $O(n^{5/2})$ time using the algorithm of Hopcroft and Karp [65]. The subsumption holds iff the cardinality of this matching equals the cardinality of Π_1's in-list. Assuming that action subsumption takes constant time, the algorithm for plan class subsumption is $O(n^{5/2})$.

3.5.2 Subsumption with Policy Constraints

In this section, we extend the partial plan language to include, in addition to the in-list, a collection of monotonicity constraints of the form (δ, av, ev). Because the policy constraints do not interact with the action constraints, the subsumption algorithm is separable into two parts. Π_1 subsumes Π_2 iff both

1. the in-list for Π_1 subsumes that of Π_2 according to the algorithm of Section 3.5.1, and

2. for all monotonicity constraints $(\delta_{i,1}, av_{i,1}, ev_{i,1})$ in the description of Π_1, there exists a (not necessarily distinct) $(\delta_{j,2}, av_{j,2}, ev_{j,2})$ associated with Π_2 such that:

    (a) $\delta_{i,1} = \delta_{j,2}$ or $\delta_{j,2} = 0$,

    (b) $av_{j,2}$ subsumes $av_{i,1}$, and

    (c) $ev_{j,2}$ subsumes $ev_{i,1}$.

Note the reversal of subsumption polarity for the variables in monotonicity constraints. For action constraints, it is weaker to assert that a more general action type is included in the plan. Under the definition of monotonic policy constraints (3.2), in contrast, generality in the variables leads to stronger constraints. For example, asserting that **presence⟨vessel-repair⟩** increases in the test result variable is more restrictive than asserting that **presence⟨CABG⟩** does.

Pairwise comparison of monotonicity constraints is sufficient as long as it is not possible for one constraint to be subsumed by a group of others without being subsumed by a single member of the group. This condition would be violated if such a group subsumption were possible for action and event variables. For example, if $\mathcal{X}(av_1) \subseteq \mathcal{X}(av_2) \cup \mathcal{X}(av_3)$ but $\mathcal{X}(av_1) \not\subseteq \mathcal{X}(av_2)$ and $\mathcal{X}(av_1) \not\subseteq \mathcal{X}(av_3)$, pairwise comparison of monotonicity constraints would lead to an incomplete subsumption algorithm. Although this situation can be expressed with NIKL's *covers* relation [74], that facility is not used in the SUDO-PLANNER knowledge base.

Because the mapping of monotonicity constraints need not be one-to-one, the second stage of the algorithm requires only $O(n^2)$ event variable subsumptions. Taking these primitive subsumptions as constant, the overall plan class subsumption complexity remains $O(n^{5/2})$.

3.5.3 Subsumption with Conditionals

Π_1 subsumes Π_2 iff $\Pi_1[e_i]$ subsumes $\Pi_2[e_i]$ for each e_i appearing in an explicit conditional constraint on Π_1. Unfortunately, determining the effective constraints under each condition (the $\Pi[e_i]$) is difficult because of interactions between monotonicity and conditional constraints. A constraint conditional on e_i may influence $\Pi[e_j]$ even if e_i and e_j have no taxonomic relation.

For example, let e_i = **cardiac-cath-result(3vd)**. The conditional constraint e_i : **CABG(true)** asserts that **CABG** is performed if catheterization indicates three-vessel CAD. Suppose we post this constraint in conjunction with the monotonicity constraint that CABG policy be increasing in CAD extent (3.3). Because the monotonicity constraint implies a threshold policy and the conditional constraint tells us that **3vd** is above the threshold, we can infer the CABG policy for values of CAD extent more severe than **3vd**. Consider the condition e_j = **cardiac-cath-result(lmd)**, where **lmd** stands for left main disease, a severe form of CAD (**lmd** > **3vd**). The monotone policy constraint entails that e_i : **CABG(true)** subsumes e_j : **CABG(true)**, a result that does not follow from the conditional constraints alone.

The following algorithm ignores this potential interaction and is therefore incomplete. It assumes that the conditional constraints are arranged in a taxonomy according to the conditioning events. The classifier should update this taxonomy as the constraints are posted.

The algorithm constructs a description of the partial plan class $\Pi_1[e_i]$ by merging the in-lists and policy constraints associated with each event subsuming e_i. It merges in-list elements as described in Section 3.4.1 and simply conjoins the policy constraints. For each e_i relevant to Π_1, the subsumption algorithm computes $\Pi_2[e_i]$ by classifying e_i in Π_2's conditional event lattice and proceeding as above. If $\Pi_1[e_i]$ subsumes $\Pi_2[e_i]$ for all e_i, then Π_1 subsumes Π_2.

Despite the separability assumption, the algorithm is sound (all derived subsumptions are valid) because the constraints in Π_2 are individually stronger than those of Π_1. Therefore, any properties of plans holding by virtue of constraint interactions in Π_1 must also hold in Π_2.

The complexity of this algorithm is dominated by subsumption computations on the conditional partial plans; the time needed to construct them can be ignored in asymptotic analysis. In the worst case, the events are linearly arranged so that each constraint is inherited by all successors. Since there are a linear number of conditional subsumption computations on the same order of constraints, the complexity of the overall subsumption algorithm in this situation is $O(nn^{5/2}) = O(n^{7/2})$.

3.5.4 Extensions

Further work should explore the development of a complete algorithm for plan class subsumption with conditional constraints. In addition, there are several extensions to the constraint language that would provide significantly greater expressive power.

The constraint language cannot express relations among actions in the plan. For example, it would be convenient to link the roles of several actions to assert that they share a common instrument. The language would also be enriched if it permitted expression of some kinds of temporal relations among actions.

Unfortunately, it appears that admitting any interactions or relations among different actions renders the problem combinatorial. The separability of action constraints led to a tractable algorithm because they could be matched action-by-action. The tractability of monotonicity constraints is due to their universality. In contrast, the intractability of nonlinear plan subsumption (see Section 2.7) lies in the addition of an operator for constraining a transitive relation. The relation in this case is interpreted as step ordering; other isomorphic interpretations lead to similar intractability. In extending the expressive power of the constraint language, caution is required to minimize the concomitant degradation of computational feasibility.

4 Qualitative Probabilistic Networks

The qualitative probabilistic network formalism is part of SUDO-PLANNER's domain modeling language for representing the relationships among actions and events. This chapter is a self-contained description of the formalism. Chapters 5, 6, and 7 describe in detail how qualitative probabilistic networks support tradeoff formulation in SUDO-PLANNER.

4.1 Introduction

Many knowledge representation schemes, including the various flavors of "causal networks" [111, 126, 168], qualitative physical models [7], and belief networks [114], model the world as a collection of states, events, or other ontological primitives connected by links that describe their interrelationships. The representations differ widely in the nature of the fundamental objects and in the precision and expressiveness of the relationship links.

Qualitative probabilistic networks (QPNs) occupy a region in representation space where the objects are arbitrary variables, and the relationships are qualitative constraints on the joint probability distribution among them. This area is important for AI research because the relation among variables is often uncertain due to incomplete knowledge or modeling, and because strictly numeric representations are inappropriately precise for many applications. Excess precision leads to knowledge bases applicable in only narrow domains and to diminished modularity because interactions increasingly arise at finer levels of detail [58, 177].

The qualitative relationships expressible in the QPN formalism are designed to afford robustness yet permit a reasoner to deduce useful properties about optimal assignments to the specially designated decision variables in the network. These "useful properties" are facts that enable a planner to reduce the search space of possible courses of action. The nature of these decision properties and the qualitative relationships leading to them are developed in the body of this chapter.

4.1.1 Motivation

The primary purpose of qualitative probabilistic networks is to support dominance-proving for tradeoff formulation in SUDO-PLANNER. In addition, the analysis of QPNs offers potential benefits in two other areas.

Probabilistic semantics for a common knowledge base construct. Relations similar in intent to those expressible in QPNs have been applied widely in AI knowledge bases without serious attempts at formalization, probabilistic or otherwise. The analysis below suggests how such constructs might be interpreted and in some cases dictates how they *must* be interpreted to justify inferences drawn by associated reasoners.

Qualitative reasoning methods for domains where signs of associations are not guaranteed, and functional relations are not deterministically fixed. Many applications of qualitative reasoning are not faithful to the underlying assumptions behind a "qualitative differential equations" interpretation. Taking an explicit probabilistic approach reveals the possible pitfalls of such violations. This issue is discussed further in Section 4.8.4 below.

4.1.2 Preview of the Chapter

Section 4.2 formally introduces qualitative probabilistic networks, relates them to numeric graphical probabilistic representations, and presents an example from the domain of digitalis therapy. The digitalis example illustrates the use of *qualitative influences*, qualitative relations describing the sign (direction) of the relationship between a pair of variables.

The next four sections elaborate the semantics, properties, and application of qualitative influences. A formal probabilistic definition for them is motivated and developed in Section 4.3. Section 4.4 describes inference mechanisms that are sound with respect to this definition and presents an efficient algorithm for answering queries about the qualitative influences holding among arbitrary variables in the network. Section 4.5 considers alternative probabilistic semantics and shows that the definition of Section 4.3 is the weakest satisfying the inference mechanisms of Section 4.4. Application of these techniques to the digitalis example is the subject of Section 4.6.

Qualitative synergies, which describe the qualitative interaction among influences, are defined, defended, and analyzed in Section 4.7. This section also presents graphical algorithms for reasoning about synergies in QPNs similar to those for qualitative influences. Analysis of the digitalis model enhanced with synergy assertions demonstrates that useful properties of the preferred therapy plan follow from purely qualitative assertions.

Section 4.8 contrasts the qualitative probabilistic network representation with related work in AI, decision theory, and statistics. The relevance of these results to previous qualitative reasoning applications is also discussed. A perspective on the significance of this work is offered in the final section.

4.2 Qualitative Probabilistic Networks

4.2.1 Network Models

A network model is a graph-like structure with nodes that represent variables and edges and hyper-edges that describe relationships among them. In a probabilistic model, the values of variables as well as their interrelationships are uncertain, defined by a probability distribution over the joint value space. Probabilistic network models have attracted much recent attention in AI, for example in Pearl's work on belief networks [114] and related formalisms [18, 86, 148]. The network formalism developed here is accurately viewed as a qualitative abstraction of *influence diagrams* [68], which are belief networks with additional constructs to support decision-making. In particular, all properties holding of a belief network or influence diagram by virtue of structure alone are also true of the corresponding QPN. Some QPN terminology, notation, and even solution concepts (by analogy) are borrowed from Shachter's work on influence diagram evaluation [136, 137].

Formally, a qualitative probabilistic network is a pair $G = (V, Q)$. V is the set of *variables*, or vertices of the graph. Q is a set of *qualitative relationships* among the variables. The qualitative influences and synergies in Q correspond to directed edges and hyper-edges, respectively, in the graph G. To be a valid QPN, G must be acyclic with respect to influence edges.

Variables, named by lower-case symbols, are associated with a set of possible values, for example, boolean for propositional event variables, or real intervals for continuous parameters. Unlike most numeric schemes, there is no practical requirement to reformulate the value spaces into discrete, finite sets. Let $X(a)$ denote the domain of variable a. The domain of a tuple of variables is the product space of the individual domains, for example, $X(\langle a, b \rangle) = X(a) \times X(b)$. The tuple is written as a set when the ordering is insignificant. Subscripted symbols denote values in the domain of a variable.

The variable set V may contain one special variable v, called the *value node*.[1] Relationships involving v express preferences over the other variables.

It is also useful to distinguish a set $D \subseteq V - \{v\}$ of *decision variables*. A decision-making program takes variables in D to be under its control and therefore focuses on deriving the implications on v of choosing different values for them. The remainder of the variables in the network are random variables not under direct control of the decision maker.

Qualitative relationships express constraints on the joint probability distribution over the variables. Unlike the numeric conditional probabilities specified in belief networks and influence diagrams, they are not generally sufficient to determine the exact distribution. In fact, in a purely qualitative network the absolute likelihood of any joint event is completely unconstrained! Nevertheless, the qualitative relationships are carefully designed to justify the deduction of a class of *relative* likelihood conclusions that in turn imply useful decision-making properties. Note that nothing prevents us from building hybrid models combining qualitative relationships with those more precise, although the present work does not pursue that possibility.

There are two types of qualitative relationships in QPNs. *Qualitative influences* describe the direction of the relationship between two variables. *Qualitative synergies* describe interactions among influences. These concepts form the basis of the QPN formalism

---

[1]This name is unfortunate because v actually represents a *utility function*, often distinguished in decision theory from the *value function*. Nevertheless, the term is retained because it is well entrenched in the vocabulary of influence diagrams.

and are developed in detail below.

4.2.2 Example: The Digitalis Therapy Advisor

The development of QPN concepts is illustrated with a simple causal model taken from Swartout's program for digitalis therapy [155]. The model, shown in Figure 4.1, is a fragment of the knowledge base that Swartout used to re-implement the Digitalis Therapy Advisor [51] via an automatic programmer.

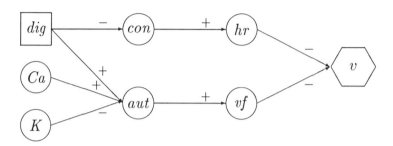

Figure 4.1: Part of the causal model for digitalis therapy. The sign on a link from node a to node b indicates the effect of an increase in a on b.

In the figure the circular nodes represent random variables. The rectangular node is a decision variable, in this case denoting the dosage of digitalis (dig) administered to the patient. The value node v is drawn within a hexagon and represents the utility of the outcome to the patient. Qualitative influences among the variables are indicated by dependence links, annotated with a sign denoting the direction of the relationship. The link asserts that the variables are related monotonically, in a precise probabilistic sense elucidated below.[2]

According to the model, digitalis negatively influences conduction (con) and positively influences automaticity (aut). The former is the desired effect of the drug, because a decrease in conduction *decreases* the heart rate (hr), which is considered beneficial for patients with tachycardia, the population of interest here. The desirability of lower heart rates is represented by the negative influence on the value node, asserting that lower rates increase expected utility. This is obviously true only up to a point; a universal objective of therapy, after all, is to keep heart rates significantly above zero. Of course, conclusions drawn from these models must be qualified by the underlying assumption that the variables remain within the monotonic range of these relationships.

The increase in automaticity is an undesired side-effect of digitalis because this variable is positively related to the probability of ventricular fibrillation (vf), a life-threatening cardiac state. Calcium (Ca) and potassium (K) levels also influence the level of automaticity.

There are no links into the decision variable because the digitalis dosage is considered by the model to be under direct control.

---

[2]Discussion of qualitative synergies holding in this example is deferred to Section 4.7.

A qualitative encoding of this model is appropriate for the knowledge base of a general digitalis therapy program because a numeric description would require additional context information or be inaccurate. While the exact probabilistic relationships among these variables vary from patient to patient, the *directions* of the relations are reliably taken as constant. Conclusions drawn from this model are therefore valid for a broad class of patients.

The conclusions we would like our programs to derive from the digitalis model are those taken for granted in the description above. For example, we unthinkingly assumed that the effects of digitalis on conduction and of conduction on heart rate would combine to imply that digitalis reduces the heart rate. Further, because lower heart rates are desirable, digitalis is *therapeutic* along the upper path. Conversely, it is *toxic* along its lower path to the value node. The tradeoff between therapy and toxicity cannot be resolved by mere qualitative influences.

The immediate task of this chapter is to develop a semantics for these qualitative influences that justifies the kinds of inferences we require while providing the maximum robustness. In the sections below, I provide such a semantics in terms of a probabilistic definition for qualitative influences. In Section 4.5 we will see that this definition is the weakest in a reasonable class that justifies the conclusions mentioned above.

4.3 Qualitative Influences Defined

4.3.1 Influence Notation

The qualitative links in the digitalis model above can be represented formally as edges in the graph annotated by sign. Let $S^\delta(a, b, G)$ denote the assertion that a qualitative influence of a on b in direction (that is, sign) δ holds in graph $G = (V, Q)$.

Definition 4.1 (Qualitative influence edges) $S^\delta(a, b, G) \equiv (a, b, \delta) \in Q$, *for all* $\delta \in \{+, -, 0, ?\}$.

By convention, S^0 links are left implicit in graphical displays of the network. They would also typically be left implicit—inferable via a closed-world assumption—in data structures representing qualitative networks. For example, a representation of the QPN of Figure 4.1 would explicitly record $(dig, con, -)$ in Q, but would leave $(dig, vf, 0)$ implicit in the absence of a signed link.

The *pred* function selects only the predecessors exerting nonzero influence on a variable.

Definition 4.2 (predecessors)

$$pred_G(b) \equiv \{a \mid (a, b, \delta) \in Q, \text{ for some } \delta \in \{+, -, ?\}\},$$
$$pred_G^*(b) \equiv \bigcup_{c \in pred_G(b)} [\{c\} \cup pred_G^*(c)].$$

Note that for all $d \in D$, $pred_G(d) = \emptyset$. The subscript G is omitted when its value is clear from context.

4.3.2 Probabilistic Semantics for Qualitative Influences

Consider two variables, a and b. Informally, when a and b denote boolean events, a qualitative influence is a statement of the form "a makes b more (or less) likely." This binary case is easy to capture in a probabilistic assertion. Let A and $\bar{A}$ denote the assertions $a = \mathbf{true}$ and $a = \mathbf{false}$, respectively, and similarly, B and $\bar{B}$.

Definition 4.3 (binary S^+) *We say "a positively influences b" (stochastically) and write $S^+(a, b, G)$, iff for all $x \in X(pred_G(b) - \{a\})$ such that x is consistent with both A and $\bar{A}$,[3]*

$$\Pr(B|Ax) \geq \Pr(B|\bar{A}x). \tag{4.1}$$

In Definition 4.3, the *context* x ranges over all consistent assignments to the variables other than a that influence b. (Henceforth, x in a formula will be understood as universally quantified over the values of predecessor variables.) Thus, S^+ is analogous to Forbus's qualitative proportionality, α_{Q+} [42], which is an inequality on partial derivatives, also universally quantified over contexts. We need to include the *ceteris paribus* condition here and in the definitions below so that qualitative relations will be applicable in situations where x is partially or totally known. If we had stated the S^+ definition in marginal terms ("on average, a positively influences b"), it would not be valid to apply it in specific contexts.

Because its definition refers to a specific predecessor set, S^+ holds in a particular network; programs that alter the structure of the network may exhibit non-monotonicity in S^+ relative to its first two arguments [52]. In the following I omit the third argument only when the intended network is unambiguous or inessential.

Conditions analogous to (4.1) and those following define negative and zero influences; I omit them for brevity. S^0, an assertion that (4.1) holds with equality, is the familiar concept of conditional independence of a and b given b's direct influences. We could rule out the independent case with strict versions of S^+ and S^-, but discussion is limited to non-strict influences in this work.

$S^?$ always holds. It is included explicitly only so that we can represent S^0 implicitly in the lack of an influence assertion.

For dichotomous variables, it is not hard to show that Bayes's rule implies that (4.1) is equivalent to

$$\Pr(A|Bx) \geq \Pr(A|\bar{B}x). \tag{4.2}$$

In the terminology of Bayesian belief revision, (4.1) is a condition on *posteriors*, while (4.2) is a condition on *likelihoods*. Notice that $S^+(a, b)$ is simply an assertion that the *likelihood ratio* is greater than or equal to unity.

Formalizing the intuitive idea that "higher values of a make higher values of b more likely" is not quite as straightforward when a and b take on more than two values. An obvious prerequisite for such statements is some interpretation of "higher." Therefore, we require that each random variable appearing in an S^+ or S^- assertion be associated with

---

[3]We can safely ignore cases where the conditional probabilities are undefined because these are impossible contexts.

an order $\geq$ on its values. This relation has the usual interpretation for numeric variables such as "potassium concentration"; for variables like "automaticity," an ordering relation must be contrived.

The more troublesome part of defining positive influences is specifying what it means to "make higher values of b more likely." Intuitively, we want a statement that the probability distribution for b shifts toward higher values as a increases. To make such a statement, we need an ordering on cumulative probability distribution functions (CDFs) F_b over b that captures the notion of "higher."

However, probability distributions cannot be straightforwardly ordered according to the size of the random variable. Different rankings result from comparison of distributions by median, mean, or mean-log, for example. We require an ordering that is robust to changes of these measures because the random variables need be described by merely *ordinal* scales [80]. An assertion that calcium concentration positively influences automaticity should hold whether calcium is measured on an absolute or logarithmic scale, and regardless of how we measure automaticity.

An ordering criterion with the robustness we desire is *first-order stochastic dominance* (FSD) [178]. FSD holds for CDFs F_b and F_b' iff for any given value b_0 of b, the probability of obtaining b_0 or less is smaller for F_b than for F_b'. That is, F_b FSD F_b' iff

$$\forall b_0 \ F_b(b_0) \leq F_b'(b_0). \tag{4.3}$$

A necessary and sufficient condition for (4.3) is that for all monotonically increasing (that is, order-preserving) functions ϕ,

$$\int \phi(b_0) dF_b(b_0) \geq \int \phi(b_0) dF_b'(b_0). \tag{4.4}$$

That is, the mean of F_b is greater than the mean of F_b' for *any* monotonic transform of b. For further discussion and a proof that (4.3) is equivalent to (4.4), see [41].

We are now ready to define qualitative influences.

Definition 4.4 (S^+) *Let $F_b(\cdot|a_ix)$ be the CDF for b given $a = a_i$ and context x. Then $S^+(a, b)$ iff*

$$\forall a_1, a_2. \ a_1 \geq a_2 \Rightarrow F_b(\cdot|a_1x) \ \text{FSD} \ F_b(\cdot|a_2x). \tag{4.5}$$

Definition 4.4 is a generalization of Definition 4.3 under the convention that **true** > **false** for binary events.

Like (4.1), (4.5) is a condition on posteriors. A comparable definition of S^+ in terms of likelihoods must imply FSD of the posteriors for *any prior distribution* F_b. That is, we allow that there may be a context x inducing any distribution on b. Milgrom [100] proves that the following condition is necessary and sufficient for (4.5) to hold for any $F_b(\cdot|x)$.

$$\forall a_1, a_2, b_1, b_2. \ a_1 \geq a_2 \wedge b_1 \geq b_2 \Rightarrow \frac{f_a(a_1|b_1x)}{f_a(a_1|b_2x)} \geq \frac{f_a(a_2|b_1x)}{f_a(a_2|b_2x)}. \tag{4.6}$$

In (4.6), $f_a(\cdot|b_ix)$ is the probability density function for a given b_i and x.

This condition is known in statistics as the Monotone Likelihood Ratio Property (MLRP) [4]. The necessity of MLRP for (4.5) is established by the special case of dichotomous events. That (4.6) is a generalization of (4.2) is more clearly seen by rewriting the latter as

$$\frac{\Pr(A|Bx)}{\Pr(A|\bar{B}x)} \geq 1 \geq \frac{\Pr(\bar{A}|Bx)}{\Pr(\bar{A}|\bar{B}x)}. \tag{4.7}$$

For a demonstration of the sufficiency of MLRP, see Milgrom [100].

It is convenient to adopt special notation for influences on the value node v. The value node is related to its predecessors by a *utility function* $u : X(pred(v)) \rightarrow \Re$ [77].

Definition 4.5 (U^+) *The variable a positively influences utility, $U^+(a)$, iff*

$$\forall a_1, a_2.\ a_1 \geq a_2 \Rightarrow u(a_1, x) \geq u(a_2, x). \tag{4.8}$$

The definition of $U^+(a)$ is a special case of $S^+(a, v)$ taking into account the deterministic relation (a degenerate probability distribution) between v and its predecessors in the network.

4.4   Indirect Relationships

Edges in a graph of influence links constrain the direct relationship between pairs of variables. Our next step is to design inference mechanisms to derive the indirect relationships that follow from patterns of local influences.

First, let us define the *canonical direction* between two variables to be the strongest qualitative influence derivable from those explicitly appearing in Q. The canonical direction can be easily computed from Q by preferring an explicit 0 to the other δs (which are always consistent with 0 because the conditions are non-strict), preferring $+$ or $-$ to ?, and replacing the conjunction of $+$ and $-$ with 0.

Definition 4.6 (dir) *Let $\Delta = \{\delta \mid (a, b, \delta) \in Q\}$. The canonical direction of influence of a on b, $dir(a, b, G)$, is given by*

$$dir(a, b, G) = \begin{cases} undefined & if\ b \in pred_G^*(a) \\ 0 & if\ \Delta = \emptyset,\ 0 \in \Delta,\ or\ \{+, -\} \subseteq \Delta \\ + & if\ \Delta = \{+\}\ or\ \Delta = \{+, ?\} \\ - & if\ \Delta = \{-\}\ or\ \Delta = \{-, ?\} \\ ? & otherwise. \end{cases}$$

If $dir(a, b) = ?$ then a and b are dependent in an unknown, varying, or context-dependent direction.

4.4.1 Probabilistic Dependence in Graph Representations

Definition 4.7 (dep) *The dependency graph, dep(G), of G = (V, Q) is*

$$dep(G) = (V, E), \quad where \ (a, b) \in E \ \text{iff} \ dir(a, b, G) \neq 0$$

The dependency graph simply encodes the pattern of nonzero influences without distinguishing the signs on the links. Pearl [117] has characterized the expressiveness of these graphs with respect to the dependency structure of probability distributions. Some results of this work and terminology developed there will prove useful in analyzing the properties of QPNs.

In a directed acyclic graph representation, two variables are conditionally independent given any set of other variables that *d-separates* them in the graph.

Definition 4.8 (d-separation, Pearl [112]) *Two variables a and b are* d-separated *by a set of variables S in a directed acyclic graph iff for every* undirected *path from a to b either:*

1. *there is a node $s \in S$ on the path with at least one of the incident edges leading out of s, or*

2. *there is a node t on the path with both incident edges leading in, and neither t nor any of its successors are in S.*

The concept of d-separation is illustrated by the network of Figure 4.2.

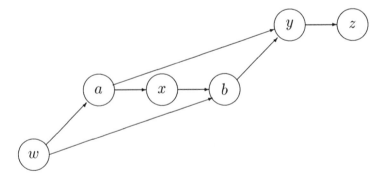

Figure 4.2: Variables a and b are *d-separated* by $\{w, x\}$ but by no other subset of $\{w, x, y, z\}$.

The following implication of Definition 4.8 is useful in justifying the inference rules for QPNs presented below.

Lemma 4.9 *If $b \notin pred_G^*(a)$ then a and b are d-separated in dep(G) by any S such that $pred_G(b) \subseteq S \subseteq \{s | b \notin pred_G^*(s)\}$.*

For convenience, all proofs are relegated to Appendix B.

Taking $S = pred_G(b)$, this result is the basis for our closed-world assumption that $dir(a, b, G) = 0$ if there are no explicit influences in Q. If in addition there are no directed paths from b to a, we adopt the default influence $S^0(a,b)$. In Pearl's terminology, this assumption is valid when $dep(G)$ is an I-map—a graph for which all d-separations are true conditional independencies.

4.4.2 Network Transformations

We answer queries about relations among separated variables in a QPN by transforming the graph into one where the variables of interest are related directly. The method is based on Shachter's algorithm for evaluating numeric influence diagrams [136] by repeated reductions and arc reversals. Each manipulation preserves the probabilistic relationships—qualitative in our case—holding among variables in the possibly smaller set V. It is possible via sequences of these manipulations to answer queries about the relationships among any subset of variables in the network [137].

The two basic network transformation operators are reduction (red) and reversal (rev). The reduced network $red(b,G)$ is the qualitative probabilistic network obtained by splicing variable b out of G and adjusting qualitative influences as dictated by Theorem 4.11 below. The reversed network $rev(a,b,G)$ is obtained from G by replacing $(a,b,\delta) \in Q$ with the influence (b,a,δ) and updating other influences as specified in Theorem 4.12.

Let $G' = (V',Q')$ be the result of one of these transformation operations. For simplicity we adopt the convention that Q' contains only the canonical directions. The relation between Q and Q' is described in Section 4.4.3 below. Both the red and rev operations preserve essential properties of the networks:

- $dep(G')$ is acyclic.

- $dep(G')$ is an I-map.

4.4.3 Variable Reductions

It can be demonstrated for the binary case that, in the absence of direct links from a to c, $S^+(a,b,G) \wedge S^+(b,c,G) \Rightarrow S^+(a,c,red(b,G))$. The ability to perform inference across influence chains is an essential property of a qualitative algebra. From the digitalis model, for example, we would like to deduce that increasing the dose of digitalis decreases the heart rate but increases the likelihood of ventricular fibrillation. Indeed, most programs with models like this would make such an inference. Fortunately, the definition offered above for S^+ implies transitivity for multi-valued as well as binary variables.

Theorem 4.10

$$S^{\delta_1}(a,b,G) \wedge S^{\delta_2}(b,c,G) \wedge S^0(a,c,G) \Rightarrow S^{\delta_1 \otimes \delta_2}(a,c,red(b,G)),$$

where $\delta_i \in \{+,-,0,?\}$ and $\otimes$ denotes sign multiplication, described by Table 4.1.

Application of Theorem 4.10 requires that no direct influences exist between a and c. A more general specification of the result of variable reduction is the following:

$\otimes$	+	−	0	?
+	+	−	0	?
−	−	+	0	?
0	0	0	0	0
?	?	?	0	?

$\oplus$	+	−	0	?
+	+	?	+	?
−	?	−	−	?
0	+	−	0	?
?	?	?	?	?

Table 4.1: The $\otimes$ operator for combining influence chains and the $\oplus$ operator for combining parallel influences. For example, $+ \otimes - = -$. The operations commute, associate, and distribute like ordinary multiplication and addition.

Theorem 4.11

$$S^{\delta_1}(a,b,G) \wedge S^{\delta_2}(b,c,G) \wedge S^{\delta_3}(a,c,G) \Rightarrow S^{(\delta_1 \otimes \delta_2) \oplus \delta_3}(a,c,red(b,G)), \qquad (4.9)$$

where $\oplus$ denotes sign addition, also described in Table 4.1.

Theorem 4.10 is really a corollary of Theorem 4.11 with $\delta_3 = 0$, the identity element for $\oplus$.

This result tells us how to update the direction between pairs of predecessors and successors of a reduced variable. When the reduced variable has at most one successor, Theorem 4.11 covers all necessary changes to the network. When there are multiple successors, however, the removal may render them dependent, as the modified network does not contain the original d-separating set. To reflect these dependencies, we must add new influences among these variables. One way to compute the new relations is to reverse all but one of the successor links according to the procedure of the next section, then perform reduction as described above.

We can solve some special problems using reduction transformations exclusively. If the variables can be ordered for reduction so that they have at most one successor when reduced, the updating rule of Theorem 4.11 is sufficient. For example, to find the qualitative influence of a on b given a set of variables W for any $a \in pred^*(b)$ and $pred^*(a) \subseteq W \subseteq pred^*(b)$ we need only splice out all other variables in the network. The restrictions on a and W ensure that the variables can be ordered for simple reduction. Because each application of reduction rule (4.9) reduces the number of influence edges (including zeroes) in the network by one, the complexity of this procedure is $O(|V|^2)$.[4] This contrasts with the corresponding problem for numeric probabilistic networks, which is NP-hard [19]. Some sample reduction sequences are displayed in Table 4.2.

4.4.4 Influence Reversals

The procedure developed above is valid when a precedes b in the network and the variables of W are intermediate between the two. Often, however, the network is such that the

---

[4]Since it is possible to construct cases where this algorithm requires $\Omega(|V|^2)$ operations, its overall complexity is $\Theta(|V|^2)$.

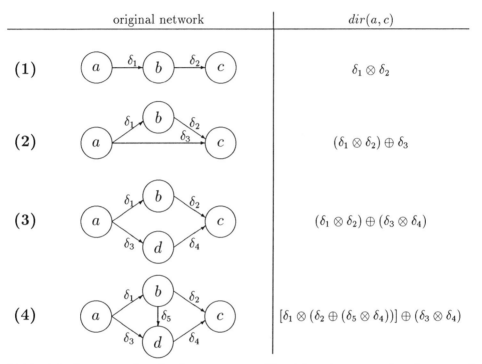

Table 4.2: Some sample reduction sequences. The right column contains the expression for $dir(a,c)$ in the network obtained by removing nodes between a and c. Fragments (1) and (2) correspond to the situations of Theorems 4.10 and 4.11, respectively. When $a \in pred^*(b)$, the relation with all intermediate variables reduced is simply the sign sum of all directed paths from a to b.

qualitative influence of a on b cannot be determined by any sequence of single-successor reductions. In such cases we need to perform one or more reversals in the network before or after applying the methods of the previous section.

In reversing a qualitative influence link, we must preserve the essential properties mentioned in Section 4.4.2 above. To ensure acyclicity, we can reverse the influence from a to b only if there are no other directed paths between them. Reversal is also precluded if a is a decision variable. To guarantee that the dependency structure is valid after reversal (that is, $G' = rev(a, b, G)$ is an I-map), we generally have to insert additional links. As demonstrated by Shachter [137], it is sufficient that each of the two variables gain the other's predecessors:

$$pred_{G'}(a) = pred_{G'}(b) = pred_G(a) \cup pred_G(b).$$

The definition for $S^\delta(a, b)$ (4.4) explicitly refers to the predecessors of b. Therefore, when the predecessor structure changes we need to recompute the influences that may be affected. The following result describes the influences holding after reversal.

Theorem 4.12 Let $G' = rev(a, b, G)$. G' inherits all the qualitative influences of G except:

1. $dir(a, b, G')$ is undefined.

2. $dir(b, a, G') = dir(a, b, G)$.

3. $\forall w \in pred_{G'}(b)$,

$$dir(w, b, G') = [dir(w, a, G) \otimes dir(a, b, G)] \oplus dir(w, b, G).$$

4. $\forall w \in pred_{G'}(a) - \{b\}$,

$$dir(w, a, G') = \begin{cases} dir(w, a, G) & \text{if } dir(w, b, G) = 0 \\ ? & \text{otherwise} \end{cases}$$
$$= dir(w, a, G) \oplus (dir(w, b, G) \otimes ?).$$

This transformation is illustrated in Figure 4.3.

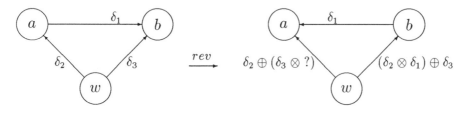

Figure 4.3: Influence reversal.

Some information may be lost in the process of reversing influences. For example, let $G'' = rev(a, b, rev(a, b, G))$, the network obtained by reversing an influence then reversing it again. Application of Theorem 4.12 twice yields the result depicted in Figure 4.4. Although the link from a to b is correct, the reversal process weakens the other links. More generally, the prospect of information lost suggests that the strategy for transforming a network may have significant impact on the strength of conclusions obtained. Analysis of this and related issues can be found in another paper focusing on inferential properties of QPNs [175].

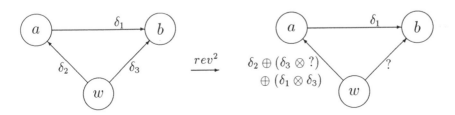

Figure 4.4: Information lost in a double reversal of the influence from a to b.

4.5 Necessity Results

The preceding sections establish that the FSD condition for S^+ (Definition 4.4) is sufficient to support essential inferences such as the chaining of influences. In this section I present some simple desiderata for a qualitative influence definition that entail the *necessity* of FSD for these properties.

4.5.1 Posterior Conditions

I start by specifying the form such definitions must take. To capture the intent of "higher values of a make higher values of b more likely" in a probabilistic semantics, it seems reasonable to restrict attention to conditions on the posterior distribution of b for increasing values of a. Therefore, I postulate that a definition of $S^+(a, b)$ must be of the form

$$\forall a_1, a_2.\ a_1 \geq a_2 \Rightarrow F_b(\cdot | a_1 x)\ R\ F_b(\cdot | a_2 x), \tag{4.10}$$

where R is some relation on CDFs. This condition is exactly (4.5) with FSD replaced by the more abstract relation.

There are two basic desiderata that severely restrict the possible Rs. First, S^+ must satisfy Theorem 4.10. Without the ability to chain inferences, the qualitative influence formalism has little computational value. Second, the condition must be a generalization of the original specification of S^+ for dichotomous variables (Definition 4.3). With only two possible values this appears to be a minimal monotonicity condition. These criteria lead to a sharp conclusion.

Theorem 4.13 *Let $S^+(a, b)$ be defined by (4.10). Given the following conditions:*

1. *Theorem 4.10*

2. *For binary b, $a_1 \geq a_2$, and x,*

$$F_b(\cdot|a_1x) \; R \; F_b(\cdot|a_2x) \Leftrightarrow \Pr(B|a_1x) \geq \Pr(B|a_2x)$$

the weakest R is FSD.

The force of this result is weakened somewhat by the *a priori* restriction of definitions to those having the form of (4.10). Many statistical concepts of directional relation (based on correlation or joint expectations, for example) do not fit (4.10) yet appear to be plausible candidates for a definition of qualitative influence. *Quadrant dependence* [87] holds between a and b when[5]

$$\forall a_1, a_2. \; a_1 \geq a_2 \Rightarrow F_b(\cdot|a \leq a_1) \text{ FSD } F_b(\cdot|a \leq a_2). \tag{4.11}$$

Lehmann proves that quadrant dependence is necessary but not sufficient for *regression dependence*, which is his terminology for (4.5) without the quantification over contexts x. As quadrant dependence is weaker, yet still exhibits transitivity,[6] it seems to be an attractive alternative to regression dependence. To justify our choice of the latter, we must consider the decision-making implications of probabilistic models.

4.5.2 Decision-Making with Qualitative Influences

The prime motivation for adopting a probabilistic semantics is so that the behavior of our programs can be justified by Bayesian decision theory [134]. A decision of d_1 over d_2 (that is, such a choice of assignments to decision variables) is valid with respect to a QPN if the network entails greater expected utility for the former. The most useful distinctions to make in designing a qualitative representation are those that will support inferences about properties of the valid decisions.

For example, if a positively influences utility (Definition 4.5) and there are no *indirect* paths from decision variable a to the value node, then a choice of a_1 over a_2 is valid iff $a_1 \geq a_2$.[7] Decision-making power is enhanced if we can deduce new influences on utility from chains of influences in the network. Our definition of qualitative influence is necessary as well as sufficient for such inferences.

Theorem 4.14 *Suppose $U^{\delta_2}(b, G)$ and $U^0(a, G)$. A necessary and sufficient condition for $U^{\delta_1 \otimes \delta_2}(a, red(b, G))$ is $S^{\delta_1}(a, b, G)$ as in Definition 4.4.*

Figure 4.5 depicts this situation with $\delta_2 = +$.

---

[5]This is actually the condition Lehmann proposes as a strengthening of quadrant dependence. The basic quadrant dependence fixes a_1 at a's maximal value.

[6]For transitivity we need to quantify over contexts in (4.11). The proof parallels that for Theorem 4.10.

[7]The existence of other paths from a to utility would leave open the possibility that the net influence of a is negative. For example, we could summarize the therapeutic effect of digitalis through conduction and heart rate as a direct positive influence. But this might be outweighed by the indirect negative influence of digitalis via automaticity.

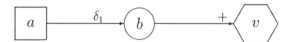

Figure 4.5: Chaining utility influences. The influence $\delta_1 = +$ in G is necessary and sufficient for $U^+(a, red(b, G))$.

Theorem 4.14 demonstrates that while conditions weaker than S^+, such as quadrant dependence, may be sufficient for propagating influences across chains, they are not adequate to justify *decisions* across chains. For choosing among alternatives, the relevant parameter is the utility function evaluated at a point; utilities conditioned on intervals of the decision variable (as in quadrant dependence) do not have the same decision-making import.

4.5.3 Simpson's Paradox

Because qualitative influences are based on simple intuitive relationships, they may provide insight into qualitatively counterintuitive situations. One celebrated example is Simpson's paradox, in which a factor is shown to have positive impact on some result in all contexts (precisely the definition of S^+), yet its overall influence is negative.

In an instance presented by Blyth [5], patients given an experimental treatment have an increased chance of survival in each of two test cities. However, when the statistics from the cities are pooled, it turns out that patients with the treatment have a *decreased* survival probability. How is this possible? In this example, the population of $city_1$ have a significantly better prognosis and patients from $city_2$ are more likely to be treated. Thus, a treated patient is more likely to come from $city_2$ and is therefore less likely to survive.

A QPN modeling this example would have qualitative influences $S^+(treat, survive)$, $S^+(city, survive)$ (adopting the convention $city_1 > city_2$), and $S^-(treat, city)$. Reducing *city* according to (4.9) leads to the ambiguous conclusion $S^?(treat, survive)$, indicating that Simpson's paradox is a possibility in this circumstance.

If there had been no interaction between the likelihood of treatment and the patient's residence, or if the interaction had been in the other direction, Simpson's paradox could not arise. The following is a direct consequence of the QPN update rules, Theorems 4.11 and 4.12.

Corollary 4.15 *Suppose $V = \{a, b, c\}$ and $S^+(a, c, G)$, and let $\delta_{a,b}$ be $dir(b, a, G)$ or $dir(a, b, G)$, whichever is defined. A necessary condition for Simpson's paradox to apply for a and c with respect to b is:*

$$\delta_{a,b} \otimes dir(b, c, G) \in \{-, ?\}.$$

Although the phenomena surrounding Simpson's paradox are well understood, QPNs provide a convenient language for expressing these enabling conditions.[8] With a, b, and c standing for *treat*, *city*, and *survive*, respectively, the result applies directly to the example above. (Incidentally, if the residence of the patient is known at the time of a treatment decision, the model correctly mandates that the treatment should be administered.)

4.6 Back to the Digitalis Model

To summarize the discussion of qualitative influences thus far, let us return to the digitalis example presented in Section 4.2.2. We are interested in computing the effect of the decision variable, *dig*, on utility. The network of Figure 4.1 reduces to the one depicted in Figure 4.6a, which further reduces to that of 4.6b.

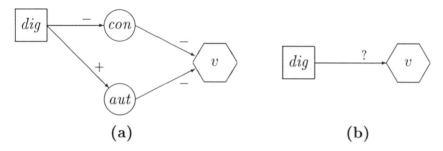

(a) **(b)**

Figure 4.6: Reduction of the digitalis model. (a) Digitalis is therapeutic in its effect on conduction but toxic via the influence on automaticity. (b) The overall effect of digitalis cannot be resolved with qualitative influences.

The result, not surprisingly, is ambiguous. Purely qualitative influences are too weak to determine optimal decisions in the presence of true tradeoffs. Nevertheless, the QPN is sufficient to determine some influences (for example, calcium on ventricular fibrillation), and uncovers the source of indeterminacy in others.

In the next section, a second type of qualitative relationship is introduced: qualitative synergy. Synergies complement influences by constraining the interactions among probabilistic influences. Although synergies cannot resolve the tradeoff of Figure 4.6b, they can provide useful facts about the relation of the optimal digitalis dosage to other variables in the model.

4.7 Qualitative Synergy

Swartout's XPLAIN knowledge base includes the "domain principle" that if a state variable acts synergistically with the drug to induce toxicity, then smaller doses should be given

---

[8]See Neufeld and Horton [107] for a discussion of Simpson's paradox in the context of another formalism based on probabilistic inequalities.

for higher observed values of the variable [155]. This fact could be derived by a *domain-independent* inference procedure given a suitable definition for qualitative synergy. Two variables synergistically influence a third if their joint influence is greater (in the sense of FSD) than separate, statistically independent influences. In the digitalis example, we need to assert that digitalis acts at least independently with Ca and K deviations in increasing automaticity. For the desired result, we also need the fact that heart rate and ventricular fibrillation are synergistic in their influence on utility. (This synergy is due to our indifference to heart rate—indeed it is undefined—for patients in fibrillation. The relation of this indifference to synergy is clarified in Section 4.7.7 below.)

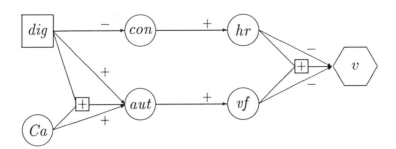

Figure 4.7: The digitalis model with synergy. A boxed sign indicates that the inputs are qualitatively synergistic in their influence on the output.

Figure 4.7 illustrates the QPN for digitalis enhanced by synergy assertions. Potassium (K) is omitted for simplicity; its implications are analogous (with sign reversal) to those for calcium. Qualitative synergies are indicated by a boxed sign with multiple inputs and a single output. The input variables are synergistic in the designated direction in their influence on the output variable.

4.7.1 Synergy Notation

Qualitative synergies are the second type of qualitative relationship represented in Q for a QPN $G = (V, Q)$. As qualitative influences are directed edges augmented by sign, qualitative synergies are directed hyper-edges with a sign label. A qualitative synergy assertion that the variables in $T \subset V$ are synergistic in direction δ on variable w is written $Y^\delta(T, w, G)$.

Definition 4.16 (Qualitative synergy hyper-edges) $Y^\delta(T, w, G) \equiv (T, w, \delta) \in Q$.

4.7.2 Qualitative Synergy Defined

A formal definition of qualitative synergy must capture the informal intuition expressed above that the "joint influence is greater than separate statistically independent influences." This will be the case when the effect of varying one variable is enhanced by simultaneous variation of the other.

70

The joint influence of two variables a and b on a third, c, is expressed by the conditional cumulative distribution for c, $F_c(\cdot|ab)$. To compare magnitude of "influence," we need some reference points. One way to measure a difference in influence is to take the difference of two conditional CDFs. Two variables are synergistic if the difference associated with raising one is greater (in the sense of FSD) for higher values of the second.

Definition 4.17 (qualitative synergy, Y^δ) *Variables a and b are synergistic on c in network G, written $Y^+(\{a,b\},c,G)$ iff*
$$\forall a_1, a_2, b_1, b_2, c_0.\ a_1 \geq a_2 \wedge b_1 \geq b_2 \Rightarrow$$

$$F_c(c_0|a_1 b_1 x) - F_c(c_0|a_2 b_1 x) \leq F_c(c_0|a_1 b_2 x) - F_c(c_0|a_2 b_2 x). \tag{4.12}$$

Replacing $\leq$ in condition (4.12) by $\geq$ or $=$ defines sub-synergy or zero synergy (Y^- and Y^0), respectively. If the variable set T in $Y^\delta(T,w,G)$ contains more than two elements, the condition above holds for all pairs of variables in T.

As usual, x ranges over assignments to the other predecessors of c.

The inequality (4.12) quantified over c_0 can be viewed as stochastic dominance of the respective distributions of CDF differences. The condition means that raising a from a_2 to a_1 has a greater effect for higher values of b. Note that the inequality is symmetric in a and b.

If $S^0(a,c)$, then $Y^0(\{a,w\},c)$ follows immediately for any variable $w \in pred^*(c)$ because of conditional independence. With conditional independence, $F_c(\cdot|a_1 wx) = F_c(\cdot|a_2 wx)$ for all w and x, therefore both sides of equation (4.12) are zero.

Lacking an explicit synergy assertion for two or more variables that are predecessors of another, the prudent closed-world assumption is $Y^?$: no constraint on their interaction.[9] Although it is reasonable to assume S^0 in the absence of knowledge to the contrary, in this case, the variables are tied by a common immediate successor. They are *not* d-separated by this successor, and interactions in situations with this pattern are quite common.

Fortunately, there are several prototypical patterns of systematic interaction that might alleviate the burden of specifying qualitative synergies. One that has attracted some interest in the literature on numeric probabilistic networks is the "noisy OR gate" model proposed by Pearl [114, Chapter 4].

In the noisy OR model, the binary-valued predecessors of a binary "effect" variable are considered separate possible causes of the effect. Each "cause" variable is associated with a parameter p_i representing the probability of the effect given that this variable is true and all other predecessors are false. We can compute the rest of the conditional probabilities for y under the assumption that the "inhibiting events" that prevent Y given each Z_i are independent. For effect variable y with predecessors $z_1, \ldots, z_n$, the conditional probabilities are:

$$\Pr(Y|z_1 \ldots z_n) = 1 - \prod_{\{i|Z_i\}} (1 - p_i). \tag{4.13}$$

---

[9]In the examples of this section, all synergies are specified explicitly.

Regardless of the magnitudes of the p_is, the noisy OR model entails sub-synergy, Y^-. To see this, consider the Y^- condition ((4.12) with the inequality reversed) for the special case of binary variables. $Y^-(\{z_j, z_k\}, y)$ iff:

$$\forall x \in X(\{z_i | i \neq j \land i \neq k\})$$
$$\Pr(Y | Z_j Z_k x) - \Pr(Y | \bar{Z}_j Z_k x) \leq \Pr(Y | Z_j \bar{Z}_k x) - \Pr(Y | \bar{Z}_j \bar{Z}_k x). \qquad (4.14)$$

Let

$$p_x = \prod_{Z(x)} (1 - p_i), \text{ where } Z(x) = \{i | Z_i \text{ in assignment } x\}.$$

Then from the noisy OR model (4.13),

$$\Pr(Y | Z_j Z_k x) - \Pr(Y | \bar{Z}_j Z_k x) = p_x p_j (1 - p_k), \text{ and} \qquad (4.15)$$
$$\Pr(Y | Z_j \bar{Z}_k x) - \Pr(Y | \bar{Z}_j \bar{Z}_k x) = p_x p_j. \qquad (4.16)$$

Because $0 \leq p_k \leq 1$, the expression in (4.15) is no greater than that of (4.16), satisfying the binary Y^- condition (4.14). Figure 4.8 illustrates the relation between a numeric probabilistic network using the noisy OR model and its corresponding QPN.

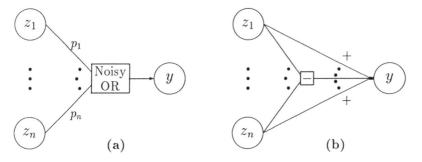

Figure 4.8: (a) The "noisy OR" model, and (b) its corresponding qualitative abstraction.

It is also easy to verify that Henrion's generalizations of the noisy OR model [59] entail Y^-. Intuitively, a noisy OR is sub-synergistic because, as with deterministic OR gates, raising an input has less effect when other inputs are already raised. In contrast, a model based on a probabilistic generalization of "gating conditions" (see Rieger and Grinberg [126]) would be synergistic because an increase in one variable enables the effect of the other. More generally, we should expect non-"?" synergy results from canonical models because any representation that specifies an n-way influence in terms of $O(n)$ parameters must employ some systematic assumption about interactions.[10]

---

[10]Dempster's rule of combination is also sub-synergistic under an analogous definition of synergy in terms of belief functions [139]. A demonstration of this requires further assumptions regarding how to interpret conditioning as evidence combination.

4.7.3 Supermodularity, Y^δ, and Monotone Decisions

The Y^δ definition relates closely to the concept of *supermodular* functions [128, 161].

Definition 4.18 (supermodularity, Ross [128]) *A function g such that, for all $a_1 \geq a_2$ and $b_1 \geq b_2$:*

$$g(a_1, b_1) + g(a_2, b_2) \geq g(a_1, b_2) + g(a_2, b_1) \tag{4.17}$$

is called supermodular. *If (4.17) holds with equality, then g is* modular, *and if the inequality is reversed, g is* submodular.

The most important property of supermodular functions, from our perspective, is that they imply *monotone decisions*. Let the function $a_g(b)$ choose the value of a that maximizes g for the given b.

$$a_g(b) = \arg\max_a g(a, b).$$

It can be shown that $a_g(\cdot)$ increases monotonically in b if g is supermodular (see Ross [128, p. 6]).

The following result clarifies the connection between Y^δ and supermodularity.

Lemma 4.19 $Y^+(\{a, b\}, c)$ *(respectively Y^- and Y^0) holds iff the function*

$$e_\phi(a, b|x) = \int \phi(c_0) f_c(c_0|abx) dc_0$$

is supermodular (submodular, modular) in a and b for all increasing functions ϕ and contexts x.

The function e_ϕ is the expectation of c under the monotonic transform ϕ. The equivalence between *sub*modularity for all c (Definition 4.17, the Y^+ condition) and *su*permodularity of expectations for all ϕ is reminiscent of the correspondence between the FSD condition (4.3) and increasing expectations for all ϕ (4.4).

Once again, it is useful to define special notation for synergistic influences on the value node.

Definition 4.20 (Y_U^δ) *Variables a and b are synergistic on utility, $Y_U^\delta(\{a, b\}, G)$, for $\delta = +, -, 0$, iff u is supermodular, submodular, or modular, respectively, in a and b.*

Note that $Y_U^\delta(T, G)$ is weaker than $Y^\delta(T, v, G)$, as the condition on u need not hold for all monotonic transformations.

In the terminology of utility theory, δ-modularity expresses *multiattribute risk aversion, proneness,* or *neutrality* as δ is $-$, $+$, or 0, respectively [34, 125]. Multiattribute risk neutrality is equivalent to additive separability for u [40], as suggested by the form of the modularity condition (4.17).

The correspondence between Y_U^δ and supermodularity is useful because of the monotone decision property of supermodular functions. Consider the situation of Figure 4.9. There we have $Y_U^+(\{a, b\})$ even though $dir(a, v) = dir(b, v) = ?$. Qualitative influences alone tell us nothing about which value we should choose for the decision variable a. Positive synergy, on the other hand, implies that if b is observable, our policy should be to choose higher values of a for greater values of the observed b. While this still does not reveal the exact value of the optimal a, it dictates the *form* that our strategy should take.

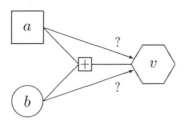

Figure 4.9: Synergistic influence on utility. Even though $U^?(a)$ and $U^?(b)$ we can deduce that the optimal choice of a is increasing in b.

4.7.4 Propagation of Synergies in Networks

The mechanisms for deducing indirect synergies that hold in a QPN are analogous to the network transformation techniques for qualitative influences developed in Section 4.4. In particular, we can extend qualitative synergies through qualitative influences by variable reduction.

Theorem 4.21 *Synergies can be extended along qualitative influences by reduction according to the following:*

$$Y^{\delta_1}(\{a,b\},c,G) \wedge S^{\delta_2}(c,d,G) \wedge S^0(a,d,G) \wedge S^0(b,d,G) \Rightarrow$$
$$Y^{\delta_1 \otimes \delta_2}(\{a,b\},d,red(c,G)).$$

This reduction is depicted in Figure 4.10.

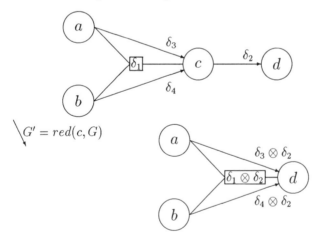

Figure 4.10: Propagation of synergy through qualitative influences. Values for $dir(a,d,G')$ and $dir(b,d,G')$ follow from Theorem 4.10. The new synergy $Y^{\delta_1 \otimes \delta_2}$ is the result of Theorem 4.21.

Like Theorem 4.10, Theorem 4.21 requires that there be no direct influences among the variables newly linked in the reduced QPN. The next result provides the reduction rule for the more general case.

Theorem 4.22

$$Y^{\delta_1}(\{a,b\},c,G) \wedge S^{\delta_2}(c,d,G) \wedge Y^{\delta_3}(\{a,c\},d,G) \wedge Y^{\delta_4}(\{b,c\},d,G)$$
$$\wedge S^{\delta_5}(a,c,G) \wedge S^{\delta_6}(b,c,G) \wedge Y^{\delta_7}(\{a,b\},d,G) \Rightarrow$$
$$Y^{(\delta_1 \otimes \delta_2) \oplus (\delta_3 \otimes \delta_6) \oplus (\delta_4 \otimes \delta_5) \oplus \delta_7}(\{a,b\},d,red(c,G)). \tag{4.18}$$

Theorem 4.22 generalizes Theorem 4.21 because $S^0(a,d,G) \wedge S^0(b,d,G) \Rightarrow \delta_3 = \delta_4 = \delta_7 = 0$ by conditional independence.

Note that the signs of direct influences from a and b to d do not affect the synergy propagation, though the signs of influences on c do. This more complicated situation is illustrated in Figure 4.11 below.

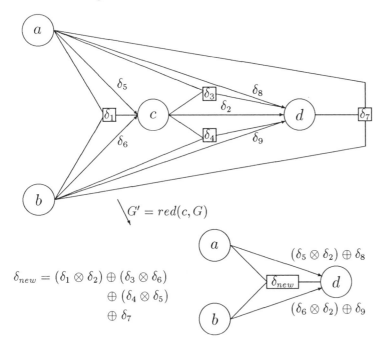

Figure 4.11: Variable reduction with parallel synergies.

A special case of the foregoing results demonstrates how to propagate synergies *backwards* through qualitative influences. Upon reduction, a variable's predecessors assume its role in all synergies, with modified signs reflecting the direction of the predecessor's influence.

Corollary 4.23

$$Y^{\delta_3}(\{a,c\},d,G) \wedge S^{\delta_6}(b,c,G) \wedge S^0(a,c,G) \Rightarrow Y^{\delta_3 \otimes \delta_6}(\{a,b\},d,red(c,G)).$$

The result follows from the assignment $\delta_1 = \delta_5 = \delta_7 = 0$ in Theorem 4.22. (The zero synergy of a and b on c, δ_1, follows from the zero influence of a on c, δ_5.) Application of Corollary 4.23 is illustrated in Figure 4.12.

75

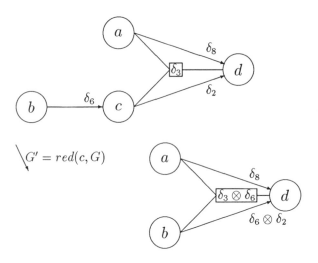

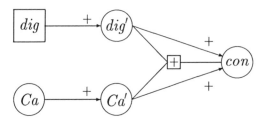

Figure 4.12: Backwards propagation of synergies through qualitative influences.

For an example of the use of backwards propagation, consider a synergy relation from the digitalis model. In the more detailed model of Figure 4.13, the effects of variables *dig* (digitalis dosage) and *Ca* (measured serum calcium) would be mediated by *dig'* and *Ca'*, the actual concentrations of digitalis and calcium in the bloodstream. Even though the synergy assertion is in terms of the physiological parameters, we can deduce synergy on the practically relevant proxy variables by reduction according to Corollary 4.23.

Figure 4.13: An elaboration of a digitalis model fragment. Variables *dig* and *Ca* represent dosage and measurement, respectively, while the primed versions are actual concentrations. The unprimed variables are synergistic by reduction of *dig'* and *Ca'*.

Though the definition for Y_U^δ differs from Y^δ, the synergy update rule (4.18) also holds when *d* is the value node and Y_U is substituted for Y as appropriate. In fact, for backwards propagation the Y_U^δ condition is *exactly* preserved.

Theorem 4.24 *Given* $S^{\delta_6}(b, c, G)$ *and* $S^0(a, c, G)$, $Y_U^{\delta_3}(\{a, c\}, G)$ *is both necessary and sufficient for* $Y_U^{\delta_3 \otimes \delta_6}(\{a, b\}, red(c, G))$.

A canonical decision situation with the above form is the estimation problem from statistics. The problem is to choose an estimate *a* of the true "state of nature" θ given only an observation z that is statistically related to θ. Karlin and Rubin [75] demonstrate that if

1. the optimal estimate is increasing in θ (the monotone decision property of Section 4.7.3),

2. utility decreases away from the optimum, and

3. z is related to θ by the MLRP (the likelihood condition for S^+ (4.6), Section 4.3.2),

then a and z also satisfy the monotone decision property.

By representing the estimation problem as the QPN of Figure 4.14, we see that the sufficiency part of Theorem 4.24 is a similar result, with the monotone decision property replaced by the stronger condition of qualitative synergy. Synergy seems justified for the estimation problem because the relative value of a higher estimate increases with the state of nature.

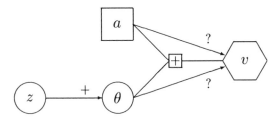

Figure 4.14: A qualitative probabilistic network for the estimation problem.

The applicability of the setup in Figure 4.14 goes well beyond estimation. Suppose the state of nature θ represents an unobservable disease severity and the decision variable a the aggressiveness of therapy. Choosing a therapy level is similar to estimating the severity of disease, as more serious conditions call for stricter treatments. It is essential that a program be capable of inferring the qualitative implications for therapy of any symptom z related to disease severity in a known direction.

4.7.5 Synergy Reversal

Synergies must also be updated upon reversal of a link. Consider a reversal of the influence from c to d in the network of Figure 4.11 (top half). Synergies on d are revised (or newly created) according to the following rule.

Theorem 4.25

$$Y^{\delta_1}(\{a,b\}, c, G) \wedge S^{\delta_2}(c, d, G) \wedge Y^{\delta_3}(\{a,c\}, d, G) \wedge Y^{\delta_4}(\{b,c\}, d, G)$$
$$\wedge S^{\delta_5}(a, c, G) \wedge S^{\delta_6}(b, c, G) \wedge Y^{\delta_7}(\{a,b\}, d, G) \Rightarrow$$
$$Y^{(\delta_1 \otimes \delta_2) \oplus (\delta_3 \otimes \delta_6) \oplus (\delta_4 \otimes \delta_5) \oplus \delta_7}(\{a,b\}, d, rev(c, d, G)).$$

After reversal, the possibility of interactions with d render all synergies on c ambiguous. Synergies on variables other than c or d are unaffected by the operation.

4.7.6 Landmark Values

The monotone decision property can be used to develop a concept of *landmark values* for QPNs analogous to the landmark value concept in qualitative simulation [82]. A landmark value is any distinguished point in the domain of a variable. Their usefulness to qualitative reasoning accrues when landmark values of several variables correspond in a meaningful way or the point has some other qualitative significance for the application.

In QPNs, the interesting landmarks are optimal values of decision variables and the corresponding values of observable non-decision variables. Suppose that in the disease-severity interpretation of Figure 4.14, the variable z represents an observable symptom with a specially designated "normal" value of z^*. There is a corresponding landmark value of the decision variable, a^*, representing the optimal level of therapy given $z = z^*$. The value of a^* may be known to the program, especially if there is documented experience with z-normal patients, everything else being equal. Even if its exact value is not known, or if it depends on other variables, the a^* concept has meaning as a landmark value in terms of its optimality property.

Suppose further that a patient presents with an elevated z-value of $z' > z^*$. The qualitative implication drawn from our model is that the corresponding optimal therapy a' is increased, $a' \geq a^*$, all else being equal. As correspondences in the quantity space [42] are known in finer detail, the program can determine optimal strategies with increasing precision.

4.7.7 Synergy in the Digitalis Example

To complete our discussion of qualitative synergy, let us return to the digitalis model of Figure 4.7. As promised, I start by justifying the synergy relation between hr and vf.

Consider two heart rates, $hr_1 \geq hr_2$, and the two values of the binary variable vf. The synergy condition, $Y_U^+(\{hr, vf\})$, is an instantiation of Definition 4.20:

$$u(hr_1, VF) - u(hr_2, VF) \geq u(hr_1, \overline{VF}) - u(hr_2, \overline{VF}). \tag{4.19}$$

Given VF, the heart rate is irrelevant (and ill-defined because ventricular fibrillation is a state where the heart is not contracting regularly). Therefore, the left-hand side of (4.19) is zero. For patients *not* in fibrillation, lower heart rates are preferable, by $U^-(hr)$, at least within the range considered here. This implies that the right-hand side of (4.19) is negative, satisfying the inequality.

By applying the results of Section 4.7.4, we can successively reduce any variables positioned between the ones of interest. Figure 4.15 shows the result of removing all but dig, Ca, and v. The final step, transformation from the fragment of Figure 4.15a to that of 4.15b, requires parallel combination of synergies using Theorem 4.22.

The final result of the exercise is that while the value of administering digitalis is ambiguous, by $U^?(dig)$, we can deduce that the optimal dosage is a decreasing function of calcium, by $Y_U^-(\{dig, Ca\})$. The more detailed model of Figure 4.13 showed us that this result holds whether we are talking about the actual substance concentrations in the bloodstream or about the amounts administered and measured by imperfect means.

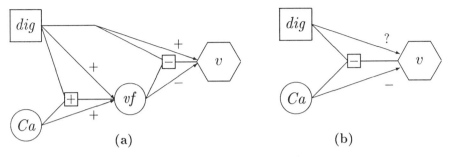

Figure 4.15: Transformation of the digitalis model with synergy: (a) collapsing the therapeutic pathway and consolidating the toxic, (b) final situation after reduction of *vf*.

Inferences of this sort play a central role in therapy planning and in the development of consultation systems via automatic programming [103, 155]. For planning, this type of result is a constraint on the class of admissible plans, significantly pruning the search space [173]. This is an especially useful kind of constraint for the automatic generation of a consultation system because the qualitative form of the solution corresponds to the structure of part of the target code.

The digitalis dosage d^* for patients with normal calcium—a distinguished point in the quantity space for Ca—is a landmark value as described in Section 4.7.6. Sub-synergy implies that the dosage for a patient with calcium above normal should be lower than d^*. This is essentially the strategy of the digitalis program produced by Swartout's XPLAIN system [155], where a domain principle mandates that dosage should be adjusted according to "drug sensitivities." QPNs provide a more general and principled language for encoding domain knowledge, from which policies such as this can be derived.

4.8   Related Work

The QPN representation and reasoning techniques presented here borrow many concepts from other work in AI and decision theory. The most obvious debt is to research in numeric probabilistic networks, especially that of Pearl [114] and Shachter [136]. This work also relates to other efforts by similarity of purpose. In the following sections I compare it with research in qualitative probability, ordering relations on random variables, and non-monotonic and qualitative reasoning.

4.8.1   Qualitative Probability

The central task in designing a qualitative probability representation—indeed in the design of a qualitative representation for anything—is choosing the important qualitative distinctions to make. For example, a straightforward mapping of techniques from qualitative physics might suggest that we carve up the $[0, 1]$ probability scale into a quantity space by choosing a small set of designated reference points. For example, the set of points

{.01, .05, .5, .95, .99} might be chosen as especially significant.

Such a scheme is a "non-starter" because it is only by coincidence that the important qualitative thresholds for any problem will align themselves with the fixed boundaries in the probabilistic quantity space. Furthermore, it is not clear that the types of manipulations typically performed on probabilities will respect these boundaries in a systematic fashion. For example, Bacchus's inheritance reasoner [3] cannot chain inferences about typicality. Attempts to construct qualitative notions of *absolute* probability (see, for example, the work of Halpern and colleagues [54, 55]) are likely to encounter similar problems.[11] Unlike the scales of physical parameters, the probability interval does not appear to have values (except the endpoints) that are universally interesting or even of special significance within a domain. And the *qualification problem* [143] is inevitably important here because one can almost always think of conditions that would bring the probability of any non-analytic event outside any given non-universal range.

This suggests that it might be more appropriate to base qualitative probability concepts on *relative* likelihoods. A relative likelihood logic permits statements that one formula is more likely than another [35, 46]. Absolute probability is subsumed by a scheme of this type given a set of special formulas corresponding to canonical chance situations (such as experiments with an idealized coin) of all probabilities.

The qualitative relationships presented here can be viewed as a special case of relative likelihood where only assertions about the comparative probability of particular conditional events are permitted. Both S^δ and Y^δ are limited to comparisons of the likelihood of a given event under different conditions. For the binary case, S^δ induces a quantity space on the *likelihood ratio* (4.7) with a distinguished value of one.

There are three primary advantages to restricting the formalism to these special likelihood comparisons. First, information in the constraints is substantially—though not completely—preserved by the transformation operations presented in Sections 4.4 and 4.7, a necessary prerequisite for tractable inference. (See Blyth [6] for examples of difficulties with some other seemingly reasonable qualitative likelihood comparisons.) Second, the ability to deduce decision properties suggests that these comparisons are making some of the significant qualitative distinctions. And third, the *ceteris paribus* condition in the definitions reduces the impact of the qualification problem, as does the embedding of the formalism in closed-world networks.

The enterprise of qualitative probability is not necessarily hostile to quantitative probability. In Savage's axiomatization of Bayesian decision theory [134, Chapter 3], the qualitative likelihood ordering logically precedes development of quantitative probability measures.[12] The existence of a numeric representation for likelihood is only a convenient fact that simplifies much of the theory and supports some direct applications. The em-

---

[11] For a more fundamental argument about the limitations of this approach, see the recent work of Xiang et al. [182].

[12] The same is true of an earlier treatment by Koopman [79]. Strictly speaking, the qualitative theory is more general than the quantitative one, which typically requires some sort of additivity axiom. This is not, however, a motivation for the present work (indeed, the proofs assume additivity), which stresses advantages for knowledge representation and computation.

phasis to date on numerical probability representations in applied decision theory and AI is due in part to technological history; there is no fundamental requirement of probability or utility theory that we focus exclusively on the precise extreme of the representation spectrum.

4.8.2 Relations on Random Variables

Philosophers have long attempted to develop mathematical definitions of causality, occasionally producing probabilistic interpretations. Motivated by a more limited set of concerns, I have ignored in this treatment temporal properties, mechanisms, and other issues salient to causality. These matters aside, Suppes [154] proposes a probabilistic condition for binary events that is equivalent to S^+ (4.1) without the context quantification. For multi-valued variables, Suppes suggests quadrant dependence (4.11). A cause is considered spurious if the probabilistic relation can be explained by a prior common cause. The concept of spuriousness can be partially captured in QPNs by distinguishing qualitative influences inferred via arc reversals (spurious) from those derivable solely from reductions along influence chains (genuine). This is similar in spirit to the approach of Simon [145], and is equivalent to the distinction emphasized by Pearl [113] between causal and evidential support.

As suggested previously, ordering of random variables has also attracted considerable interest in statistics [4, 87, 128] and decision theory [178]. Milgrom [100] demonstrates the application of MLRP to theoretical problems in informational economics.

The key difference between the S^+ definition proposed here and previous work is that we obtain transitivity by requiring the condition to hold in all contexts. Humphreys [71] proves a special case of Theorem 4.10 to the effect that binary qualitative influences along Markov chains (graphs where each node has a single predecessor, thereby eliminating context) can be combined by sign multiplication. In contrast, Suppes demonstrates that the causal algebra induced by his condition—defined only at the margin—does not possess the transitive property. A causal algebra either lacking sound reduction rules like those of Section 4.4.3 or restricted to simple Markov chains would have little value for knowledge representation.

Considerably less attention has been devoted to relations of probabilistic synergy. The supermodularity concept of Section 4.7.3 has not, to my knowledge, previously been interpreted in a probabilistic context. However, a constraint similar in spirit to sub-synergy was exploited by NESTOR [18, page 102], a diagnostic program based on probabilistic inequalities. (NESTOR used qualitative influences to bound probability intervals as well.) And we saw in Section 4.7.2 that several canonical probabilistic models proposed for AI programs are special cases of Y^δ.

4.8.3 Non-Monotonic Reasoning

There has been considerable interest of late in probabilistic accounts of non-monotonic reasoning [115]. Recently, Neufeld [106] proposed a probabilistic semantics for defaults based on a relation equivalent to strict binary S^+ without the context quantification. His reasoner derives consequences of an *inference graph* of defaults and logical relations by applying properties of the probabilistic relation and conditional independencies implicit in the graph's structure.

Although the use of qualitative probabilistic relations for non-monotonic inference is interesting, I am skeptical about the ultimate potential of any purely probabilistic approach. Likelihood is only one of many criteria for believing [32]; a satisfactory semantics for defaults must encompass the full range of factors determining whether adopting a particular state of belief is cognitively and computationally rational [31, 144].

4.8.4 Qualitative Reasoning

It might appear at first glance that the very imprecision sanctioned by qualitative mechanisms obviates the need to consider explicitly uncertainty underlying the models. This position, however, confounds the weakness of inferences and input specifications with other kinds of variability in the model. The distinction is crucial because the latter might undermine the soundness of conclusions drawn from qualitative knowledge bases.

The interpretation of a set of qualitative physical relationships as "qualitative differential equations" (see Kuipers [82], for example) treats each relationship as a constraint on some "true" functional relationship that holds over time. To assert that $b = M^+(a)$ (in Kuipers's notation) is to claim that there exists an increasing function f such that $b_t = f(a_t)$ for all t. This is incompatible with a probabilistic interpretation, even though f is only loosely constrained. A qualitative influence assertion of $S^+(a, b)$, on the other hand, leaves open the possibility that the relationship is non-deterministic (f might vary over time) and does not prohibit an increase in a from coinciding with a decrease in b.

Application of qualitative-physics inference mechanisms in a probabilistic environment is dangerous because they tend to take as impossible what is merely unlikely. For example, Forbus's measurement interpretation algorithm for Qualitative Process theory [43] prunes away the qualitative behaviors that are inconsistent with observations of the system. If the dynamics of the system are really probabilistic (I do not claim that this is the case for Forbus's application), then this step is not valid because no behaviors are truly inconsistent. In such a situation, measurements serve to change the likelihoods of various behaviors but never to rule them out. This difference is vital in a critical application because some highly unlikely behaviors may nevertheless be important enough to demand attention from the reasoner.

Though we cannot prune measurement interpretations, we might be able to perform some pruning on the plan space using the techniques presented above. A particular measurement does not in general reveal any facts about the other model variables with certainty, yet it may allow us to deductively conclude that some decision variables (perhaps dials in the control room) should be adjusted in particular directions.

4.9 Conclusion

4.9.1 Summary

A QPN model represents qualitative constraints on the probabilistic relationships among a set of variables. In this chapter I have defined and analyzed two basic constraint types: qualitative influences that express direct relationships between variables, and qualitative synergies that express interactions among influences. The probabilistic definitions justify sound graph-based inference procedures that answer queries about the qualitative relationship of any subset of variables in the model. Qualitative relationships involving the special value variable v dictate structural properties of the optimal assignment to decision variables.

Despite the ubiquity of constructs similar to qualitative influences in knowledge representation mechanisms, there has been little study of the semantics of these statements. Previous work either denies the probabilistic nature of the relationships among variables in the model or takes for granted the ability to draw inferences by chaining influences in the network. I have defined a positive qualitative influence of a on b as an assertion that, in all contexts, the posterior probability distribution for b given a is stochastically increasing (in the sense of FSD) in a. A series of results provides theoretical support for this S^δ definition:

- S^δ justifies reduction of variables by influence chaining. Reduction of any subset of variables can be performed in $O(|V|^2)$ time.

- S^δ permits some nontrivial conclusions upon influence reversal.

- S^δ is the weakest posterior condition that justifies chaining of influences.

- S^δ is necessary and sufficient for chaining *decisions* across influences.

Two variables a and b are positively synergistic on c if the posterior distribution for c is increased more (in the sense of FSD) upon a positive change in a for higher values of b. This Y^δ definition has several computationally and decision-theoretically useful properties:

- Canonical models such as the "noisy OR" often entail Y^δ.

- Y^δ is equivalent to supermodularity on expectation with respect to all monotonic transformations.

- Y^δ_U implies the monotone decision property.

- Synergies may be propagated forwards or backwards along qualitative influences. They also may be nontrivially updated upon influence reversal.

- Any non-redundant sequence of reductions and reversals is computable in polynomial time.

Together, the two qualitative relationships provide a simple yet powerful modeling language. A planner is often able to derive important facts about the qualitative structure of optimal strategies from only weak premises on the qualitative relationships in the domain.

4.9.2 Discussion

Though powerful in some respects, the qualitative relationships are also quite limited. As we saw in Section 4.6, qualitative influences are unable to resolve true tradeoffs because parallel influences of different sign are indeterminate in combination $(+ \oplus - = ?)$. Indeed, "unresolvable in a QPN" might be the best available formal definition of a tradeoff situation.

Thus, a QPN decision model can support planning "up to tradeoffs." To proceed beyond that point, we would need more precise knowledge of these relations. I see no insurmountable barriers to the development of hybrid representations that augment QPNs with stronger constraints, up to and including constraint to exact numeric values. As mentioned above, features of such a hybrid scheme were explored by Cooper in the NESTOR project [18]. While NESTOR's basic representation was probability intervals, it applied constraints similar to qualitative influences and synergies to bound the result of certain combination operations.

Finally, evaluation of QPNs as a knowledge representation must also take into account the feasibility of constructing knowledge bases of reasonable complexity. For reasons of modularity and precision, QPNs should be substantially easier to generate than their numeric counterparts. This prospect is explored further in the next two chapters, which describe SUDO-PLANNER's knowledge base and its procedure for constructing QPNs from the KB.

5 Effects of Actions

The representation of effects is a central issue in planning research and is perhaps the factor that most distinguishes different designs. The topic requires special attention in this work because traditional representations cannot accommodate actions with uncertain effects. Mechanisms from previous work in planning under uncertainty have limited applicability for SUDO-PLANNER because the descriptions of effects were not specifically designed to support dominance-proving.

The first three sections in this chapter address basic issues that loom large in efforts to design a representation for the effects of actions. The distinction between terminological and assertional knowledge has implications for the role of effects in characterizing actions in a knowledge base. The frame problem remains an obstacle in the quest for tractable action representations that are formally sound. Finally, a realistic action representation must provide for context-dependent effects, though AI planners have traditionally lacked this facility.

The discussion of basic issues prepares the way for a presentation of SUDO-PLANNER's representation. Effects in SUDO-PLANNER are based on the qualitative relations of Chapter 4. Section 5.4 describes the knowledge base constructs for specifying effects and discusses some difficulties in relating them precisely to QPN semantics. Section 5.5 introduces the Markov influence, a special construct that facilitates specification of simple temporal effect patterns. Inheritance of effect assertions in the event taxonomy is the subject of Section 5.6. Finally, Section 5.7 describes SUDO-PLANNER's mechanism for handling the information-gathering behavior of actions. SUDO-PLANNER's procedure for generating QPNs from the knowledge base of effect assertions is presented in Chapter 6.

5.1 Terminological and Assertional Knowledge

Philosophers and knowledge representation theorists sometimes emphasize the distinction between knowledge that is *definitional* for a concept and *factual* information true only by happenstance. On the AI side, for example, Woods contrasts structural (definitional) and assertional (factual) features of semantic network representations [181, Section III.J]. The KRYPTON knowledge representation system [9] realizes this distinction by explicitly separating its terminological (definitional) reasoning component ("T-box") from the assertional reasoner ("A-box").

SUDO-PLANNER's representation for actions (Section 3.2) is based on NIKL, the T-box of KL-TWO [165]. Its taxonomy of action types, therefore, is based entirely on terminological knowledge.[1] Conversely, SUDO-PLANNER uses the action definitions exclusively to generate the taxonomic relations among action types. Mixing assertional knowledge with the definitions of actions in a terminological system like NIKL interferes with classification, thereby degrading the effectiveness of taxonomic reasoning. Haimowitz et al. [53] recount other undesirable consequences of T-box abuse.

In principle, actions could be defined in part by their effects. For example, we could define **treatment** as an action that alleviates some disease, and its specialization **CAD-treatment** by value-restricting the **disease** role to **CAD**. Alternatively, actions can be defined *operationally*, that is, in terms of their objects, instruments, and procedures.

Permitting both types of definition presents a difficulty for terminological reasoning because the effects of operationally defined actions are typically not derivable from their specifications. For example, **CABG** is in fact a **CAD-treatment**, but this does not follow from its operational definition. It is unclear whether **CABG** should be classified as such in the taxonomy of Figure 5.1 because this would inhibit proper classification of its operationally defined subtypes, depending on the specification conventions and the classification algorithm.

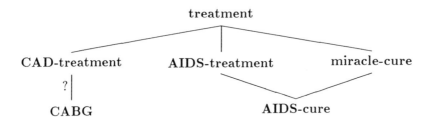

Figure 5.1: A pseudo taxonomy where actions are defined by their effects.

Defining actions by their effects makes it difficult to ensure that the agent can actually execute actions prescribed by the planner. The action type **AIDS-cure** in Figure 5.1, defined as a "treatment that cures AIDS," is perfectly coherent, but it cannot be implemented because it has no known instances (at the time of this writing). Unless the planner realizes this, it will offer vacuous recommendations whenever it encounters AIDS patients.

To prevent this potential fallacy, all information about the effects of actions in SUDO-PLANNER is treated as assertional knowledge. Definitions of actions must be "ineffective," referring only to operational features, as described above. Although nothing in SUDO-PLANNER's representation *guarantees* that definitions are operational or that action types are instantiable and implementable, banishing effects ensures that SUDO-PLANNER is not subject to the wishful-thinking delusion illustrated by the **AIDS-cure** action.

This is not to say that any scheme using "effective" definitions will produce practically worthless plans. Given a fixed knowledge base of implementable actions defined by their

---

[1]There is substantial room for philosophical controversy about whether the information in NIKL concept specifications is truly definitional. All that matters for this discussion, however, is that the reasoner interprets the specifications as definitions.

effects (as in the system of Swartout and Neches [156]), the planner will produce legitimate plans. However, if we permit the planner to construct its own action definitions dynamically from other concepts in the knowledge base (as in SUDO-PLANNER), including effect constructs can lead to non-implementable action types as above.

An alternative approach to the problem would be to explicitly represent and consider the *knowledge prerequisites* associated with each action [102]. Given a description of the agent's knowledge, the planner could recognize its inability to implement **AIDS-cure**. The "ineffective definition" principle I am advocating here is a simpler, global convention that achieves the purpose of knowledge prerequisites for an important special case.

5.2 The STRIPS Assumption

5.2.1 The Frame Problem

The classic dilemma in representing and reasoning about the effects of actions is the *frame problem* [97, 143]. The frame problem has come to stand for a variety of computational and notational complexities arising from the apparent necessity of considering the possible change in status of every proposition for each action. Actual planners circumvent these difficulties by restricting attention to propositions explicitly mentioned in action specifications, a convention first applied by STRIPS [38]. Waldinger has named this policy the "STRIPS assumption" [167]. Characterizing such policies in a formal logic has proven to be a difficult task for AI theorists [56].

The frame problem is just as important and difficult when actions have uncertain effects. However, the uncertain nature of effects requires representations quite different from those of categorical planners, and non-effects likewise require a probabilistic interpretation. While add and delete lists that specify the propositions changing truth value as a result of an action are sufficient for categorical planning,[2] uncertain environments present the possibility that arbitrary propositions may change after performing an action. The solution approach I propose for the uncertain case is similar in form to traditional techniques, with results of comparable adequacy. The presumption that actions affect directly only those variables explicitly referenced in their specifications can be formalized in terms of changes in probabilistic relations that occur when the action is performed.

5.2.2 The STRIPS Assumption for Uncertain Effects

Generally stated, the STRIPS assumption dictates that the effect of an action on the world model be completely determined by the direct effects specified in its description. We can characterize the implications of this assumption for planning under uncertainty in terms of dependency graph concepts (see Section 4.4.1). Let S_a be the set of event variables that

---

[2]That is, the truth value changes are sufficient for defining modifications to the world model. Specifying and implementing truth value change is tricky, however, because changes in status for the sentences mentioned imply changes in their logical consequents. Lifschitz demonstrates how to account for this correctly within the STRIPS framework [91].

action variable a directly affects. The STRIPS assumption for planning under uncertainty is that there exists an I-map G such that for all event variables e,

$$a \in pred_G(e) \Rightarrow e \in S_a. \tag{5.1}$$

Condition (5.1) has direct implications for probabilistic independence. By virtue of G's I-mapness and Lemma 4.9, a is conditionally independent of any $e \notin S_a$ given $pred_G(e)$. Each variable $d \in pred_G(e)$, in turn, is either a direct effect of a or is conditionally independent given its predecessors, $pred_G(d)$. Ultimately, the effect of a on e is completely determined by a's direct effects and e's relation to them. Note that we still need to describe the interaction, if any, between a and e in their joint effects. Section 5.3 discusses this issue further.

The probabilistic STRIPS assumption does *not* require that a be conditionally independent of e given the direct effects S_a, or even by any subset of S_a. In Figure 5.2, for example, a and e are d-separated (Definition 4.8) by $\{s, y\}$ but by no other variable set. The predecessor y is necessary for conditional independence of a and e even though y itself is unconditionally independent of a.

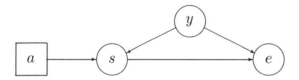

Figure 5.2: Action a is conditionally independent of e given $S'_a = \{s, y\}$ but not given any subset of its direct effects $S_a = \{s\}$.

If we enlarge the conditioning set to include predecessors of a's direct effects, however, we get another valid independence condition. Let S'_a be the set of a's direct effects plus the other variables that affect those effects:

$$S'_a = S_a \cup \bigcup_{s \in S_a} pred_G(s) - \{a\}.$$

The graphical condition (5.1) implies that a is conditionally independent of e given S'_a. In the graph of Figure 5.2, for example, $S'_a = \{s, y\}$.

In summary, we can formalize the STRIPS assumption under uncertainty in terms of probabilistic conditional independence. In particular, given a dependency graph of variables in the world model, any variable e not specified as an effect of action a must not be directly connected to a. Under this condition there may be a probabilistic dependency between a and e in some situations, but this can always be described in terms of a's and e's relations to S_a.

5.3   Context-Dependent Effects

It is not possible in general to describe the effect of an action on a single event in isolation. Typically, the effect will depend on the context in which the action is performed, including the other actions in the plan and the values of other event variables in the world model. Consideration of context requires an effect representation expressive enough to capture interaction among actions and events in their joint effects.

Traditional planning representations do not provide for context-dependent effects, except through the use of preconditions. Preconditions provide only a gross form of context dependence where the action is prohibited in designated situations. Formally, preconditions are a special case of more general specifications of effects as a function of the action in conjunction with the background situation.

Rather than saying an action cannot be performed in situations failing to meet a set of preconditions, we could specify that it does not have particular effects (usually the desired ones) unless the conditions hold. Under this interpretation, the planner can apply *put-on(a, b)*, for instance, in any situation, but the result *on(a, b)* is conditional on *cleartop(a)* and *cleartop(b)*. Otherwise, the effects of *put-on* are undefined. By placing the conditions on effects rather than on the action, we can employ actions that may have many contingent effects. In addition, the planner is free to introduce such actions into the plan without guaranteeing that the preconditions are satisfied.

Pednault has recently generalized traditional planning representations to include "secondary preconditions" for specifying context-dependent effects [119]. While "primary" preconditions can be treated as special cases of these, there may be some utility to keeping them conceptually distinct in a practical planning system.

5.4 Specification of Effects

The effects of actions in SUDO-PLANNER are encoded as qualitative relations among action and event variables. Qualitative influences describe the direct effects of an action, and qualitative synergies describe interactions among influences, or context-dependence (Section 5.3). Effects are specified simply by S^δ (qualitative influence) and Y^δ (qualitative synergy) assertions, with $\delta \in \{+, -, 0, ?\}$. S^0 assertions are implicit, by the probabilistic STRIPS assumption (5.1) of Section 5.2.2.

5.4.1 Semantics of Effect Assertions

An assertion of the form $S^\delta(av, ev)$ or $Y^\delta(av, ev_1, ev_2)$ means that action and event variables of types av and ev participate in the designated relation. Effects of events on other events are similarly specified. The knowledge base construct S^δ is distinguished from the QPN predicate S^δ in two ways:

1. There is no third argument. In QPNs, S^δ is always evaluated with respect to some network G. S^δ assertions in the knowledge base cannot refer to particular QPNs because they are, in fact, the source of QPNs assembled during planning.

2. The variable arguments are types, not instances.

A similar distinction applies to Y^δ.

Despite the rigorous probabilistic definition of qualitative relations in QPNs, the semantics of these assertions in the knowledge base are not immediately clear. The S^δ definition (4.4), for example, refers explicitly to the context x composed of the "other predecessors" of the affected variable. Without a G argument, the assertions must be given a context-independent interpretation. And because probability distributions over event variable types are undefined, the meaning of the qualitative relations must derive from the process of instantiating the types to individual variables.

A complete declarative semantics for effects in the SUDO-PLANNER knowledge base is a topic for further research. Some properties of these assertions can be presented in declarative form, however, and the description of the QPN construction algorithm in Chapter 6 provides further constraint on their interpretation. Nevertheless, the current absence of a full semantic account complicates knowledge engineering and hinders the formal analysis of SUDO-PLANNER's model construction techniques.

5.4.2 Special Constructs

It is possible, and often useful, to introduce special knowledge base constructs to capture regularities in the S^δ and Y^δ relations among instantiated event variable types. Such constructs offer notational economy by specifying patterns of effects with a single assertion. In addition, they can be used to direct the global course of model development through special handlers in the model construction procedure. An example of a special effect construct (the only one implemented in SUDO-PLANNER) is the "Markov influence" introduced in Section 5.5. By accounting for a simple but common pattern of effect over time, Markov influences help to redress the lack of temporal structure in SUDO-PLANNER's event representation.

5.5 Markov Influences

A Markov influence represents an effect that depends on the prior state of the affected variable. In other words, the value of the affected event variable after an action depends on its value before the action as well as on the value of the action variable.

For example, $CABG$ alleviates CAD, but the distribution of final CAD states also depends on the initial CAD value. To represent this directly in the knowledge base, however, we would need separate concepts for "CAD before CABG" and "CAD after CABG." Such a scheme is infeasible because it requires distinct concepts for each event variable in all potentially relevant temporal relationships to the action variable instances.

Markov influences specify state change for a variable across time periods without explicitly referring to the times involved. The form of a Markov influence assertion of av on ev is $K^{\delta_1,\delta_2}(av,ev)$, where δ_1 is the direction of influence and δ_2 is the direction of synergy between av and the prior value of ev. For example, the Markov influence of $CABG$ on

CAD is

$$K^{-,-}(\mathbf{presence}\langle \mathbf{CABG}\rangle, \mathbf{extent}\langle \mathbf{CAD\text{-}event}\rangle). \tag{5.2}$$

The first "$-$" indicates that $CABG$ stochastically decreases CAD, and the second asserts that the effect is more negative the greater the extent of the patient's original coronary disease. Figure 5.3 displays the QPN fragment generated by the Markov influence in this example.

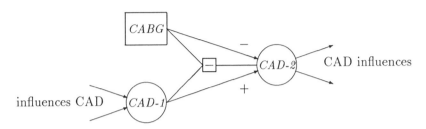

Figure 5.3: The negative Markov influence of CABG on CAD.

In interpreting K^{δ_1,δ_2} during QPN construction, SUDO-PLANNER modifies event variables and their relationships and introduces any new structure required. (Section 6.3.3 describes the interpretation procedure in detail.) For the CABG/CAD influence (5.2), SUDO-PLANNER splits **extent**$\langle \mathbf{CAD\text{-}event}\rangle$ into two QPN variables, denoted $CAD\text{-}1$ and $CAD\text{-}2$ in the figure. It adds an influence of sign δ_1 ($-$) from $CABG$ to $CAD\text{-}2$, along with a qualitative synergy of sign δ_2 connecting $CABG$ and $CAD\text{-}1$ to $CAD\text{-}2$. SUDO-PLANNER also introduces a positive influence from $CAD\text{-}1$ to $CAD\text{-}2$, based on the general assumption that the value of the affected event after the action, ev_2, is positively related to its prior value ev_1.

The $K^{\delta_1,\delta_2}(av, ev)$ relationship is called a Markov influence because the split event variable enforces a Markov independence property in the network. Specifically, influencers of the original variable ev are independent of ev_2 given the prior state variable ev_1 and the new influencer av. Similarly, variables affected by ev do not depend on the prior value ev_1 given the posterior value ev_2 and the variables that affect ev. This partitioning is demonstrated in Figure 5.3 by the delegation of all influencers to $CAD\text{-}1$ and all influences to $CAD\text{-}2$.

5.6   Inheritance of Effects

As mentioned in Section 5.4.1, effect assertions in the knowledge base refer to event variable types, while effects in QPNs relate event variable instances. The correspondence between the two is determined in part by the implications of an effect assertion on effects among taxonomically related types. That is, some of the semantical questions raised above would be answered by an account of effect inheritance.

An effect assertion of the form $S^\delta(ev_1, ev_2)$ has the intended interpretation that *all* event variables of type ev_1 have a δ influence on *some* event variable of type ev_2. Therefore, the asserted effect also holds for any subtype of ev_1 on any supertype of ev_2. Effects associated with their antecedent type are inherited downward in the event variable taxonomy.

Defining the effect relation to have a universally quantified antecedent and an existentially quantified consequent preserves the important property of closure under transitivity. This feature is essential given the chaining inference rules for QPNs developed in Chapter 4. An effect of ev_1 on ev_n derived from paths of effects from the former to the latter will have the universal/existential form if all of the component effects are of that form.

The details of inheritance and its uses in QPN construction are deferred to Chapter 6. Practical considerations in model construction as well as a set of general desiderata for reasoning at multiple levels of abstraction (Section 6.1) justify the interpretation for effect assertions described here.

5.7 Creating Observables

Although the emphasis in this chapter is on effects that change the world, it is also important to consider the information value of performing actions. SUDO-PLANNER actions generate information by creating *observable* event variables. An observable event variable EV has a corresponding function $EV(obs)$ defined for $obs \in \mathcal{O}$. A plan π cannot specify differential action on EV unless EV is observable.

An observable creation assertion of the form $CO(a_i, ev)$ specifies that variables of type ev are observable in plans that include a_i. For example,

$$CO(\textbf{cardiac-catheterization(true)}, \textbf{extent}\langle\textbf{cardiac-cath-result}\rangle)$$

asserts that performing catheterization reveals the value of the test result to the agent. The result variable exists conceptually whether the test is performed or not, but without the test the agent cannot see the result or use it to condition subsequent action.

To SUDO-PLANNER's dominance prover, observability makes an event variable eligible to appear in action policy and conditional plan class constraints. Constraints of these types are ill-defined unless the event in question can be observed.

Observable creation places a semantic constraint on plans beyond the syntactic specification of Section 3.1 (see the informal Ω_0 definition (3.1)). Specifically, the plan must order the actions so that all observables are created before they are used as conditions. This constraint ensures that we are not implicitly conditioning an observation on the value of the observation itself.

Observable-creating actions are called *tests*. The treatment of observables here differs somewhat from the representation of information dependencies in influence diagrams [68]. There the observability of events does not change but tests influence the values of the observables. One way to implement this (Ross Shachter, personal communication) is to make the observed variable EV a deterministic function of an underlying physiologic state s and a binary variable indicating whether the test was performed. The result is $EV = s$ if the test is performed, with EV a noninformative constant otherwise. In the scheme employed by SUDO-PLANNER, the test action directly causes s to be observable. The result is formally equivalent, but maintaining the distinction in the knowledge base leads to a uniform interpretation of EV. Furthermore, the separation of information-gathering and world-affecting permits the dominance prover to apply constraints on the value of information (for example, its non-negativity [48]) in determining plan class admissibility.

6 Model Construction

Customized construction of decision models at multiple levels of abstraction is SUDO-PLANNER's solution to the computational problems of adhering to decision-theoretic principles (see Sections 1.5 and 1.6). This chapter explores these issues further and describes the implemented model construction techniques. I start by outlining a challenging set of desiderata for multilevel reasoning in the general case. Although it does not satisfy the desiderata completely, SUDO-PLANNER constitutes a first step towards automatic model construction from a multilevel knowledge base.

6.1 Desiderata for Reasoning at Multiple Levels of Abstraction

As argued in Section 1.6, the interconnectedness of concepts in realistic knowledge bases dictates that we employ abstraction to avoid the requirement for exhaustive consideration of the KB before model analysis. Many researchers have proposed and developed techniques for reasoning at multiple levels of abstraction (see Section 6.5.2 for a partial review of this work). In this section, I outline a set of desiderata for multilevel reasoning schemes in the general case. Subsequent sections describe SUDO-PLANNER's multilevel representation and model generation procedure and evaluate them in terms of these desiderata.

The following list contains some key features of an ideal multilevel reasoning system.

- *Non-Reductionism.* Lower levels need not be strict refinements of upper levels. The strength of conclusions can increase in either direction.

- *Fluidity.* The knowledge base is not strictly layered. Relationships need not respect levels.

- *Multilevel Operationality.* Substantive reasoning can occur at any level. The higher levels are not merely for control and explanation.

- *Definitional Clarity.* The representation has a clear semantics and the inference procedure, a transparent description.

- *Coherence.* Conclusions are consistent across abstraction levels.

Conceptually, these desiderata are orthogonal. Practically, they interact considerably, in that satisfying some may render others more or less easy to achieve. I discuss the desiderata and their interdependencies in the sections below. I place particular emphasis on non-reductionism and fluidity because these have had the largest influence on the design of SUDO-PLANNER.

6.1.1 Non-Reductionism

The simplest theoretical approach to abstraction is to regard the lower levels as refinements of the upper, thereby defining upper level concepts as versions of those below that ignore certain distinctions (see Hobbs [62], for example). Indeed, the submergence of detail is the usual meaning of the term "abstraction." Enforcing this criterion in practice, however, can lead to infeasible information requirements and fails to capture some known phenomena in multilevel reasoning.

Reductionism imposes a strong constraint on the knowledge in a multilevel system: conclusions derivable at a given level must also follow from models at deeper levels. While this property may hold in some cases, in others the local information associated with low-level concepts will not entail conclusions as strong as those obtained from the higher-level model. This weakness can be caused by several factors, including:

- Difficulty in expressing the stronger relationships with the "natural" vocabulary for the more specific concepts. For example, breaking an aggregate concept into descriptions of its components may render global properties inaccessible.

- Lack of information for instantiating the more specific concepts to obtain conclusions of comparable strength. Typically, lower-level concepts are more difficult to instantiate because they require more detail. Even though incomplete knowledge may be sufficient for the conclusions, the program may require concrete instances for tractable, "vivid" reasoning [90].

- Absence of a theory describing the relation between properties of the specific and general concepts.

- Absence of a theory of the specific concepts themselves.

A second argument against reductionism in multilevel modeling is that it is violated in the current state of human knowledge. In medical reasoning, for example, physiological knowledge can often resolve conflicts arising from application of empirical associations at the higher, clinical level in the presence of multiple disorders [157]. But in some areas of medicine our knowledge of physiological mechanisms is quite weak, perhaps supporting confident prediction of only qualitative relationships [84]. These may lead to useful conclusions in some cases, but not necessarily conclusions as strong as those obtained from shallower models. (They may not even reproduce all qualitative conclusions known at the empirical level). Proceeding downwards in the abstraction hierarchy to biochemistry almost always makes things worse because biochemical theory and our knowledge of the biochemistry underlying physiological processes is not strong enough to explain higher-level effects.

This phenomenon is by no means unique to medicine. Successful macroeconomic models typically cannot be grounded in microeconomic foundations. Even in physics—the pinnacle of reductionist science—more detailed descriptions do not always lead to stronger conclusions. For example, we typically cannot derive useful predictions from a description of a system at the quantum level.

The foregoing argument is not a philosophical objection to reductionism in principle. Until we carry out the reduction in actuality, however, a purely reductionist computational mechanism will not suffice for representing and reasoning about the body of human knowledge.

6.1.2   Fluidity

The second desideratum for multilevel reasoning is that the notion of "level" be fluid as opposed to rigid. A rigid multilevel system is one where all reasoning respects fixed level boundaries defined by the allowable relationships between concepts.

To clarify this, let us define more precisely the components of a multilevel representation. We call the basic elements *concepts* and presume that concepts are arranged in some taxonomic structure. Two concepts are *taxonomically related* if one is a descendant of the other in the taxonomy. Taxonomic relativity is the basis for statements that one concept is at a higher or lower abstraction level than another. Interpretation of the taxonomic relation may vary in different representation schemes. In NIKL (and hence SUDO-PLANNER), the taxonomies represent specialization hierarchies, where concept subsumption is defined with respect to an extensional semantics.

In addition to taxonomic relationships, a multilevel knowledge representation provides a set of *domain relations*. Depending on the purpose of the KB, these might express causal, functional, or any other useful type of information about the concepts. In SUDO-PLANNER, for example, I employ qualitative probabilistic relationships to represent the effects of actions.

A multilevel KB is *rigid* if we can partition the concepts into a set of fixed levels, such that:

1. All domain relations connect concepts at the same level.

2. No concepts at the same level are taxonomically related.

3. Taxonomic relations among concepts at different levels induce a total order on the levels.

The rigidity of a given multilevel KB can be decided by an efficient algorithm. Figure 6.1 illustrates a rigid multilevel KB. Relations among concepts respect the level boundaries as dictated above. An example of a system with a rigid KB is Patil's ABEL program for multilevel physiological reasoning [109].

A *fluid* multilevel KB (see Figure 6.2) does not enforce these restrictions. Domain relations between two taxonomically related pairs may cross, and a concept may appear in a domain relation with two or more others that are themselves taxonomically related.

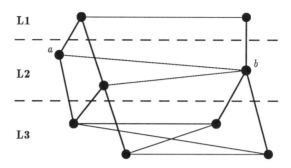

Figure 6.1: A rigid multilevel knowledge base. Thick lines indicate taxonomic relations; thinner ones denote domain relations. We can partition the KB into levels (L1, L2, L3) such that there are no inter-level domain relations and no intra-level taxonomic relations.

A fluid scheme may impose some discipline of its own on patterns of relations, but the restrictions are not as sweeping as those given above. Pople's CADUCEUS [120] is an example of a fluid multilevel KB architecture.

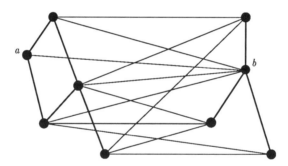

Figure 6.2: A multilevel system with a fluid knowledge base. No partitioning into levels is possible.

While we can speak of *relative* levels in a fluid KB, the notion of an *absolute* level is ill-defined. One concept is at a higher level than another if the two are taxonomically related, otherwise they are incomparable. Concepts a and b are at the same level (L2) in the rigid KB of Figure 6.1, but there is no basis for such a statement in the fluid case of Figure 6.2.

One advantage of a rigid design is the ease of controlling multilevel reasoning with uniform levels. A rigid KB necessitates choice of only a single global level, in contrast to the selection of levels required for each local region of a fluid KB.

Although it complicates the control problem, the flexibility of fluid KBs has important advantages. The appropriate depth for reasoning about individual concepts depends on the goals and characteristics of particular problems, and there is no reason to expect that the same depth is appropriate throughout the knowledge base. For example, a reasonable medical reasoning strategy might be to explore in great detail the concepts relating to the patient's chief complaint while examining peripheral concepts at a higher level. A rigid multilevel reasoner can pursue this strategy by switching between levels for different parts of the analysis. However, the rigid reasoner can never mix concepts from distinct levels *in the same model* because it cannot express inter-level relationships directly. Therefore, it cannot consider the chief complaint and the peripheral concepts *together*, unless it is willing to represent them at the same abstraction level.

Fluidity is central to SUDO-PLANNER's ability to derive useful results before exhaustively examining the knowledge base. The example model of Figure 1.8 includes specific effects of **AAA-repair** as well as high-level effects associated with its ancestor concept, **treatment**. If the level of detail of a decision model were constrained to be uniform, reasoning could not commence until the model was translated to some common denominator. For large KBs, this requirement can impose unacceptable delays on model analysis.

6.1.3 Multilevel Operationality

In some multilevel reasoning systems, all conclusions are expressed in terms of the lowest-level concepts. Structure at higher levels is used for explanation, control of reasoning, and perhaps other purposes, but it is not operational in the same sense as knowledge at the lower fringe.

For true multilevel behavior, all levels should enjoy the same operational status. The full advantages of abstraction are realized only if it is possible to avoid some low-level concepts entirely; merely postponing attention to detail provides only limited savings. The requirement that the reasoner perform all substantive inference at the lowest level smacks of reductionism and compromises the flexibility of fluid representations.

There are two senses in which SUDO-PLANNER's high-level reasoning is substantive. First, the plan graph can express dominance results about plan classes at high levels of abstraction. In fact, these results are more valuable than those about lower-level plan classes because they prune more of the search space.

Second, the benefit of fluidity cited above would not be possible if substantive reasoning were not permitted at higher levels. Reasoning about some facets of **AAA-repair** at the generality of **treatment**—even though more specific knowledge about the same effects is available—leads to useful dominance results at an earlier stage of the modeling process than would otherwise be possible.

6.1.4 Definitional Clarity

The desirability of definitional clarity in a knowledge representation is self-evident, regardless of its number of levels. Unfortunately, a precise semantics for knowledge representation schemes is sometimes difficult to produce, as Section 5.4.1 illustrates. In the case of multilevel reasoners, our other desiderata further complicate the task. A reductionist scheme is theoretically much simpler than one that violates monotonicity of conclusion strength with refinement, and rigidity in level boundaries eliminates a large class of interactions that would present definitional difficulties. In my view, the flexibility advantages of fluidity and the unreality of reductionism outweigh the current lack of clear theoretical accounts of non-reductionist, fluid multilevel reasoning systems.

6.1.5 Coherence

The final desideratum is that the KB be *coherent*. A multilevel KB is coherent if the conclusions it sanctions at different levels are logically consistent with one another. The conclusions derivable at different abstractions can be different—weaker, stronger, or incomparable because they refer to distinct domains—but they should not be contradictory.

Certain controlled forms of incoherence might be tolerable if the reasoner has special facilities to handle inter-level conflicts. For instance, some nonmonotonic inference mechanisms are designed expressly to prefer specificity, overriding the conclusions it derives from high-level premises in favor of more specific results (see especially research on inheritance systems and formalisms [133, 162]).

Inter-level coherence is usually difficult to guarantee. A purely reductionist KB is coherent by definition, though it may not always be feasible to verify reductionism. Definitional clarity makes it easier to maintain coherence, but as mentioned above, there is a strong tension between clarity and fluidity. Tension also exists between definitional clarity and nonmonotonicity [8, 56, 163], so admitting even regular incoherence is likely to compromise other desiderata.

6.2 Event Variable Knowledge Base

The action and event taxonomies of Chapter 3 constitute the taxonomic skeleton of SUDO-PLANNER's multilevel knowledge base. The KB is fleshed out with effect assertions (Section 5.4) relating actions and events across taxonomic levels.

Figure 6.3 presents a view of part of the KB supporting the running example. Effect arcs relate the simple taxonomy of primary surgical actions at the left of the diagram to the major event variables of interest. Among these are *MI* and *stroke* presence, a small cluster of *disease severity* variables, and *mortality*. All paths eventually lead to the special utility variable, *value*. The qualitative relation assertions specifying Figure 6.3 and the rest of the KB are listed in Appendix C.

As in previous figures, thick lines represent taxonomic relationships, and thinner ones, domain relations. Domain relation links in Figure 6.3 correspond to qualitative influence (S^δ) assertions in the KB. Qualitative synergy and Markov influence assertions are not shown. To avoid confusion between the two uses of qualitative relations, the diagrammatical conventions for KB graphs like Figure 6.3 differ significantly from those used in QPN figures.

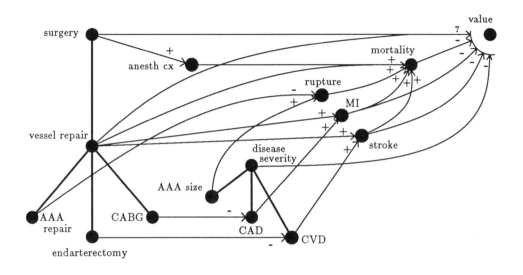

Figure 6.3: Part of SUDO-PLANNER's multilevel event variable KB.

Inspection of Figure 6.3 reveals that SUDO-PLANNER's KB is fluid, as we cannot partition the nodes into levels in a manner satisfying the rigidity conditions of Section 6.1.2. For instance, any partitioning would require that *surgery* and *vessel repair* be on different levels because of their taxonomic relation, and on the same level because of their mutual links to value.

Close inspection of the KB also reveals that it is incoherent (and therefore trivially non-reductionist). For example, there is a direct positive link from *vessel repair* to *stroke*, yet its subconcept, *endarterectomy*, has a negative effect on *stroke* through its influence on *CVD*. The apparent contradiction causes no difficulty in this case, since SUDO-PLANNER's model construction algorithm prefers the more specific path when considering *endarterectomy*. Incoherence with respect to *value*, on the other hand, would present a serious problem, causing SUDO-PLANNER's dominance prover to generate inconsistencies in the plan graph. The "?" links to *value* from *surgery* and *vessel repair* are in the KB specifically to avoid this potential error.

A full discussion of coherence requires an examination of how the KB is interpreted by SUDO-PLANNER's model construction procedure, described in Section 6.3 below. One important characteristic of the construction procedure is its treatment of inheritance. As described in Section 5.6, the intended meaning of an effect link from ev_1 to ev_2 is that each variable of type ev_1 affects some variable of type ev_2 (the universal/existential interpretation). Therefore, event variables inherit outgoing relation links from their taxonomic ancestors.

Figure 6.4 illustrates the use of inheritance in a fragment of the SUDO-PLANNER KB. In the linear taxonomy at the left, *aneurysm size* is a kind of *disease severity* variable because size is an indicator of severity for the disease "aneurysm presence." The variable

101

is further specialized by restricting the location of the aneurysm to the abdominal aorta (AAA). The same concept specialization relates the two rupture variables. All links in the figure appear as explicit assertions in the knowledge base.

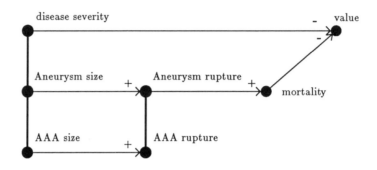

Figure 6.4: Fragment of the KB relating AAA size and value. Effect links are inherited downward in the antecedent taxonomy.

Further effect relations are implicit in the taxonomic relationships. For example, *AAA rupture* positively influences mortality, by inheritance from its parent, aneurysm rupture. In this case, inheritance provides everything that is known about the effects of *AAA rupture*.

In other cases, more specific knowledge supplements or replaces inherited information. *AAA size* positively influences *aneurysm rupture* by virtue of being an *aneurysm size*, but more specifically it influences the rupture of a particular type of aneurysm, AAA. Given the universal/existential interpretation, the local assertion is strictly stronger than that inherited from *aneurysm size*.

From the perspective of the destinations of effect links, variables inherit relations *upwards* in the taxonomy. For example, the link from *AAA size* to *aneurysm rupture* could also be inherited (at the destination end) upward from *AAA rupture*. The inheritance is redundant in this case, but in general could make a difference, for instance, if the link from *aneurysm size* did not exist.

A final possibility is that a direct link at one level could correspond to a more complex set of paths at another. For example, *aneurysm size* (and *AAA size* as well) exhibits a negative influence on *value* by virtue of being a *disease severity*. At a more specific level, *aneurysm size* influences *value* via a path through *aneurysm rupture* and *mortality*. Although the more detailed path leads to the same conclusion in this case, the direct relation leads to simpler and more efficient models. On the other hand, the detail is necessary for reasoning about interactions with other variables that share with *aneurysm size* segments of their influence path to *value*.

6.3　Model Construction in SUDO-Planner

SUDO-PLANNER's high-level behavior is a cycle of model construction and dominance proving, as illustrated by Figure 1.10. Figure 6.5 elaborates that view, revealing that the model construction cycle consists of the incremental evolution of a central QPN. From the perspective of the model constructor, the KB is an event variable graph in the general form of Figure 6.3. At each iteration, the constructor modifies the current QPN according to relations in the KB. The dominance prover analyzes the modified QPN, which then forms the basis for the next cycle of model construction. The process continues until no QPN modification operators are applicable (that is, the KB is exhausted) or it is explicitly halted by its invoker. The invoker can interrupt the model construction cycle at any time to inspect the plan graph, which is continually maintained by the plan space manager.

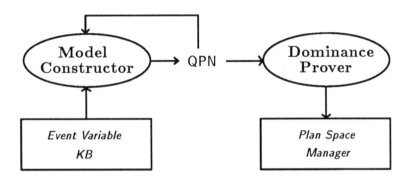

Figure 6.5: SUDO-PLANNER's model construction cycle. The QPN evolves through a sequence of incremental modifications.

This section explains the left-hand half of Figure 6.5 involving the process of constructing and modifying QPNs based on KB relations. Chapter 7 explains the dominance-proving right-hand side.

To assemble a QPN from relations in an event variable KB, the model constructor selects a subset of the variables and links from the KB graph. Selection of this subset is complicated by several factors, which form some of the central issues in model construction and modification.

Choosing variables.　In a large knowledge base, it is imperative that selectivity be exercised in assembling the set of variables. For proper focus, we require some notion of relevance. I discuss the design of justified focus mechanisms in Section 6.4.

Choosing abstractions.　Given that a particular concept is of interest, the constructor must decide at which taxonomic level to represent it with a QPN variable.

Changing abstractions. One way to modify a QPN is to change the abstraction level of some of its components. SUDO-PLANNER's elaboration mechanism (Section 6.3.1) attempts to update QPN relationships appropriately when changing levels.

Multiple inheritance. An event variable may have more than one source for inheriting effect relationships. The constructor must include mechanisms for selecting, merging, and resolving conflicts among inherited relationships.

Recording and merging conclusions from different models. In an iterative process of model modification, some of the conclusions drawn from the models might be useful in decisions about the subsequent evolutionary path. SUDO-PLANNER exploits this opportunity in a limited fashion, described in Section 6.3.2.

Because the dominance prover continually analyzes the QPN throughout its evolutionary process, each modification the model constructor applies must preserve validity. This requirement places strong constraints on the modification operators and the KB, and in fact, it is not completely met by SUDO-PLANNER's model construction mechanisms.

The model construction procedure includes two basic operations for modifying QPNs. SUDO-PLANNER alternates between *elaboration* steps that replace existing relationships with more detailed pathways, and *backward chaining* steps that extend the model to include additional related variables. The sections below present the procedures for these steps.

6.3.1   Elaboration

Elaboration introduces detail to a QPN. The multilevel operationality of SUDO-PLANNER's knowledge representation permits it to reason initially at high levels of abstraction, then refine the model to consider more specific concepts. Thanks to the KB's fluidity, refinement need not occur all at once; instead, the constructor can refine the QPN incrementally by elaborating individual links.

The elaboration process comprises three stages:

1. Choose a QPN link to elaborate.

2. Find a set of elaborating paths in the KB.

3. Merge the new structure into the QPN.

The starting point for the model construction process in our running example is the QPN of Figure 6.6a.[1] The initial QPN relates *AAA size* to *value* via the most general route in the KB. In this instance, the negative link derives from the KB relation between *disease severity* (an ancestor of *AAA size*) and *value*, as shown in Figure 6.6b.

The rest of this section describes the three stages of elaboration, illustrating the process by application to this simple QPN and to more complex networks.

---

[1]This QPN is identical to that of Figure 1.11. SUDO-PLANNER's graphical interface drew all QPN pictures for the running example appearing in this chapter (including Figure 6.6a).

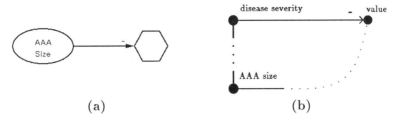

| (a) | (b) |

Figure 6.6: (a) Initial QPN for the running example. (b) The link corresponds to the most general effect of *AAA size* found in the event variable KB.

Stage 1: Choose Link to Elaborate

SUDO-PLANNER selects the QPN link to elaborate in a first-in/first-out order. It places links on a FIFO queue upon their addition to the QPN. If the queue is empty, the elaboration operator is inapplicable.

Stage 2: Find Elaborating Paths

Given a link between two QPN variables, an *elaboration* is a mutually compatible collection of paths connecting the corresponding variables in the KB. SUDO-PLANNER considers paths of length one or two only, thereby limiting the rapidity of model refinement. The individual paths may include both explicit and inherited KB relations. Two paths are *compatible* if their relations are valid when combined in a QPN. For example, SUDO-PLANNER regards as incompatible combinations that contain versions of the same variable at different taxonomic levels. True semantic compatibility is not verifiable by the model constructor.

SUDO-PLANNER tags each link in the QPN with a pointer to the event variable in the KB from which it was derived. The link in Figure 6.6a, for example, originated from *disease severity* in the KB of Figure 6.6b. To elaborate this link, SUDO-PLANNER searches for paths from *AAA size* to *value* that derive from origins more specific than *disease severity*.

As Figure 6.7 illustrates, the search for elaborating paths in the KB graph is bounded by the origin variable (in this case, *disease severity*) and the KB variable currently appearing in the QPN (*AAA size*). The source of an elaborating path must be a descendant of the origin, so that it specializes the model, and an ancestor of the QPN variable, so the relations are inherited. The path may terminate at the current destination or at any of its descendants.

There may be several candidate elaborations. Suppose, for example, that in the KB of Figure 6.7 elaborating paths emanate from nodes *a*, *b*, and *c*. SUDO-PLANNER prefers the most general elaborations because the more specific ones remain reachable in subsequent elaboration steps. Therefore, it removes the paths from *b* from consideration. But since *a* and *c* are not taxonomically related, SUDO-PLANNER includes the union of their elaborating paths.

This strategy is a form of multiple inheritance. Because there is no guarantee that the

105

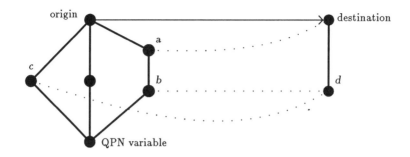

Figure 6.7: Search for elaborating paths. The dotted lines indicate that variables a, b, and c are sources of candidate elaborations.

relations inherited from different paths are consistent or compatible, this merge operation (as well as the process of merging the elaboration into the QPN, stage three) is a source of potential error in SUDO-PLANNER's model construction algorithm.

The path selected to elaborate the link in our initial QPN (Figure 6.6a) is the chain

$$aneurysm\ size \longrightarrow aneurysm\ rupture \longrightarrow value. \tag{6.1}$$

Aneurysm size is the most general variable that is a descendant of *disease severity*, an ancestor of *AAA size*, and has a path of length at most two to *value*. (The direct link from *aneurysm rupture* to *value* is inherited from an ancestor, not shown in the KB fragment of Figure 6.4.) The elaboration can be interpreted as an explanation of the original link: *AAA size* is undesirable because it positively influences *aneurysm rupture*, which is undesirable.

Stage 3: Merge New Structure

If SUDO-PLANNER finds an elaboration, it removes the original link from the current QPN. It then proceeds to the final stage of elaboration: merging the chosen elaborated paths into the model. The merge task is to determine how to modify the variables and relationships in the QPN to include the new structure.

For our initial QPN, merging is easy. A new variable, *aneurysm rupture*, is introduced to the QPN, and the elaboration path (6.1) simply replaces the original link. The KB variable *aneurysm size* is recorded as the origin of the first link, though the QPN variable remains *AAA size*. SUDO-PLANNER adds the two new links to the FIFO queue for possible further elaboration. Figure 6.8 displays the final result of the elaboration step.

In the general case, merging is more complicated. When introducing a new variable, SUDO-PLANNER must connect it to all existing QPN variables—not just those on the new paths—according to relations encoded in the KB. Performing the update correctly is tricky because the new variable may be connected to existing ones via complex and possibly redundant pathways.

When a new variable is introduced to the network, SUDO-PLANNER connects it with all existing QPN variables that are directly related to it, explicitly or via inheritance, in

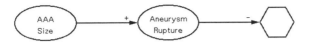

Figure 6.8: An elaboration of the initial QPN.

the KB. For example, the variable z is linked to current variable x upon introduction to the QPN of Figure 6.9a. Variables z and y remain unconnected because there is no direct link between them in the KB graph.

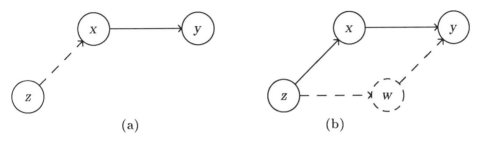

Figure 6.9: (a) Introducing z to the network. (b) The KB contains no direct relation between z and y, but includes a path through w, not currently in the QPN.

Suppose, however, that the KB contains a path from z to y via variable w, which is not represented in the current QPN. The network of Figure 6.9a then leads to the false conclusion that y is independent of z given x. We can remedy this by introducing w to the QPN along with z, adding the appropriate links as illustrated in Figure 6.9b. Although safer, this policy is unsatisfactory because introduction of a single variable is liable to trigger the migration of a large fraction of the KB into the QPN.

SUDO-PLANNER preserves the incrementalism of QPN modification by ignoring indirect connections of the sort displayed in Figure 6.9b. Typically (and necessarily to avoid unsound inferences), pathways in the KB have corresponding one-step summaries at higher taxonomic levels. In this case, we would expect z to inherit a direct link to y from some ancestor. To be conservative, we could add these *spanning links* [120] automatically, although the implemented SUDO-PLANNER includes no KB pre-processing. The spurious links included due to such a policy are of little consequence because if truly spurious they will be removed upon subsequent elaboration.[2]

When possible, SUDO-PLANNER combines taxonomically related variables. If the newly introduced variable has an ancestor in the QPN, the merge procedure tests whether the existing relations are compatible with the specialized variable. Because outgoing links are inherited, compatibility holds exactly when the links into the existing ancestor variable hold for the new variable. If compatible, the new replaces the old. Otherwise, SUDO-PLANNER attempts to merge the new relations with the old variable. Here, compatibility

---

[2] Elaboration results in simple removal if the elaborating structure is already present in the QPN.

depends only on the outgoing relations. If the merge fails in this direction as well, SUDO-PLANNER maintains both variables in the QPN. The two will be merged eventually if subsequent QPN modification presents the opportunity.

For example, the elaboration search situation of Figure 6.7 yielded paths from *a* to the existing variable *destination*, and from *c* to its descendant, *d*. SUDO-PLANNER first tries to replace *destination* with *d*, succeeding if all incoming links to *destination* hold for *d* as well. Failing that, it attempts the converse merge. In this case, *d* is replaceable by *destination* because it is a new variable with no outgoing links. Subsequent elaboration steps will trigger the reintroduction of *d*, in particular when the path from *a* is specialized to originate from *b*.

Finally, qualitative synergies are also added to the QPN during the merge stage. Whenever a node has two or more incoming links, SUDO-PLANNER checks the knowledge base for an asserted or inherited synergy among the predecessor variables. Recall that SUDO-PLANNER interprets the absence of an explicit synergy link in the QPN as "?" by default.

6.3.2 Backward Chaining

The QPN for the running example as developed to this point (Figure 6.8) is not very interesting from the perspective of planning. The semantics of qualitative influences entail that small AAAs are preferable to large ones, but tell us nothing about what we should do about them. Furthermore, no amount of elaboration applied to this relation sheds any light on action.

The second basic QPN modification operator, *backward chaining*, extends the scope of the model. In a backward chaining step, SUDO-PLANNER searches for variables in the KB that affect a particular existing QPN variable. The mechanics of this step are straightforward: choose a variable to extend back, find its predecessors in the KB, and merge the new structure according to the merge procedure described above.

The first attempt at backward chaining on the running example produces no modification because the chosen variable, *AAA size*, has no predecessors. SUDO-PLANNER next applies an elaboration step, which replaces *aneurysm rupture* with *AAA rupture*. Backward chaining on *AAA rupture* finally yields a significant QPN modification, shown in Figure 6.10.

The new QPN has the same variables as that of Figure 1.8, though it lacks the positive synergy between *AAA repair* and *AAA rupture* on *value*. Given this synergy, the dominance prover could establish that *AAA repair* is positively synergistic with *AAA size*, and therefore that the optimal repair policy is to fix the aneurysm iff it is larger than some threshold size. However, the synergy is unavailable to SUDO-PLANNER at this stage in QPN development. In the current model, *AAA repair*'s relation to *value* is inherited from its ancestor *surgery* (see the KB graph of Figure 6.3). The synergy is simply not valid at this high level. Further elaboration of the model combined with QPN inference yields the desired result later in the model construction process.

The initial stage of backward chaining is the choice of a variable to extend back. SUDO-PLANNER selects arbitrarily among the eligible, or *extensible*, variables. If no variables

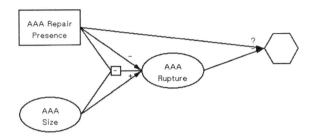

Figure 6.10: QPN after backward chaining on *AAA rupture*.

are extensible, the backward chaining operator is inapplicable. A variable is considered extensible if:

1. it is not a decision variable (these have no predecessors),

2. it has not already been extended back, and

3. it is one of the specially designated *focus variables*, it is a successor of a focus variable, or it is ± synergistic with a focus variable on *value*.

I describe the concept of a focus variable and justify its use in Section 6.4.2. Informally, focus variables are those deemed relevant based on their role in the case description or in plans under consideration. The heuristic application of focus variables to restrict the variables eligible for backward chaining directs the course of QPN evolution.[3] Although this control is not necessary to run the main example, a focus mechanism of some sort is crucial for tractable model construction from large KBs.

To implement the extensibility test, SUDO-PLANNER records instances of synergy with a focus variable as it derives them in intermediate computations of the dominance prover. This is the only semantic information about domain relations (and the only type of QPN inference) that the model construction procedure exploits. More sophisticated application of intermediate results might improve efficiency and control, but would also exacerbate the undesirable consequences of incoherence in the multilevel KB.

The second stage of backward chaining is to retrieve the QPN variable's predecessors from the KB. SUDO-PLANNER simply traces back links in the KB graph. The back extension does not consider inherited predecessor relations because these will be uncovered in subsequent elaboration.

The final stage is to introduce the predecessors to the QPN. The procedure to merge structure from backward chaining is equivalent to the merge stage for elaboration described in the previous section.

---

[3] The application of focus variables is similar in spirit to the use of *focus objects* in McAllester's ONTIC theorem prover [96].

The backward chaining strategy adopted by the model construction procedure imparts special significance to the directionality of influence relations in the event variable KB. Whether we assert that a affects b or that b affects a in the KB strongly influences the shape of QPNs produced by SUDO-PLANNER, even though the semantics of qualitative influences does not dictate this choice. As Section 4.4.4 demonstrates, QPN influences can be reversed without affecting their sign, although the reversal may change other relations in the network. SUDO-PLANNER fails to exploit this flexibility—in fact, the implementation never attempts to reverse influences—despite its demonstrated usefulness in traditional decision modeling [138].

6.3.3   Variable Mitosis for Markov Influences

An important type of backward chaining occurs when the predecessor exerts a Markov influence on the current QPN variable. As Section 5.5 describes, a Markov influence represents an effect over time, inducing a relationship between the action and the values of its affected variable before and after execution. To represent this situation in a QPN, we require separate variables for the "before" and "after" values. SUDO-PLANNER modifies the QPN by dividing the affected variable in two and updating relations as appropriate.

The variable division process, or *mitosis*, is illustrated in Figure 6.11. SUDO-PLANNER encounters a Markov influence in the process of backward chaining on *CAD extent*. The QPN fragment of Figure 6.11a displays the variables connected to *CAD extent* prior to interpreting the Markov influence.

Figure 6.11b illustrates the Markov influence itself. *CABG* influences *CAD extent*, in a manner synergistic with the prior value of the variable. The mitosis process translates this implicit distinction among the two *CAD* variables to an explicit separation in the QPN. The resulting network fragment, shown in Figure 6.11c, contains the variables *CAD-1* and *CAD-2*, denoting the *CAD extent* before and after *CABG*, respectively. The previous predecessors of *CAD—CAD history* and *catheterization result*—are attached to *CAD-1*, and the previous successor—*MI*—to *CAD-2*. The Markov influence explicitly specifies the influence of *CABG* on *CAD-2*, and its synergy with *CAD-1*. Implicit in all Markov influences is the positive relationship between the "before" and "after" variables.

The split variables are divided further if they are the object of other Markov influences. In general, the QPN may contain an arbitrary Markov chain reflecting a temporal sequence of values of the same event variable.

The presence of multiple QPN variables corresponding to a single KB variable complicates the model construction process slightly. When merging structure (during elaboration or backward chaining) involving links *into* such a variable, SUDO-PLANNER selects the head of the Markov chain. Structure containing paths *out of* a multiply represented variable is referred to the tail variable. These conventions preserve the Markovian character of the QPN's dependency graph.

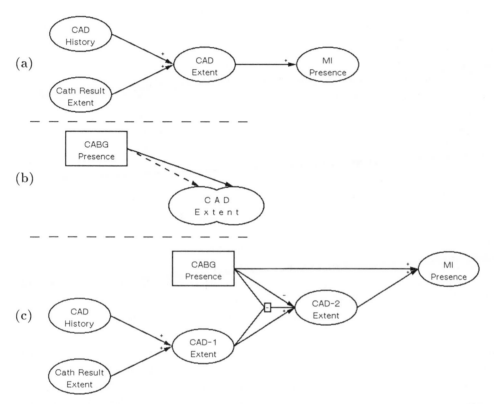

Figure 6.11: Variable mitosis. (a) The situation before mitosis. (b) The Markov influence of *CABG* on *CAD* implicitly refers to two *CAD* variables. (c) The final result: *CAD* is split into *CAD-1* and *CAD-2*, and relationships are appropriately distributed among the two.

6.3.4 The Model Construction Procedure: Conclusion

Having completed the description of SUDO-PLANNER's model construction process, we are now in a position to evaluate it in terms of the five basic desiderata for multilevel reasoning presented in Section 6.1. Of the five, SUDO-PLANNER scores better on non-reductionism, fluidity, and multilevel operationality than it does on definitional clarity and coherence. A strict judge, however, would find the system wanting with respect to all these criteria.

The event variable KB is clearly non-reductionist and fluid. However, in adopting a style of top-down refinement, SUDO-PLANNER's model construction procedure does not take full advantage of the flexibility offered. Because it generally does not record intermediate results, the dominance prover is incapable of combining partial conclusions from separate decision models. Thus SUDO-PLANNER will miss a result following from a set of KB relations unless it incorporates those relations together in a QPN.

The addition of high-level spanning links as a conservative knowledge engineering policy compromises the goal of multilevel operationality. Because SUDO-PLANNER removes the spurious relations only upon elaboration, it ends up deriving conclusions at a lower level than is strictly necessary.

As mentioned above, SUDO-PLANNER's event variable KB is neither well-defined nor guaranteed to be coherent. Further study of the semantics of KB assertions would advance definitional clarity (see Section 5.4.1), as would a more formal characterization of the model construction procedure. A better understanding of these issues is a prerequisite for an analysis of KB coherence.

The practical implication of this evaluation is that knowledge engineering is difficult. In my experience developing SUDO-PLANNER, the effect of KB modifications on the sequence of models generated was often unpredictable. Rules of thumb for debugging the KB, such as adding high-level single-step summaries of complex pathways, were discovered by trial-and-error. Only later was I able to rationalize the practice in terms of its interaction with the model construction procedure.

Some of the shortcomings of the model construction procedure are probably amenable to incremental solutions. For example, the backward bias of model extension (discussed at the end of Section 6.3.2) would be easy to balance with a forward extension operator. As another example, we could increase fluidity and coherence by permitting multiple, mutually exclusive relation sets at a single abstraction level. Such an extension requires a generalization (and a formal tightening) of the notion of compatibility regulating the merging of structure into QPNs. Section 7.5.1 discusses the possible use of spanning relations, a special case of this idea, in a qualitative approach to tradeoff resolution.

This critical view of SUDO-PLANNER's model construction performance does not reflect discouragement about the task of constructing decision models from large multilevel KBs. SUDO-PLANNER represents a first attempt to automate this task, which was intentionally framed in terms of highly ambitious (and somewhat conflicting) desiderata in order to uncover the performance boundaries. By identifying and emphasizing its limitations, I aim to stimulate research on improvements to SUDO-PLANNER's approach to knowledge representation and model synthesis.

6.4 Focus of Attention

For large KBs, controlling model construction is a significant and difficult problem. Directing model synthesis effort toward the most relevant regions of the KB requires some sort of *focus* mechanism. Unfortunately, it appears to be difficult to justify a focusing strategy based on the decision-theoretic principles underlying SUDO-PLANNER. The sections below discuss the basic issue of justified focus and present the rationalized, albeit unjustified, focus mechanism implemented in SUDO-PLANNER.

6.4.1 Justified Focus

In the most straightforward implementation of the model construction procedure, SUDO-PLANNER would start from a QPN containing only the value node and proceed to apply backward chaining and elaboration steps until it exhausted the KB or its computational resources. This unfocused approach proves unsatisfactory for any real problem. A planner with a moderately large medical knowledge base would be obliged to consider the advisability of actions ranging from taking blood pressure to prophylactic heart transplants for every patient. We need a method that focuses attention without recklessly overlooking valid therapeutic opportunities.

Ideally, we would like to ground our focus mechanism in relevance principles that justify selectivity in the application of knowledge. A sound procedure for focus of attention ignores only facts that are *irrelevant* to the task at hand [153]. For the planning task, knowledge is irrelevant iff it has no bearing on the optimal strategy.

One approach to justified focus assumes that at any time the agent's plan is optimal given the information available at that time. Under this assumption, the planner need consider only strategy modifications warranted by changes in its information state. In a medical context, the planner in effect assumes that it has been the patient's physician up to the current time, so the current plan must be what it would have recommended given the current information. When new information arrives, it is necessary to reevaluate only those previous conclusions that depend on changed facts [94].

This "status quo optimality" heuristic meshes well with the planning and execution model of Section 3.1. If the planner has converged on a singleton plan class specifying the appropriate action in every contingency, then planning is finished and only execution remains. More realistically, the planner produces plan classes specifying action for only the immediate contingencies, necessitating further planning for the unanticipated observation patterns that make up the majority of possible futures. When an unanticipated situation occurs, the planner needs consider only its difference from an anticipated situation in adapting its corresponding plan to meet the new situation.

Unfortunately, the focusing power of this heuristic is often disappointingly weak. The smallest changes in situation may dictate arbitrary alterations in strategy, requiring the modification of actions seemingly unrelated to the situation change. In medicine, for example, the advisability of a therapeutic action typically depends on the broad concept of overall state of health. For instance, consider a patient who is a candidate for a heart transplant. Suppose that in the current situation, the planner determines that the patient narrowly qualifies for this dangerous and expensive procedure. Next consider a new finding that is unrelated to heart disease or to any other cardiovascular concept but that has a slight negative influence on the patient's life expectancy. Even though its health risk is unrelated, the new finding reduces the potential benefit of a heart transplant because it lessens the survival time to be gained. Because the patient is a marginal transplant candidate and the new finding has no effect on the cost of the procedure, the observation may be grounds for reversal of the original decision.

These kinds of situations are ubiquitous in medicine, and I suspect they are common in other domains as well. In a comprehensive KB all events are related, if only because they all have some connection to *value*. This observation suggests that the opportunities to focus a planner based on true irrelevance are rare and therefore we need to explore other grounds for allocating reasoning resources in the planning task.

6.4.2 Focus Variables

SUDO-PLANNER employs a simple focus mechanism based partly on the status quo optimality heuristic discussed above. The method designates particular QPN variables as *focus variables*, thereby controlling the invocation of backward chaining as described in Section 6.3.2.

Initially, the set of focus variables comprises those marked as *changed* in the input problem description. This is a direct reflection of the assumption described above: if the current strategy is optimal, only changes in the status quo are relevant to planning. SUDO-PLANNER maintains focus by adding to the list any variable that is mentioned in dominance conditions derived in the course of planning. These variables are worthy of further inference because new dominance results about actions and observed events that appear in undominated plan classes refine the plan graph.

A QPN variable is eligible for backward chaining if it is synergistic with a focus variable on *value*. To understand the rationale for this criterion, consider the QPN of Figure 6.12. There, f is the sole focus variable and c is a candidate for backward chaining. The two variables are synergistic in direction δ_1 on *value* in this reduced QPN, that is, $Y_U^{\delta_1}(\{c, f\})$. Let d be some predecessor of c in the event variable KB, not in the current QPN. The backward chaining criterion dictates that c be extensible if $\delta_1 \in \{+, -\}$, but not if $\delta_1 \in \{0, ?\}$.

If $\delta_1 \in \{+, -\}$, then both c and its predecessor d are of interest to the planner. The synergy entails a nontrivial monotone decision relation for f and c, and for f and d as well if $\delta_2 \neq ?$. This result could be significant for one of two reasons:

1. Variable f has changed, therefore synergy with a decision variable dictates the direction to alter the status quo plan.

2. Variable f appears in the description of an active plan class, therefore the monotone decision property dictates a refinement to the plan graph.

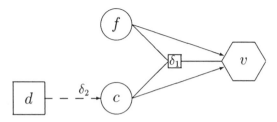

Figure 6.12: Synergy with a focus variable. $Y_U^{\delta_1}(\{c,f\})$ holds in the QPN containing variables c, f, and v. Backward chaining on c to introduce d to the network can lead to interesting results only if $\delta_1 \in \{+,-\}$.

Because f is a focus variable, one of these reasons must be in force.

Conversely, if $\delta_1 \notin \{+,-\}$, we gain nothing (with respect to f) by backward chaining on c. If $\delta_1 = 0$, then c is irrelevant to f, as is d. This is a strong case of justified focus. On the other hand, if $\delta_1 = ?$ then c and its predecessors generally are relevant. However, the ambiguous sign prevents SUDO-PLANNER from determining in what way they are relevant, and further backward chaining will never resolve the ambiguity. Hence, the model construction procedure may as well not pursue this path in the KB. To SUDO-PLANNER, futility serves as a focus justification on par with irrelevance.

To implement the extensibility criterion, SUDO-PLANNER records all known synergies with focus variables (on *value*) as they are derived in the course of dominance proving. The situation Figure 6.12 depicts holds for the QPN in some state of reduction, not necessarily in any constructed QPN or in the KB directly.

6.5 Related Work

Section 6.3.4 includes an evaluation of SUDO-PLANNER's model construction procedure in terms of the desiderata for multilevel reasoning presented in Section 6.1. In this section, I take a broader perspective and contrast the SUDO-PLANNER approach with related work on model construction and multilevel reasoning. The two topics are reviewed separately below, since SUDO-PLANNER is the first program designed to construct decision models from a multilevel KB.

6.5.1 Decision Model Construction

Most work on decision model structuring has been carried out with the intent of aiding human decision analysts (see Humphreys and McFadden [70], Keeney [76], and von Winterfeldt [166] for a mixed sample). There is a significant demand for such aids, especially as the availability of inexpensive, user-friendly software packages for personal computers makes DA technology accessible to a widening group of potential analysts. The need is particularly critical for those analysts who have less experience with the methodology and a lower level of familiarity with the underlying decision-theoretic concepts. In fact, we have incorporated some of the qualitative dominance ideas from this dissertation into BUNYAN, a program for critiquing human-generated decision models [176]. But despite some common concerns, the issues faced in attempting to fully automate the model construction task differ significantly from the problems of aiding human modelers.

In this section, I discuss the few projects that have specifically addressed themselves to automated knowledge-based formulation of decision models. Note that all of these efforts aim to build a single, complete (that is, numerically precise) decision model. In SUDO-PLANNER, a set of incomplete models contribute dominance results about various facets of the decision problem. It is important to distinguish that the standards for model construction in the two approaches. For incomplete models it is reasonable to speak of *validity*, while for complete ones *approximation* is a more appropriate standard. And because each iteration of SUDO-PLANNER's model construction cycle addresses only a subset of decision features, this approach offers better prospects for justified focus (Section 6.4.1).

In Holtzman's "intelligent decision systems" [64], the domain knowledge is primarily in the form of a general decision model, encoded as an influence diagram with assessment functions for each node of the graph. Constructing a model for a particular decision is largely a matter of reducing the template model that is built into the program. This is essentially the decision-model-as-KB approach that I rejected in Section 1.5 for reasons of scalability.

The alternative advocated in this work calls for dynamic assembly of decision models from a knowledge base of primitive components. An early example of this kind of behavior was exhibited by a program for Hodgkins disease, described by Rutherford et al. [129], that dynamically constructs decision trees from a KB specifying a variety of diagnostic tests and treatments. Its flexibility lies in the possibility of modifying the set of available tests and treatments on a case-specific basis. Hollenberg's Decision Tree Builder (DTB) [63] also generates decision trees using a medical knowledge base of diseases, tests, and treatments. Unlike the Hodgkins program, DTB is intended to handle a broad range of medical decision problems. Consequently, its representations are considerably more general, and its tree generation, correspondingly more flexible. A disease may be parameterized by *attributes*, which in turn may influence the applicability of various actions as well as the values of probabilities and utilities in the model. Tests and treatments may indicate or modify the values of disease attributes.[4] A simple control structure directs tree construction, employing a model of patient states for bookkeeping purposes.

With this kind of generation approach, it is extremely difficult to escape from exhaustive consideration of a combinatorial space of plans and events. The programs must construct strategies that include every action identified as potentially beneficial, and model every event identified as potentially relevant. The desire to avoid this behavior was the primary motivation for developing abstraction mechanisms for SUDO-PLANNER (see Section 1.6). Control of model construction remains important even with a multilevel repre-

---

[4]Incidentally, difficulties with this mechanism first brought my attention to the problem of distinguishing the values of event variables in different temporal relation to their affecting actions (J. P. Hollenberg, personal communication), handled by Markov influences and variable mitosis in SUDO-PLANNER (see Section 6.3.3).

116

sentation, as discussed in Section 6.4.

The model constructor closest in spirit to SUDO-PLANNER is Breese's ALTERID system [12, 13]. ALTERID constructs numeric influence diagrams from a KB of logical and probabilistic assertions in response to specific queries. Aside from the contrast in precision between qualitative and numeric probabilistic relationships, the KB language ALTERID uses differs from SUDO-PLANNER's in two important respects:

1. SUDO-PLANNER's KB has an explicit taxonomic dimension. Relations at different levels of abstraction may coexist in the ALTERID KB, but they are not treated specially by the reasoner.

2. ALTERID bundles predecessors of a variable together and permits multiple exclusive groupings. Backward chaining retrieves one of the specified predecessor sets, rather than a collection of individually asserted predecessors as in SUDO-PLANNER.

Because the predecessors are specified and retrieved as a group, ALTERID avoids some of the compatibility problems faced by SUDO-PLANNER. Manipulation of these compound units provides the knowledge engineer with greater control over the networks ultimately produced, at the expense of flexibility obtained by reasoning about the individual predecessors. ALTERID's provision for multiple exclusive predecessor sets is not expressible in SUDO-PLANNER, although some exclusivity can be represented by separating the structures by taxonomic levels. The ALTERID algorithm also avoids some of SUDO-PLANNER's limitations in directing the construction process: it extends models via both forward and backward chaining, and employs sensitivity analysis and other heuristics to choose the paths of extension.

In their work on story understanding, Charniak and Goldman [16] address the problem of dynamically generating belief networks for computing the probabilities of competing interpretations of phrases in the text. Production rules direct model assembly based on patterns in the current belief network and output of the parser.

Finally, in previous research I considered special mechanisms for constructing the outcome and preference portions of a decision model [171, Chapter 8]. Although this work is largely compatible with SUDO-PLANNER, I have not included any of it in the implementation. In particular, the facilities for choosing representations for health outcomes based on terminological transformations [172] should be applicable to model construction in general.

6.5.2 Abstraction

Abstraction has been studied in a variety of AI contexts. Section 3.2.1 discussed research in planning with abstraction and its relation to SUDO-PLANNER's knowledge representations for plans and actions. Researchers have also developed formal theories of abstraction *per se* [62], intended to support a variety of AI tasks. In this section I briefly review (in terms of the desiderata presented in Section 6.1) some approaches toward multilevel knowledge representation within the "causal" modeling paradigm for diagnostic reasoning. The commonality of these systems with SUDO-PLANNER lies in their explicit use of taxonomic and domain relations; the causal nature of the domain relation is inessential to this discussion. This appears to be a minimal requirement for evaluation in terms of the multilevel reasoning desiderata. Direct comparison of these programs to SUDO-PLANNER is not possible, however, as they were designed for significantly different tasks.

In a *compiled knowledge* approach [14], all of the relations encoded at high levels could in principle be derived from deeper knowledge about low-level concepts. Compilation (typically a manual operation) improves reasoning efficiency by replacing common, complicated inference patterns by direct associations. A truly compiled KB is necessarily reductionist. The system as a whole is not really multilevel unless the reasoner also has access to the deep knowledge.

In Section 6.1.2, I cited ABEL [109] and CADUCEUS [120] as examples of rigid and fluid systems, respectively. ABEL is also reductionist; it ultimately performs all of its causal reasoning at the lowest available level of abstraction.[5] Partitioning the KB into levels improves definitional clarity and thereby enhances the prospects for coherence. CADUCEUS, like SUDO-PLANNER, is non-reductionist, fluid, and operational at all levels. Although the semantics of its KB are not perfectly clear, and the KB itself is not guaranteed to be coherent, CADUCEUS appears not to suffer as badly in these respects as SUDO-PLANNER. Because it reasons directly from the KB, CADUCEUS imposes the closed-world assumption globally, rather than locally on models constructed from the KB. Finally, the hybrid ABEL/CADUCEUS approach that Patil and Senyk propose [110] appears to inherit the desirable characteristics of CADUCEUS listed above.

6.6   On Constructed Models

In this section, I step back from the specifics of QPNs and SUDO-PLANNER's methods for constructing them to examine some fundamental questions about synthetic decision models. In particular, I look at the nature of decision models, their relation to normative decision theory, and the implications for the model construction enterprise.

6.6.1   Models and Closed Worlds

One plausible operational definition for "model" is "a structure on which a closed-world assumption is invoked." In Hewitt's terminology, decision and other models are *microtheories*, the closed components of an "open system" [61]. All deduction in open systems is applied to microtheories, which are constructed by extralogical mechanisms.

Whether or not their designers employ the terminology of models or microtheories, systems that interleave inference under closed-world assumptions with non-logical processing perform what I have been calling "model construction." An example is Forbus's Qualitative Process Engine (QPE) [44], a program that constructs qualitative process models

---

[5]However, given incomplete information, ABEL's higher levels apply knowledge based on implicit assumptions not accessible to levels below. In this situation, the program can exhibit non-reductionist behavior.

from a KB of process descriptions and a specification of potentially active processes. As in QPNs, derived relations among variables in qualitative process models depend on an assumption that the set of influences is completely known. QPE accumulates active relations in *closed-world tables* before assuming the closure required to compute the net result.

6.6.2 Decision Models

The decision-theoretic formulation of a decision problem postulates an abstract set of available acts, corresponding to the set of all plans Ω, and a set of possible states of nature Θ. The axioms of expected utility [121, 134] imply the existence of a utility function $u : \Omega \times \Theta \to \Re$, such that for all $\pi_1, \pi_2 \in \Omega$,

$$\pi_1 \succeq \pi_2 \Leftrightarrow E_\theta[u(\pi_1, \theta)] \geq E_\theta[u(\pi_2, \theta)]. \tag{6.2}$$

The expected utility property (6.2) is of fundamental theoretical importance for several reasons, including:

- It grounds the theory of subjective probability in rational decision making.

- The existence of numerical representations is analytically convenient for mathematical decision theorists.

Practitioners of applied decision theory, or *decision analysis* (DA) [69, 122], cite another implication of (6.2):

- The theory can be directly implemented in prescriptive aids for practical decision making through the assessment of formal probabilistic models and utility functions.

A *decision model* is a literal translation of the theoretical entities of (6.2) to concrete symbolic structures. In specifying decision models, decision analysts usually separate the probability and utility components by identifying a special outcome descriptor c (the *consequence*, a function of π and θ) sufficient for describing preferences. The utility model is then $u(c)$ and the probabilistic model is expressed as $f_c(\cdot|\pi)$ without explicit reference to θ.

Although modeling schemes differ in form and expressive power, all represent a choice situation in terms of the basic decision-theoretic concepts of alternative acts, uncertain events, and preferences. In standard DA methodology, analysts assess these elements by interpreting real and hypothetical choices of the decision maker in terms of (6.2). As Tversky [164] and others have noted, this procedure presumes the theory has some descriptive validity, a matter deserving considerable skepticism.

Stated in the abstract, the components of decision theory are completely general, and its arguments normatively compelling.[6] Despite their structural correspondence, however,

---

[6] This is not to deny that the tenets of Bayesian decision theory have been and continue to be highly controversial—in statistics and philosophy as well as AI. I will not recount the dispute here; nevertheless, my opinion is that the majority of the objections apply to narrow applications of the theory rather than to the fundamentals themselves. The majority of objectors, of course, have differing opinions. For elaboration, see the discussion below and previous writings [177].

the generality and normativeness of the basic decision-theoretic formulation does not automatically transfer to particular decision models. The rational agent axiomatized by decision theory is an idealization; decision models can only approximate its preferences and beliefs.

The next section explores the nature of this idealization, using Savage's concept of a "small world." Section 6.6.4 examines the implications of these observations for the enterprise of building computational agents based on decision-theoretic principles.

6.6.3 Small Worlds

Decision models fall short of capturing the ideal agent for two related reasons. First, as *models*, they are imperfectly related to the reality they are intended to represent [147]. Second, the decision problems they model constitute only a slice of the overall decision situation faced by the agent. This latter issue is the problem of small worlds.

Savage [134, page 83] points out that in the decision-theoretic formulation, the ideal rational agent

> ... has only one decision to make in his whole life. He must, namely, decide
> how to live, and this he might in principle do once and for all.

Choice of this lifelong policy is the agent's *grand-world* decision problem. Decision theorists and analysts following (and including) Savage rightfully regard grand-world decision modeling as unrealistic, and instead focus on isolated decision situations called *small worlds*. The problem of small worlds is to justify this focus—to determine when it is legitimate to apply the machinery of decision theory to isolated slices of the grand-world decision.

Savage attacked this problem formally by describing the correspondence between the small and grand worlds. Because the grand world is a refinement of the small world, states in the latter map to classes of states in the former. Thus, small-world consequences correspond to distributions over grand-world consequences. A small world that obeys the axioms of expected utility is called a *pseudo-microcosm*. Decisions based on a pseudo-microcosm are valid when the utility of small-world consequences is equal to their expected utility in the grand world, and the probability of small-world states is the same as the grand-world probability of the corresponding class. If these correspondences hold, then the small world is called a *microcosm*. Savage shows that pseudo-microcosms need not be microcosms, though he expresses the opinion that "the possibility of being taken in by a pseudo-microcosm that is not a real microcosm is remote" [134, page 90].

Details of the technical criteria for determining whether a small world is microcosmic are inessential to the present discussion (in fact they have not been completely characterized).[7] Examination of decision modeling experience suggests that even if the small worlds can be formally cast as microcosms, the myopic view from the small world is likely to result in models that fail to respect features that are expressible only in more refined worlds. For example, failure to account for portfolio effects is one way to get

---

[7] For a lucid presentation and a concrete example of a non-microcosmic pseudo-microcosm, see Shafer's reexamination of Savage's arguments, as well as the commentaries on Shafer by Lindley and Dawid [141].

"taken in by a pseudo-microcosm." Decomposing a grand-world decision into a series of small-world choices often leads to models that do not reflect the reduction in risk due to diversification from the perspective of the global portfolio choice.

Whether we attribute the portfolio effect distortions to pseudo-microcosmic effects or simply to inaccurate modeling, the source of the problem lies in the isolated nature of small-world decision making. As Section 6.6.1 notes, reasoning with decision models requires a closed-world assumption; closing a small world is tantamount to ignoring features relevant only in the grand world. Thus, choosing the scope of small worlds to avoid bias is critical to the legitimacy of decision modeling. Unfortunately, the basis for such a choice is not well-understood by decision theorists.

SUDO-PLANNER's dominance-proving architecture is unique in embracing the concept of grand-world decision making. A dominance-proving planner, as described in Section 2.4.1, is a grand-world decision maker if its plan space comprises lifelong policies rather than short-term strategies. Such a plan space is conceivable within a constraint-posting framework because—unlike the basic decision-theoretic formulation—acts are composite objects described as combinations of primitive acts. Decisions are distinctions among plan classes rather than selections of particular acts. In decision theory, acts are atomic and decisions are selections. Hence, it is not possible in decision theory to make a near-term decision without either committing to long-term decisions or proceeding as though the near-term is the only term via a small-world construction. A constraint-posting planner, in contrast, can make a near-term decision without the pretense that it has solved its ultimate decision problem.

We can consider SUDO-PLANNER a grand-world planner in this sense because its universal plan class (Section 3.1) does not limit the scope of plans. In domain modeling, however, SUDO-PLANNER is just as dependent on small worlds as traditional DA systems. As Figure 6.13 illustrates, the models SUDO-PLANNER constructs to evaluate the effects of actions are small worlds. Specifically, they represent consequences at a level of abstraction coarser than the ultra-fine grand-world ideal. It appears to me that this relation will inevitably be approximate, and thus that small-world decision models are unavoidable.

The tenuous relationship between decision models and the decision-theoretic ideal is transparent when we view our models as imperfect representations of worlds that are small to begin with. Those recognizing the problem have drawn differing conclusions about its implications for decision-theoretic applications, in both DA and AI. In the next section, I examine some of these arguments and present the view behind the design of SUDO-PLANNER and its mechanisms for constructing decision models.

6.6.4 Constructive Decision Theory

Shafer has argued persuasively that the value of a theory of probability judgment depends on its *constructive* utility, that is, on factors that determine its usefulness for developing mental arguments, evaluating evidence, and expressing and explaining beliefs [140, 142]. Shafer's objections to Bayesian decision theory stem in part from its treatment of preferences and beliefs as conceptually innate and its consequent emphasis on elicitation rather

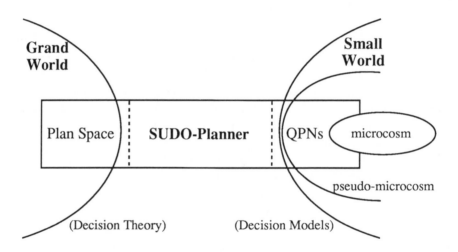

Figure 6.13: SUDO-PLANNER plans in the grand world using small-world decision models. The QPNs it generates will generally be pseudo-microcosms, faithful to the grand world only if they are also microcosms.

than synthesis. Moreover, in his view [141, page 485], "the problem of small worlds serves as a demonstration of how far [Savage's] normative approach was from a sensible, constructive approach to decision."

My conclusion in Section 1.5 that decision models are not suitable knowledge bases is an endorsement for the constructive point of view. Once we undertake to design agents without explicit *a priori* decision models, it is clear that constructive issues will be influential. The lack of an established set of principles for decision model construction, a *constructive decision theory*, increases the difficulty of this endeavor.

Although I agree with Shafer about the goals of constructive decision theory, we diverge sharply in approach. Where Shafer has emphasized comparison of alternative probability calculi (in particular, Bayesian probability versus Dempster-Shafer belief functions [139]), I would focus on more comprehensive representation issues and procedures for constructing decision models from KBs. Furthermore, there is no need to cast this effort as a new foundation for normative behavior; the rational agent of decision theory remains a useful idealization for anchoring our constructive concepts [177].

Perhaps the most appealing path to a constructive decision theory is to broaden our rationality concepts to incorporate constructive factors. This is essentially the approach of Good, who introduces "type II" rationality as the extension of Bayesian rationality where the cost of computation is taken into account [49]. This principle is difficult to apply, however, as we are usually unable to precisely characterize the necessary computation. The full analysis requires consideration of an agent's decisions about its own cognitive make-up, which can lead to infinite regress if we are not careful. (See Doyle for a discussion of some issues in what he calls *rational self-government* [30].)

6.6.5 Constructed Models: Conclusion

Once we take into account the dynamic process of synthesizing decision models, the overall procedure is no longer guaranteed to be normative. Nevertheless, the relation to Bayesian decision theory is valuable as a comparative standard. Principles of model construction can be evaluated on this basis, to the extent that we can measure the potential distortion of alternative construction strategies.

Little research to date has addressed constructive decision-modeling issues, especially from a computational perspective. In this chapter, I have identified some basic problems in representing and reasoning with the knowledge SUDO-PLANNER uses for constructing QPNs. The description of SUDO-PLANNER's mechanisms represents a first step toward solving these problems and developing a set of principles for automated decision model synthesis.

7 Dominance Proving

This chapter completes the description of SUDO-PLANNER by describing its dominance prover (the right-hand half of Figure 6.5). This module (1) derives and (2) records dominance conditions entailed by a given QPN. The first two sections of this chapter describe these tasks. SUDO-PLANNER's dominance prover supports planning up to tradeoffs, but its qualitative techniques are insufficient for resolving the tradeoffs identified. The remainder of the chapter considers approaches toward surmounting the tradeoff barrier in ways compatible with SUDO-PLANNER's dominance-proving architecture and its existing qualitative methods.

7.1 Reducing the QPN

The relation of QPN variables to the value node determines their decision-theoretic properties. The dominance prover derives these properties by transforming the original QPN to one where these relationships are direct. The reduction operator of Chapter 4 renders indirect relations direct by removing intermediate variables from the QPN and updating the remaining qualitative relations according to Theorems 4.11 and 4.22. Reduction is the sole QPN inference rule applied by SUDO-PLANNER's dominance prover.

The reduction process proceeds backwards from the value node. At each iteration, SUDO-PLANNER chooses a predecessor w of *value* such that $pred(w) \neq \emptyset$. It then constructs $red(w, G)$ by splicing w from the graph and recomputing the qualitative relations for each combination of predecessors and successors of w using formulas (4.9) and (4.18).[1] After each reduction, the dominance prover inspects the QPN for decision-theoretic implications and records the results as described below. The procedure terminates when all remaining variables have *value* as sole successor.

For example, at one point the model construction process produces the QPN of Figure 7.1a. The candidates for reduction are *long-term morbidity* and *mortality*. SUDO-PLANNER chooses one of these and reduces it, adding its predecessors to the potential reduction candidates. The program proceeds to reduce nodes one-by-one until it reaches the configuration of Figure 7.1b.

As shown in Section 4.4.3, reducing an arbitrary subset of the variables in a QPN can be performed with $\Theta(|V|^2)$ applications of the rule for updating qualitative influences (4.9), where $|V|$ is the number of variables in the network. Each influence update may require

---

[1]The implementation of these reductions is non-destructive; the original QPN is required for modification in the model construction cycle of Chapter 6.

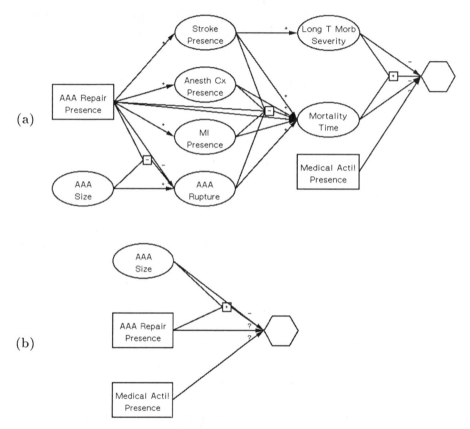

Figure 7.1: (a) The QPN before reduction. (b) The completely reduced QPN.

up to $O(|V|)$ applications of (4.18) to compute the new synergies (one for each potentially synergistic partner), bringing the overall worst-case complexity to $O(|V|^3)$.

7.2 Recording Dominance Results

Between reductions, SUDO-PLANNER inspects the QPN for relations implying dominance among plan classes. There are two ways that a QPN can manifest such implications, both involving qualitative relations with the value node. First, an action variable av may be directly related to $value$, $U^\delta(av)$ for $\delta \in \{+,-\}$. If av has no other paths to $value$, this implies that the optimal value of av in the plan is its maximum or minimum value, depending on δ (see Section 4.5.2). Second, av may be synergistic on $value$ with a potentially observable event variable ev, $Y_U^\delta(\{av, ev\})$. In this case, the optimal av policy is monotone in ev if ev is observable, by the monotone decision property (Section 4.7.3).

Let $av = r_j\langle a_i\rangle$, the action variable describing role r_j of action concept a_i. The first case can be expressed as a dominance condition by constraining plans with actions of type a_i to those with its subtype where r_j is restricted to the extreme value of its range. Let r_j^δ denote this extreme value, r_j^+ for the maximum and r_j^- the minimum. For example, $\mathbf{presence^+} = \mathbf{true}$ and $\mathbf{dosage^-} = 0$. The subtype of a_i, written $a_i(r_j^\delta)$, is obtained by value restricting r_j to r_j^δ. SUDO-PLANNER creates this concept in NIKL, which classifies it automatically in the action taxonomy.

To express the dominance result $D(\Pi_2, \Pi_1)$, SUDO-PLANNER must create the two plan classes. The dominance prover defines Π_1 by posting an action constraint (see Section 3.4.1) of type a_i on the universal plan class Ω. Π_2 is similarly defined by an action constraint of type $a_i(r_j^\delta)$. The plan space manager classifies both classes in the plan graph. The $U^\delta(r_j\langle a_i\rangle)$ condition implies that any plan in Π_1 can be improved (in a non-strict sense) by revising $r_j\langle a_i\rangle$ toward its extremum, therefore Π_2 dominates Π_1 by Definition 2.1. $D(\Pi_2, \Pi_1)$ is a restriction because $\Pi_2 \subseteq \Pi_1$.

The second type of dominance result is the monotone policy constraint justified by qualitative synergy. For example, in the reduced QPN of Figure 7.1b, AAA $repair$ is positively synergistic on $value$ with AAA $size$. (The $Y^?$ synergies holding between other pairs are implicit in the QPN graph.) $Y_U^+(\{AAA\ repair, AAA\ size\})$ implies that the optimal AAA $repair$ policy is increasing in AAA $size$, which is asserted to be observable in the description of this particular case.

The method for recording this fact on the plan graph is analogous to the action constraint procedure described above. Let Π_1 be the class of plans where $\mathbf{AAA\text{-}repair}$ is under consideration, defined by posting an action constraint of type $\mathbf{AAA\text{-}repair}$ on Ω. SUDO-PLANNER creates Π_2 from Π_1 by posting an additional monotone policy constraint of the form[2]

$$(+, \mathbf{presence}\langle\mathbf{AAA\text{-}repair}\rangle, \mathbf{size}\langle\mathbf{AAA\text{-}event}\rangle).$$

---

[2]The notation $role\langle a_i\rangle$ is used for KB event variables to distinguish them from their corresponding QPN variables. For instance, $\mathbf{presence}\langle\mathbf{AAA\text{-}repair}\rangle$ corresponds to the QPN variable AAA $repair$.

The dominance condition $D(\Pi_2, \Pi_1)$ asserts that plans where **AAA-repair** is under consideration can be restricted to threshold policies on **size⟨AAA-event⟩**.

SUDO-PLANNER must also ensure that the event variable in a monotone policy constraint is observable in the plan class restricted by the dominance result. An event variable is *freely observable* (observable without an explicit test action) if it is an action variable or, like *AAA size* in the example above, it is asserted to be so in a particular case. If the event variable ev in the $Y_U^\delta(\{av, ev\})$ condition is not freely observable, SUDO-PLANNER retrieves from its KB the set of action types asserted to render ev observable: $\{a_i \mid CO(a_i, ev)\}$ (see Section 5.7). As above, let Π_1 be the plan class where av's action type is under consideration. For each action a_i in the set of observable creators, SUDO-PLANNER generates the plan class $\Pi_{1,i}$ by posting an action constraint of type a_i on Π_1. The dominance prover adds conditions of the form $D(\Pi_{2,i}, \Pi_{1,i})$ to the plan graph, where $\Pi_{2,i}$ is obtained from $\Pi_{1,i}$ by posting the monotone policy constraint (δ, av, ev).

For example, at a later point in the model construction cycle, the dominance prover obtains the result $Y_U^-(\{AAA \; repair, cath \; result\})$. (The conclusion follows from *AAA repair*'s negative synergy with CAD and the positive relation between CAD and *cath result*.) As shown in Figure 7.2, SUDO-PLANNER must ensure that the monotone policy constraint is only in force when *cath result* is observable, that is, when cardiac catheterization has in fact been performed.

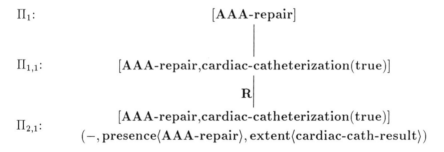

Figure 7.2: A plan graph fragment created to record a dominance result. The *AAA repair* policy is decreasing in *cath result* whenever the latter is made observable by catheterization.

The dominance prover performs one additional task during inspection of reduced QPNs. Any variables having known synergies with focus variables are marked as such. As described in Section 6.3.2, this is one of the criteria for directing the course of backward chaining in the model construction process.

7.3   The Tradeoff Barrier

The dominance-proving methods described above, in concert with the model construction procedure of the previous chapter, comprise SUDO-PLANNER's algorithm for planning up to tradeoffs. Although QPNs are powerful enough to justify an important class of commonsense decisions, the inherent weakness of the $\oplus$ operator prevents SUDO-PLANNER from reaching conclusions when the contributing factors conflict. This is the hallmark of a tradeoff situation.

Tradeoffs are dominance-proving dead ends for SUDO-PLANNER. Qualitative relations of sign "?" tend to proliferate, as a single unknown link renders ambiguous any composite pathway that spans it ($? \otimes \delta = ? \oplus \delta' = ?$, for any $\delta \neq 0$). If a decision problem involves a tradeoff, so do any decisions for which it is a subproblem.

7.3.1 Example: A Subtle Tradeoff

The seriousness of the tradeoff barrier is illustrated by a subtle tradeoff encountered by SUDO-PLANNER in the running example. At one point in the model construction process, the dominance prover is presented with the QPN of Figure 7.3.[3] SUDO-PLANNER's task is to derive the synergy between *CAD* and *AAA repair* on *value*.

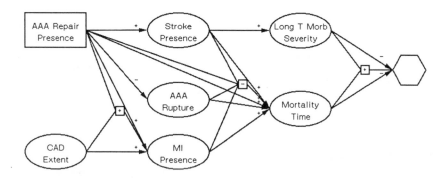

Figure 7.3: A subtle tradeoff. Although *AAA repair* and *CAD* interact in their influence on *MI*, SUDO-PLANNER's dominance prover cannot derive a synergy on *value*.

As shown in the figure, *CAD* and *AAA repair* have a direct positive synergy on *MI*. This means that increasing *CAD* increases the risk of *MI* due to the AAA surgery. While *CAD* increases the risk of *MI* in any event—a fact represented separately by the $S^+(CAD, MI)$ link—the expected increase is greater in the case of aneurysm surgery. Because *MI* is undesirable, the Y^+ relation to *MI* is an argument for a Y^- relation on *value*, and therefore for avoiding *AAA repair* in the presence of higher values of coronary disease. This is the justification given informally in Section 1.2 for the conclusion that *AAA repair* should be a threshold policy on *CAD*.

This factor is highlighted by the partly reduced QPN of Figure 7.4. If we could ignore the direct influence of *AAA repair* on *value*, then $Y_U^-(\{AAA\ repair, CAD\})$ would hold by simple propagation of synergies through influences (Theorem 4.21). Of course, we are not permitted to recklessly ignore this direct relation. Other effects of *AAA repair* may interact with *MI* and are therefore relevant to repair policy given *CAD*.

---

[3]The QPN depicted here is simplified for expository purposes. Figure 7.3 displays the essential variables and qualitative relations, suppressing those that do not affect the analysis.

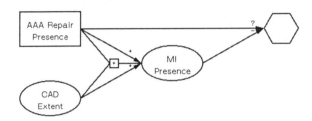

Figure 7.4: Partly reduced version of the QPN above. SUDO-PLANNER cannot derive the synergy between *AAA repair* and *CAD* on *value* because of *AAA repair*'s unresolved synergy with *MI*.

Three basic factors contribute to the synergy relation between *CAD* and *AAA repair*:

1. The positive interaction between the two variables on *MI*. As argued above, the increase in surgical risk presented by *CAD* supports a conclusion of Y_U^-.

2. *AAA rupture* is negatively synergistic with *MI* on *mortality*. Intuitively, this relation holds because a decrease in the rupture rate has a smaller impact on survival when the patient's life expectancy is already reduced by *MI*. In fact, all of the influences on *mortality* in this example are sub-synergistic, for the same reason that the noisy OR model implies Y^- (Section 4.7.2). In this case, the negative synergy combined with *CAD*'s positive influence on *MI* implies that the benefit of *AAA repair* in reducing ruptures is less important as *CAD* increases. Thus, this factor also supports Y_U^-.

3. On the flip side, the other influencers of *mortality* (such as *stroke*) also have less impact when *CAD* and therefore *MI* are increased. In this respect, a greater extent of *CAD* tends to decrease the mortality risk attributable to *AAA repair*, thereby supporting the conclusion Y_U^+.

The disagreement in sign between the second and third factors above is the reason that $Y_U^?(\{AAA\ repair, MI\})$ holds in the QPN of Figure 7.4 $(- \oplus + = ?)$. Combining this indeterminate synergy with the other relations in the figure leads to the inconclusive conclusion $Y_U^?(\{AAA\ repair, CAD\})$ in the completely reduced QPN.

We cannot resolve these factors qualitatively because they represent a genuine tradeoff. The argument that the *AAA repair* policy should be increasing in *CAD* because worse coronary disease decreases the importance of surgical risks is not spurious in the least: there are many examples in medicine and elsewhere where "having less to lose" is a legitimate basis for taking riskier action. Nor is this effect necessarily subordinate to the direct interaction. If we were considering a cause of mortality that interacted only slightly with *AAA repair*, this factor would hold sway.

7.3.2 Beyond the Tradeoff Barrier

This tradeoff indeed represents a dead end, preventing SUDO-PLANNER from drawing conclusions about any events or actions affecting CAD: observed CAD *history*, *cath result*, and $CABG$ in this example. We know in this case that the first factor easily outweighs the other two, but this fact is not expressible in the QPN of Figure 7.3. This situation is particularly frustrating because given $Y_U^-(\{AAA \ repair, CAD\})$, SUDO-PLANNER could go on to derive useful dominance results involving these other variables.

In the next two sections, I consider the possibility of transcending the tradeoff barrier. Section 7.4 discusses methods for incorporating externally resolved tradeoffs into the tradeoff formulation process. A variety of approaches for generating these tradeoff resolutions are investigated in Section 7.5.

7.4 Externally Resolved Tradeoffs

Though the process of tradeoff resolution may depend on precise, absolute knowledge, the end result is essentially qualitative. The product of a tradeoff resolver is simply the sign δ (with $\delta = ?$ signifying failure) of the originally indeterminate relation. Given the resolution δ, SUDO-PLANNER can proceed from the dead end as if δ had been derived with its own qualitative methods.

7.4.1 A Black-Box Interface

Because a tradeoff formulator like SUDO-PLANNER can apply resolutions without knowing their pedigree, QPN-based inference complements other dominance-proving mechanisms. For example, if an external source determines that factor one (from Section 7.3.1) prevails over factor three, SUDO-PLANNER can conclude that $AAA \ repair$ and CAD are negatively synergistic on *value*, and can go on to produce dominance results depending on that fact.

As Figure 7.5 illustrates, SUDO-PLANNER regards an external tradeoff resolver as a black box. When the attempt to add qualitative values results in ambiguity, SUDO-PLANNER presents the situation to the resolver. If resolution is successful, the resolver returns a non-"?" δ and SUDO-PLANNER proceeds from there.

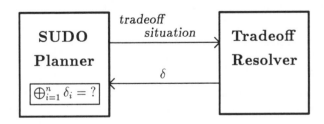

Figure 7.5: Black-box interface with an external tradeoff resolver.

7.4.2 Tradeoff Stubs

I have implemented a simple stub tradeoff resolver to demonstrate SUDO-PLANNER's ability to recover from dead ends. All qualitative relations in SUDO-PLANNER's KB are tagged with an identifier to facilitate reference to tradeoff situations. When sign addition is indeterminate, the stub resolver consults its list of answers to see if the present situation was anticipated. A total of five stub resolutions are required for the running example, including the conclusion that Y_U^- holds in the tradeoff presented in Section 7.3.1.

7.4.3 Resolver Candidates

Virtually any program that solves decision problems involving partially satisfiable goals can play the role of tradeoff resolver in the diagram of Figure 7.5. The ideal candidates are those that exploit knowledge difficult to express in SUDO-PLANNER's representation scheme yet can report their results in its qualitative terms.

Forms of knowledge suitable for resolving medical tradeoffs range from physiological models, like that in Long's program for heart failure [93], to representations of clinical trial studies, as proposed by Rennels [124]. The nature of tradeoff resolution knowledge in other domains is similarly unconstrained. Therapy predictions produced from the heart failure program [92] take the general form of qualitative influences, though the underlying model uses numeric relations.

The resolver's knowledge representation may itself be qualitative, though to complement SUDO-PLANNER it must make different qualitative distinctions, employ separate knowledge sources, or apply more powerful inference techniques. The feasibility of generating qualitative relations from other types of qualitative models is supported by the existence of programs performing similar tasks. For example, Downing's qualitative sensitivity analysis [27], and Weld's comparative analysis [170] both derive relations among variables from models describing *absolute* qualitative behavior.

7.5 Qualitative Tradeoff Resolution

The phrase "qualitative tradeoff resolution" is oxymoronic in the sense that qualitative unresolvability is my proposed definition for a tradeoff. But the meaning of "qualitative" is always relative to a set of qualities, hence varying the quality basis leads to different standards of what is qualitative. The implication for SUDO-PLANNER's task is that tradeoffs from one perspective may be non-tradeoffs from another. A tradeoff formulator should have the ability to select perspectives and reconcile the consequences of alternate viewpoints.

The following sections are speculative discussions of extensions to SUDO-PLANNER that could provide a more powerful tradeoff resolution capacity. They work by manipulating the notion of "qualitative" in one of the following ways:

1. Changing perspectives. Find another perspective or level of description in which the tradeoff is qualitatively resolved.

2. Introducing new qualitative distinctions. Other qualitative concepts can provide additional dominance-proving opportunities.

3. Modulating the degree of precision.

7.5.1 Spanning Influences and Synergies

A *spanning relation* is a domain relation that summarizes a body of network structure by directly connecting its endpoints. In a multilevel representation, the spanning relation coexists with the structure it summarizes at the same abstraction level. To interpret spanning relations, a reasoner needs the ability to maintain multiple exclusive views of a single relationship, perhaps using techniques similar to those employed by ALTERID [12] or CADUCEUS [120], mentioned in Section 6.5.

Formally, a spanning influence from a to b of sign δ asserts $S^\delta(a, b, G)$, where G is the network where all variables on pathways between a and b have been reduced. Spanning synergies are defined analogously. A spanning link mechanism is one that can reason about such relationships in the same model that contains the intermediate variables. A generalized spanning link mechanism would permit the G argument to vary arbitrarily across simultaneously considered qualitative relations. The answer to a query is the strongest result obtainable through transformation operators applied to any G.

Spanning links provide a means to express in the KB information currently encoded in tradeoff stubs. For example, if we know that the positive influence paths from a to b outweigh the negative ones, we can add $S^+(a, b)$ as a spanning link to express this fact. Even if $dir(a, b) = ?$ in the most detailed G, the spanning link can provide the stronger answer directly.

The implementation of spanning links, particularly the necessary adaptation of SUDO-PLANNER's model construction algorithm, presents some interesting problems. Modifying the assertion language to encompass spanning links is itself a significant extension, since the current representation never explicitly refers to G. It appears that a successful treatment of spanning links will require a clarification of the semantical issues raised in Section 5.4.1.

7.5.2 Negligibility Reasoning

The "order of magnitude" techniques [21, 123, 169] recently investigated in qualitative physics present another possibility for tradeoff resolution. In the case when one parallel influence can be declared *negligible* with respect to another—for example, the mildly unpleasant taste of an orally-administered drug relative to its curative powers—indeterminacy can be avoided by simply ignoring the former when in conflict with the latter.

Asserting that a factor is negligible means quite literally that it can be neglected without loss of validity. Researchers in qualitative physics have formalized this notion in terms of nonstandard analysis [22], an axiomatic framework for infinitesimal quantities. In the planning task, the standard for negligibility is in a factor's effect on the ultimate decision. Further work is required to formalize this standard in terms of infinitesimal quantities, and to relate these quantities to the probabilities and utilities that define QPN relations.

7.5.3 Further Qualitative Distinctions

Distinguishing deterministic from probabilistic relationships can enhance the qualitative conclusions derivable from a probabilistic network. For instance, Geiger has shown that a modified version of d-separation (called *D-separation*) that takes this distinction into account reveals a larger set of conditional independence relations when the network contains deterministic variables [116]. Deterministic versions of the other qualitative influences (S^+ and S^-) also provide added inferential power.

Michelena and Agogino [99] have recently investigated network models called *monotonic influence diagrams* that encode functional relationships of this type in graphical models based on probabilistic networks. Their inference procedure exploits techniques from the theory of constrained optimization to derive properties of optimal decisions via graphical manipulations similar to those for QPNs. It would be straightforward to substitute their procedures for standard QPN operators whenever functional relationships are identified by the model.

Other specializations of the qualitative relations defined here may prove useful. For example, I noted in Section 4.7.2 that the noisy OR model was a special case of negative probabilistic synergy. Explicitly recognizing that case (or using it as a new distinguished value in the quantity space of likelihood ratios) can strengthen the results of qualitative inference. In particular, some of the ambiguity introduced in influence reversal can be eliminated when the variables are known to interact in a noisy-OR fashion. Consider the reversal situation of Figure 4.3 and suppose that b is the noisy OR of a and w. Using the normal update rule (Theorem 4.12), the influence of w on a after reversal is ambiguous. However, the added constraint of the noisy OR permits us to conclude that the updated influence is negative, as long as this is consistent with the original link from w to a. More precisely, it can be shown (though the proof is not included here) that $S^{\delta_2}(w, a, G)$ implies $S^{\delta_2 \oplus \delta_4}(w, a, rev(a, b, G))$, where δ_4 is "$-$" for the noisy OR relation and "$+$" for the negated noisy OR ("noisy NOR").

7.5.4 Incorporating More Precise Information

Another broad tradeoff resolution strategy is to introduce more precise forms of information into the dominance-proving process. Extending a model to include partial or complete descriptions of the magnitudes of probabilities and utilities enlarges the set of decidable comparisons.

At the heart of any tradeoff is an unresolvable inequality on expected utilities. Though deciding this inequality based on an arbitrary set of constraints is intractable, a considerable body of research on AI and decision theory addresses restricted versions of this problem. For example, Sacks describes an algorithm for inequality proving based on algebraic constraints [132]. Other work has focused on special properties of classes of probabilities and utility functions (for a sampling, see [39, 57, 171, 178]). The work of Fertig and Breese on interval influence diagrams [37] is particularly promising for our purposes because their representation shares with QPNs the underlying probabilistic network framework.

Researchers in qualitative reasoning have also begun to consider mechanisms that employ precise knowledge to resolve ambiguities inherent in the original qualitative representations [83, 180]. Work along these lines should also be applicable to qualitative probabilistic reasoning.

8 The Complete Example

Our running example, the AAA/CAD/CVD case, has been presented piecemeal through-out this report. In this chapter I assemble the fragments into a more cohesive, chronological description of SUDO-PLANNER's performance on this problem.

8.1 Input Specification

The case, introduced in Section 1.2, is simply stated: a patient with a known history of CAD and CVD presents with a large AAA. From a medical perspective, of course, this description is exceedingly sketchy. Nevertheless, the description is sufficient to specify the relevant tradeoff formulation task, and any further information could not be exploited by SUDO-PLANNER.

The encoding of the case for input to SUDO-PLANNER is also quite simple. The status quo optimality heuristic of Section 6.4 dictates that the planner focus on changes to the current state. In this case, the underlying assumption is that the current therapy appropriately takes into account the patient's CAD and CVD, therefore planning should focus on strategy modifications warranted by the new finding, AAA.[1] Therefore, the input to SUDO-PLANNER specifies that **size⟨AAA-event⟩** be represented in the initial QPN, and that it be a focus variable.

The case description also specifies that the variable **size⟨AAA-event⟩**, as well as **history⟨CAD-event⟩** and **history⟨CVD-event⟩**, is freely observable. The initial find-ings of the case are eligible to appear in conditional plans without additional test actions to reveal their values.

That is the complete SUDO-PLANNER input for the running example. Realistic medical cases would specify many more changes and observations.

8.2 The Evolving QPN

Snapshots of the QPN in various stages of development appear throughout the previous two chapters. Figure 8.1 recapitulates the first few stages of QPN evolution, described in Section 6.3. In the initial QPN (Figure 8.1a), *AAA size* negatively influences *value* by

---

[1]Relaxing this assumption merely entails consideration of a broader set of findings. In this example, we could reexamine the current strategy by treating CAD and CVD as if they had just been discovered, like the AAA. The result is a blunter focus.

virtue of being a *disease severity*. This relationship is elaborated in Figure 8.1b, revealing that the undesirability of the aneurysm is due to its potential for rupture. Further elaboration (not shown) specializes *aneurysm rupture* to *AAA rupture*. Backward chaining on this variable introduces *AAA repair* to the QPN (Figure 8.1c), presenting the first opportunity to reason about possible action.

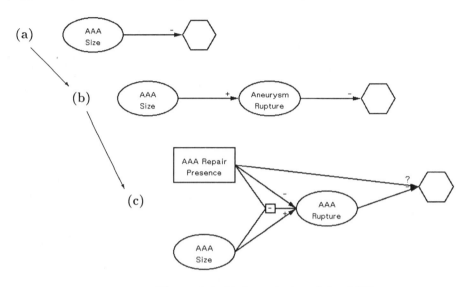

Figure 8.1: Early evolution of the QPN.

At this point, however, SUDO-PLANNER cannot determine anything about the *AAA repair* policy because the synergy between *AAA repair* and *AAA rupture* on *value* is indeterminate. A sequence of further elaboration and backward chaining steps replaces the direct relation from *AAA repair* to *value* with a collection of paths through such intermediate variables as *stroke*, *MI*, and *mortality*, which together account for the negative effects of the vessel surgery. Most of the new structure arises from elaboration; *mortality* and *value* are the only variables extended back in the process. The resulting QPN is illustrated in Figure 7.1a of the previous chapter. As demonstrated by the reduction of Figure 7.1b, this model is sufficient to justify our first dominance result: the *AAA repair* policy should be monotonically increasing in *AAA size*.

Backward chaining on *MI* introduces *CAD* to the network, producing the QPN partially depicted in Figure 7.3. As described in Section 7.3.1, SUDO-PLANNER cannot resolve the synergy between *AAA repair* and *CAD* on *value*, due to a subtle tradeoff involving the effects of *CAD*. This conflict is resolved by one of SUDO-PLANNER's tradeoff stubs (Section 7.4.2), allowing the model construction process to continue. A similar tradeoff involving *CVD* (introduced by backward chaining on *stroke*) also requires a stub for resolution.

Resolving these synergies renders the two disease variables extensible. *CVD* is the next variable selected for backward chaining. Because *endarterectomy* is related to *CVD* by a

Markov influence, the variable undergoes a mitosis process as described in Section 6.3.3. The resulting QPN is illustrated in Figure 8.2.

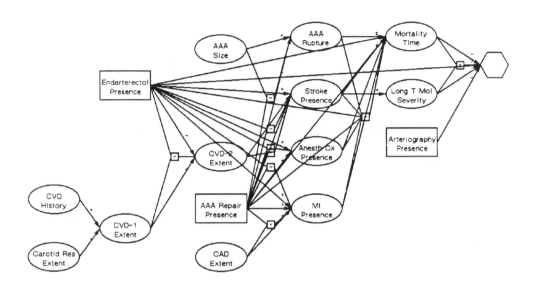

Figure 8.2: The QPN after backward chaining on *CVD*. The variable is divided in response to the Markov influence from *endarterectomy*.

By backward propagation of synergies (Corollary 4.23), SUDO-PLANNER's dominance prover can establish at this point that *CVD*'s predecessors, *CVD history* and *carotid arteriography result*, are negatively synergistic with *AAA repair* on *value*. The arteriography result is observable only if the test is performed; SUDO-PLANNER adds the action variable to the QPN as shown in Figure 8.2. Figure 8.4 (next section) illustrates the plan graph at this stage of the model-construction/dominance-proving process.

Backward chaining on *CAD* leads it to undergo mitosis and introduces structure parallel to that for *CVD* (see Figure 6.11). After elaboration removes a few spurious high-level links, the KB is exhausted and the model construction cycle terminates.[2] The final QPN is depicted in Figure 8.3.

8.3 Dominance Results

SUDO-PLANNER invokes the dominance prover on every QPN produced in the evolutionary sequence described above. It obtains the first dominance result from the QPN of Figure 7.1,

---

[2]If the KB were much larger, running the process exhaustively would be infeasible. Because plan graph validity is invariant, however, the planner can be halted at any time for inspection of its dominance results.

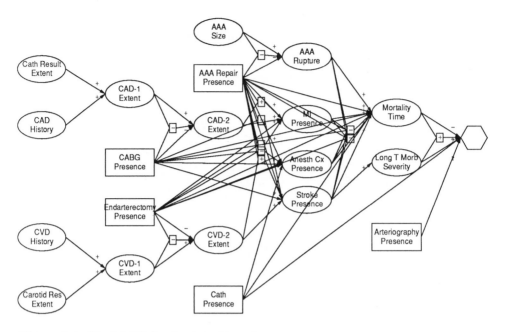

Figure 8.3: Final QPN for the AAA/CAD/CVD example (repeated from Figure 1.12).

and the next two after backward chaining on *CVD* to produce the QPN of Figure 8.2. The intermediate plan graph recording these three restrictions is shown in Figure 8.4. The restriction of Π_1 to Π_4 corresponds to the dominance result encoded by the plan graph fragment of Figure 7.2.

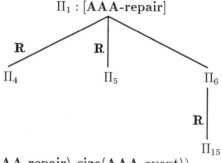

key:
Π_4 : $(+, \text{presence}\langle \textbf{AAA-repair}\rangle, \text{size}\langle \textbf{AAA-event}\rangle)$
Π_5 : $(-, \text{presence}\langle \textbf{AAA-repair}\rangle, \text{history}\langle \textbf{CVD-event}\rangle)$
Π_6 : $[\textbf{carotid-arteriography(true)}]$
Π_{15}: $(-, \text{presence}\langle \textbf{AAA-repair}\rangle, \text{extent}\langle \textbf{carotid-arteriography-result}\rangle)$

Figure 8.4: The plan graph after reducing the QPN of Figure 8.2. Plan classes are described by the constraint distinguishing them from their parents.

As the dominance prover derives further results, it creates and classifies the necessary plan classes and posts the dominance conditions on the plan graph. Figure 8.5 depicts the final plan graph, SUDO-PLANNER's terminating output for this example. The plan graph contains dominance results corresponding to each of the intuitive tradeoff formulation conclusions discussed in Section 1.2.

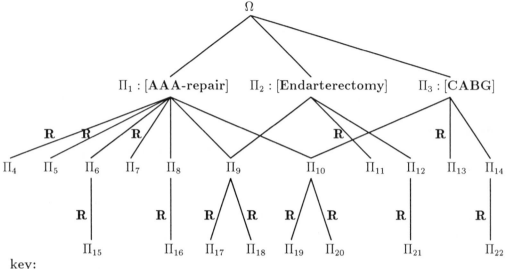

key:

Π_7 : $(-, \text{presence}\langle\mathbf{AAA\text{-}repair}\rangle, \text{history}\langle\mathbf{CAD\text{-}event}\rangle)$

Π_8 : $[\mathbf{cardiac\text{-}catheterization(true)}]$

Π_{11}: $(+, \text{presence}\langle\mathbf{endarterectomy}\rangle, \text{history}\langle\mathbf{CVD\text{-}event}\rangle)$

Π_{12}: $[\mathbf{carotid\text{-}arteriography(true)}]$

Π_{13}: $(+, \text{presence}\langle\mathbf{CABG}\rangle, \text{history}\langle\mathbf{CAD\text{-}event}\rangle)$

Π_{14}: $[\mathbf{cardiac\text{-}catheterization(true)}]$

Π_{16}: $(-, \text{presence}\langle\mathbf{AAA\text{-}repair}\rangle, \text{extent}\langle\mathbf{cardiac\text{-}cath\text{-}result}\rangle)$

Π_{17}: $(+, \text{presence}\langle\mathbf{AAA\text{-}repair}\rangle, \text{presence}\langle\mathbf{endarterectomy}\rangle)$

Π_{18}: $(+, \text{presence}\langle\mathbf{endarterectomy}\rangle, \text{presence}\langle\mathbf{AAA\text{-}repair}\rangle)$

Π_{19}: $(+, \text{presence}\langle\mathbf{AAA\text{-}repair}\rangle, \text{presence}\langle\mathbf{CABG}\rangle)$

Π_{20}: $(+, \text{presence}\langle\mathbf{CABG}\rangle, \text{presence}\langle\mathbf{AAA\text{-}repair}\rangle)$

Π_{21}: $(+, \text{presence}\langle\mathbf{endarterectomy}\rangle, \text{extent}\langle\mathbf{carotid\text{-}arteriography\text{-}result}\rangle)$

Π_{22}: $(+, \text{presence}\langle\mathbf{CABG}\rangle, \text{extent}\langle\mathbf{cardiac\text{-}cath\text{-}result}\rangle)$

Figure 8.5: The final plan graph. Plan classes Π_9 and Π_{10} are defined by the union of their parents' constraints. All leaf plan classes dominate (and therefore restrict) their parents.

8.4 Performance

The entire process takes roughly two minutes of real time on a Symbolics 3650.[3] The code is not optimized, and no extensive metering has been performed to determine the

---

[3]This figure assumes that the KB is pre-loaded and that the graphical display of QPNs is disabled.

allocation of computation time. SUDO-PLANNER appears to spend most of its time in redundant or superfluous dominance proving that could be avoided without degrading performance.

8.5   Discussion

This example illustrates SUDO-PLANNER's tradeoff formulation performance on a realistic, albeit small, medical decision problem. The program successfully plans up to tradeoffs, failing to resolve only genuine qualitative conflicts. Some of these are quite subtle; the competing factors became apparent to me only upon analysis of the QPN reduction. Given resolutions for these, SUDO-PLANNER proceeds to derive all of the desired results.

Two aspects of the example are disappointing. First is its fragility: small modifications to the KB can produce seemingly chaotic change in the course of QPN evolution and sometimes lead to weakened dominance results or even invalid ones if incompatible KB relations are brought into the model. I ascribe this defect to the cognitive complexity of the model construction procedure and the difficulty of predicting the implications of closed-world assumptions. Second, SUDO-PLANNER fails to take maximal advantage of abstraction, producing dominance results later in the process than necessary. As mentioned in Section 6.3.4, this is a by-product of the conservative knowledge engineering policy of including indeterminate high-level relations to prevent improper assumptions of independence.

The AAA/CAD/CVD case is the only complete, working SUDO-PLANNER example. In the process of implementing the program I have constructed several other QPN examples, including the digitalis model of Chapter 4. The difficulty of knowledge engineering mentioned above precluded development of a more comprehensive KB supporting a variety of model construction examples. This is not simply the traditional "knowledge acquisition bottleneck"; rather, it reflects the unpredictability of SUDO-PLANNER's QPN generation procedure. Improving its robustness is a prerequisite for widening the scope of SUDO-PLANNER.

Above all, the example serves as a demonstration of plausibility for the basic components of the SUDO-PLANNER approach: dominance proving, QPNs, and decision model construction from a multilevel KB. Weaknesses in SUDO-PLANNER exposed by the example provide a starting point for efforts to improve tradeoff formulation technology.

9 Conclusion

I conclude with an assessment of what this research has achieved and some remarks about what remains to be accomplished.

9.1 Summary of Contributions

The two central elements of this work are the dominance-proving architecture of Chapter 2 and the QPN formalism of Chapter 4. I have implemented these ideas in SUDO-PLANNER, a program that formulates tradeoffs by constructing decision models from a multilevel KB of qualitative relations. The following sections summarize these contributions, and enumerate some other products of this project scattered throughout the monograph.

9.1.1 A Dominance-Proving Architecture for Planning with Partially Satisfiable Goals

In the classical framework, planners search for a course of action guaranteed to achieve a specified goal predicate. As I argue in Section 1.4, this formulation of the task is fundamentally inadequate to account for partial goal satisfiability, including the special case where the effects of actions are uncertain. Although numerous researchers have developed planners to handle some of its aspects, no comprehensive computational framework for the more general problem has yet emerged.

The dominance-proving architecture is an attempt to fill that void. As presented in Chapter 2, the architecture's criterion for choice among plans is highly general; in particular it admits a Bayesian approach to preferences and belief without imposing *ad hoc* restrictions on the form of utility functions and probabilities. It goes beyond pure decision theory, however, in addressing the assembly of plans from more primitive descriptions of action. The architecture prescribes a division of computational labor among three components: the plan space manager, dominance prover, and domain problem solver. The plan graph representation of the search space supports techniques from traditional planning, in particular hierarchical (constraint-posting) planning and dependency maintenance.

The generality of the dominance-proving architecture precludes a final evaluation based solely on the results of this project. SUDO-PLANNER is one instance of a dominance-proving planner, developed specifically for the tradeoff formulation task. Other instances, defined by alternate choices in the design of plan class representation, domain modeling language, and dominance prover, should be expected to exhibit a variety of planning behaviors.

9.1.2 QPNs: A Formalism for Qualitative Probabilistic Influences and Synergies

Qualitative probabilistic networks are representations for constraints on probabilistic relations among a set of variables. The formalism provides constructs for two types of constraint:

- Qualitative influences describe the direction of the relation between a pair of variables.

- Qualitative synergies describe the direction of interaction among influences.

Both qualitative relations have rigorous probabilistic definitions that justify sound inference procedures based on efficient network transformations. Because the semantics for qualitative influences and synergies are based on relative, rather than absolute, statements about conditional probabilities, QPNs can be used to derive properties of the relative values of alternative plans. In particular, the relation of variables to the special *value* variable determine qualitative properties of the optimal decision, which can be exploited directly by a dominance-proving planner. I summarize the formal properties of QPNs in Section 4.9.1.

Qualitative relations directly support tradeoff formulation. In fact, resolvability in QPNs is perhaps the best available criterion for a formal tradeoff definition. As argued in Section 1.1, knowledge for tradeoff formulation is more abstract, modular, and robust than that required for general decision making. QPNs provide a mechanism to exploit these properties as far as possible before resorting to the less convenient forms of knowledge needed to solve the residual planning problem.

9.1.3 Other Contributions

In developing the main ideas above and building the SUDO-PLANNER implementation, I have been led to address a variety of peripheral topics. Those figuring prominently include:

- Identification of the tradeoff formulation task and its role in planning (Section 1.1).

- Design and analysis of knowledge representations for plan classes, actions, and the effects of actions (Chapters 3 and 5). Development of a subsumption algorithm for the plan constraint language (Section 3.5).

- Model construction at multiple levels of abstraction (Chapter 6).

  - Desiderata for multilevel reasoning (Section 6.1).

  - Exploration of issues in the automatic construction of decision models (Sections 6.4 through 6.6).

- Interpretation of the STRIPS assumption for actions with uncertain effects (Section 5.2.2).

- A theoretical approach to decision making in Savage's "grand world" (Section 6.6.3).

9.2 Limitations of SUDO-Planner

The design of SUDO-PLANNER reflects an emphasis on decision problems substantially different from those typically considered in AI planning research. As such, the domain relations expressible in its KB and the conclusions derivable by its inference procedure are novel to the field. Conversely, SUDO-PLANNER's mechanisms fail to cope with many issues that traditional systems handle routinely. Most of these omissions are not critical; straightforward extensions to SUDO-PLANNER would attain the desired capabilities. Others, however, do not have clear remedies.

In the sections below, I discuss two glaring limitations of SUDO-PLANNER's competence. Several additional shortcomings of this work have been reported in foregoing chapters:

- The limited expressive power of the plan constraint language (Section 3.5.4).

- An unsatisfactory semantics for effect assertions in the KB (Section 5.4.1).

- The fragility of the model construction algorithm (Section 6.3.4).

9.2.1 Tradeoffs

The tradeoff barrier is an obvious boundary of SUDO-PLANNER's decision-making abilities. Sections 7.3 through 7.5 discuss the nature of this obstacle and propose some approaches toward overcoming it.

The subtle tradeoff of Section 7.3.1 suggests that—though close inspection reveals that this situation contains genuinely conflicting factors—the QPN formalism does not correspond exactly to our intuitive notion of tradeoff. Further theoretical and empirical analysis is required to allocate blame for this mismatch to inferential weakness, omission of critical qualitative distinctions, and various cognitive elements. The first step is to develop a precise characterization of the completeness of QPN inference mechanisms, that is, the potential for spurious ambiguity.[1]

9.2.2 Time

No theory of planning is complete without an adequate treatment of temporal relations among actions and events. SUDO-PLANNER's representations for plan classes, actions, and events, however, are entirely atemporal. Failing to deal with time is one of the major shortcomings of SUDO-PLANNER.

Most planners handle simple sequencing among actions. For typical medical decision problems, such a mechanism is not nearly adequate and barely provides an advantage over no temporal reasoning at all. For example, in patients presenting with symptoms of appendicitis, there is a tradeoff between performing an appendectomy immediately or waiting and observing the patient to better establish the diagnosis. Waiting avoids

---

[1]Kuipers has carried out an analogous analysis of qualitative simulation [82], concluding that spurious qualitative behaviors are in fact produced by local inference schemes.

some unnecessary surgeries while increasing the risk of untreated disease. In this planning problem, the ordering of actions is already known; the task is to determine the optimal waiting time as a function of the observations.

To attack this problem with SUDO-PLANNER, one would have to treat its temporal aspect as just another domain-dependent characteristic of the situation. Because they enjoy no special status in the planner, references to time must be expressed within the existing representations for action and event variables. In this case, we can include a **time-of-surgery** role in the specification of the action **appendectomy**. The filler for that role is a time variable whose effects can be represented via the mechanisms described in Chapter 5.

SUDO-PLANNER does supply one construct specifically to account for time relations: the Markov influence assertion of Section 5.5. Markov influences implicitly encode the temporal ordering among an action and the value of an event variable before and after its application.

But even a large set of representation constructs like Markov influences combined with vigorous use of special time-related roles is no substitute for an explicit uniform treatment of time within the planner and in the representation for effects of actions. Failing to recognize that the **time-of-surgery** role of **appendectomy** is related to other temporal measures in the KB and plan graph inevitably leads to significant missed inference opportunities.

Temporal reasoning is likely to pose special problems in the dominance-proving architecture because of its emphasis on deriving properties of plan classes. In categorical planning, plans with partial temporal descriptions require the planner to establish that facts hold in all consistent completions, a problem known to be difficult [25]. It remains to be seen whether techniques from traditional planning can be adapted to this framework, or, for that matter, whether the dominance-proving task will admit some special solutions not available in the traditional case.

9.3 Further Work

The preceding chapters contain numerous digressions outlining plans and speculations about future work. This section elaborates on a few of these possibilities.

9.3.1 Extending the Dominance Prover

There are a few straightforward extensions to the SUDO-PLANNER implementation that should enlarge the dominance prover's scope without presenting conceptual difficulties. One would be to incorporate explicit reasoning about landmark values, as described in Section 4.7.6. For example, CAD_0 might be an important landmark value for CAD, representing no coronary disease or perhaps the normal extent of CAD for a given population. A medical KB would also be likely to include the value of z^*, the normal threshold value on AAA $size$ above which AAA $repair$ is indicated. The threshold z^* is a rule of thumb, valid as a decision criterion only for patients with no extenuating circumstances. Thus, use of z^* implicitly assumes $CAD = CAD_0$, among other things. Suppose a patient presents with CAD worse than CAD_0 and a AAA smaller than z^*. The patient's coronary disease is an "extenuating circumstance" for the *AAA repair* decision, but we know from SUDO-PLANNER's plan graph that extensive CAD only decreases our willingness to perform aneurysm surgery. Since the patient's AAA is below the nominal threshold, we can conclude that it is also below the revised threshold and therefore the optimal plan does not prescribe aneurysm repair.

The reasoning scenario presented above makes use of dominance results produced by the current version of SUDO-PLANNER. Hence, extending SUDO-PLANNER to handle landmark values would not require changes in either the QPN formalism or the model construction process.

A second extension of the dominance prover is the incorporation of explicit conditioning of qualitative relation assertions and dominance results. Maintenance of context-dependent conclusions (such as the conditional dominance relations of Definition 2.3) can be implemented directly in a standard TMS. SUDO-PLANNER's plan class representation already provides for conditional constraints (Section 3.4.3), although its subsumption algorithm for plan classes with conditionals is incomplete (Section 3.5.3).

Other extensions—involving new qualitative relations, plan class constraints, or trade-off resolution capabilities—are more fundamental, requiring significant modifications of SUDO-PLANNER's existing mechanisms. I expect that further work on SUDO-PLANNER will explore each of these directions.

9.3.2 Temporal Representations

Designers of temporally competent dominance-proving planners need to address three basic representation requirements. A temporal knowledge representation must include facilities to express:

1. the temporal relation among actions and observations in plans,

2. effects of action over time, and

3. time preference for the occurrence of events, including the temporal resolution of uncertainty [81].

The first item involves extensions of the plan constraint language, while the second and third are the responsibility of the domain modeling language.

There is no reason to develop languages for expressing temporal relations among actions in a plan unless the planner has some basis for distinguishing the effects of the different temporal patterns of action. The first step in adding temporal concepts to SUDO-PLANNER, therefore, should be to extend the QPN formalism to include conditions on relations among variables over time. One approach is suggested by Cox's investigations of a temporal version of first-order stochastic dominance [20]. Because atemporal FSD is the basis for the existing QPN relations, such a condition is a promising candidate for a smooth extension into the temporal dimension.

A contrasting approach is to add temporal structure to the event variables rather than to the relations. This is the path taken in a representation scheme I designed for a proposed health outcome knowledge base [172]. The KB design is organized around a taxonomy of temporal patterns, orthogonal to the health-related characteristics of the concepts. Given a temporal semantics for the pattern-definition constructs (perhaps in the spirit of Allen [1]), relations on these variables have clear temporal interpretations. The same constructs could then be applied to the specification of temporal characteristics of actions as well.

9.3.3 Critiquing Based on the Dominance-Proving Architecture

Perhaps the most immediate application of the dominance-proving architecture should be to *critiquing systems* [101, 174], programs that analyze a user's proposed plan rather than generate solutions from scratch. A dominance-proving planner critiques by exploring the plan-space neighborhood of the given plan or plan class. Dominance results involving plan classes that encompass the user's proposal suggest incremental improvements to be recommended by the critiquer.

The user's strategy focuses the dominance-proving planner on a narrow slice of the search space that might have received only fractional attention in unrestricted search. Though the planner may not have gotten there in the first place, it is possible that once there it can derive an abundance of useful results.

A proposed plan often implicitly contains resolutions of tradeoffs that would have caused SUDO-PLANNER to hang. This might be attributable to more domain knowledge, more information about the case context, or greater willingness to make assumptions or guesses. Assumptions inferred from the proposal can be asserted in the planner's KB, in much the same way as results are incorporated from black-box tradeoff resolvers in the framework of Section 7.4. Further refinements or modifications to the plan justified by its implicit assumptions are valid dominance results that should be reported in the critique.

We have incorporated some of these ideas in BUNYAN, a program for critiquing medical decision trees [176]. One of BUNYAN's "critiquing principles" is to alert the analyst to decision models that contain qualitatively dominated strategies. Although the program does not perform explicit dominance proving, the criteria for detecting dominance are based on qualitative probabilistic relations holding between abstract concepts of medical decision problems.

9.3.4 Tradeoff Resolution

Section 7.5 outlines four approaches toward resolving tradeoffs in ways compatible with SUDO-PLANNER's existing dominance-proving mechanisms:

1. Spanning relations.

2. Negligibility reasoning.

3. Functional relations.

4. Higher-precision knowledge.

Pursuit of each of these directions should be part of a full-scale assault on SUDO-PLANNER's tradeoff barrier.

9.4 Outlook on SUDO Planning

The central task that this research attacks—planning for partially satisfiable goals—is so pervasive, and the need for comprehensive AI approaches so acute, that partial solutions are well worth striving for. The same holds for other major issues addressed by SUDO-PLANNER: qualitative probability, multilevel knowledge representation, and decision model construction. It is a virtual certainty, then, that others will take up these problems, whether or not they adopt techniques from SUDO-PLANNER.

However, the outlook for SUDO-PLANNER: THE PROGRAM is quite dim. In this chapter and throughout the monograph I have chronicled numerous defects of SUDO-PLANNER that preclude it from direct application to realistic planning problems. SUDO-PLANNER is merely a demonstration vehicle, providing an instance of the dominance-proving architecture for planning with partially satisfiable goals, and a testbed for the application of qualitative probabilistic networks to problems of decision making under uncertainty. Future tradeoff formulators will surely operate much differently, as researchers discover and exploit regularities in problems and domains. And dominance-proving planners of the future will emphasize tradeoff resolution to the point that resemblance to SUDO-PLANNER will be slight at best.

In contrast, I find it easy to be optimistic about the prospects for SUDO-PLANNER: THE APPROACH. The full range of dominance-proving planners has not yet been explored, nor has the variety of possible uses for QPNs. The SUDO-PLANNER experience to date has been encouraging; however, much work remains before we can evaluate with confidence the utility of these ideas in establishing a principled basis for automated decision making.

A Notation

Listed below are brief descriptions of notational symbols employed in the body of this thesis, with references to the pages where they are introduced or defined. For symbols with more than one interpretation, the appropriate choice should always be clear in context.

a^* A landmark value of variable a, either specially designated as such or determined to correspond to landmark value of some other variable (p. 78).

a_i 1. An action in the action alphabet A (p. 21).
2. A generic action type (p. 42).
3. A specific value taken on by variable a: $a_i \in X(a)$. Used in conditional probability expressions as an abbreviation for the proposition $a = a_i$ (p. 59).

$a_i(vr)$ The action type formed by value-restricting some role of a_i to vr (p. 42).

$a_g(b)$ A function that returns the value of a maximizing $g(a,b)$ (p. 73).

A 1. An alphabet of actions for a simple plan language (p. 21).
2. The proposition interpreted as $a = \textbf{true}$, where a is a boolean variable in a QPN (p. 58).

A^* The set of strings in the alphabet A, or a wildcard in a regular expression (p. 21).

$\bar{A}$ The proposition $a = \textbf{false}$ (p. 58).

$\mathcal{A}$ The universal action class. $\mathcal{A} = \mathcal{X}(\textbf{action})$ (p. 42).

$\mathcal{A}_i$ A generic set of actions. $\mathcal{A}_i = \mathcal{X}(a_i)$ (p. 42).

action   The root of the action taxonomy (p. 42).

$\arg\max_a$ The value of a that maximizes the associated expression (p. 73).

av An action variable type (p. 43).

AV An action variable instance of type av (p. 43).

$AV(\pi)$ The value of action variable instance AV in the unconditional plan π (p. 43).

c The consequence descriptor in decision analysis used as argument to the utility function (p. 119).

$\underline{c}$ The minimal value of variable c (p. 157).

$CO(a_i, ev)$ A creates-observable assertion. Performing an action of type a_i renders event variable ev observable (p. 92).

D 1. Dominance relation over plan classes (p. 23).

$\mathcal{P}_E$	The plan classes accepted by the executor (p. 41).
$pred$	Predecessor function (p. 57).
Q	The set of qualitative relations in a QPN (p. 55).
r_j^δ	The extreme value in role r_j's range, maximum if $\delta = +$ and minimum if $\delta = -$ (p. 127).
R	A generic relation on CDFs (p. 66).
R_δ	Ordinal comparison relation holding for undefined terms by default (p. 46).
$\mathbf{R}$	Annotation on a plan graph link indicating a restriction relation (p. 10).
$\Re$	The real numbers (p. 27).
$red(b, G)$	The network obtained by reducing b from G (p. 62).
$rev(a, b, G)$	The network obtained by reversing a and b in G (p. 62).
$result$	Function returning the state resulting from performing a plan in a given state in the situation calculus (p. 23).
$role\langle a_i \rangle$	The action variable formed from concept a_i and role $role$ (p. 43).
s_i	The initial situation in situation calculus planning (p. 23).
S_a	Set of event variables directly affected by action a (p. 87).
S_a'	Set of event variables directly affected by action a, plus any other variables that affect those in S_a (p. 88).
S^δ	A qualitative influence assertion (pp. 57, 58, 59).
u	The utility function (pp. 60, 119).
U^δ	Qualitative influences on utility (p. 60).
v	The specially designated value node in a QPN (p. 55).
V	The set of variables in a QPN (p. 55).
x	Context variable in qualitative relation definition (p. 58).
$X(a)$	The domain of variable a (p. 55).
$\mathcal{X}(c)$	The extension of a (NIKL) concept c (p. 42).
Y^δ	A qualitative synergy assertion (pp. 70, 71).
Y_U^δ	Qualitative synergy on utility (p. 73).
δ	A qualitative direction, one of $+$, $-$, ?, or 0 (pp. 46, 57).
(δ, av, ev)	A monotonic policy constraint in direction δ between av and ev (p. 46).
θ	A state of nature (pp. 76, 119).
Θ	The set of possible states of nature (p. 119).
π	A plan (p. 23, defined in Section 3.1).
$\pi[e_i]$	A partial plan function defined only on the extension $\mathcal{E}_i$ of e_i (p. 47).
Π	A plan class or partial plan (p. 21).

$\Pi^\delta(av, ev)$	The plan class where av is a monotonic function (with direction δ) of ev (p. 28).
$\Pi[e_i]$	A class of partial plan functions defined only on the extension $\mathcal{E}_i$ of e_i. (p. 47).
ϕ	A monotonic transform (p. 59).
ω	A course of action in Ω_{exe} (p. 39).
Ω	The universal plan class, or set of all syntactically valid plans (p. 21).
Ω_0	The set of (semantically) legal plans (p. 40).
Ω_{exe}	The set of executable courses of action (p. 39).
$\succ$	Strict preference relation over plans (p. 23).
$\succeq$	Non-strict preference relation over plans (p. 23).
$\sim$	Indifference relation over plans (p. 23).
$\otimes$	Sign multiplication operator (Table 4.1, p. 63).
$\oplus$	Sign addition operator (Table 4.1, p. 63).

B Proofs of QPN Results

Lemma 4.9 *If $b \notin pred_G^*(a)$ then a and b are d-separated in $dep(G)$ by any S such that $pred_G(b) \subseteq S \subseteq \{s | b \notin pred_G^*(s)\}$.*

Proof: Two variables are d-separated iff every undirected path between them is blocked according to one of the conditions of Definition 4.8. Every path between a and b must pass through one of b's predecessors or one of its successors. Because $pred_G(b) \subseteq S$, the paths through the predecessors are blocked by the first condition. Consider a path through a successor of b. Let t be the first variable on the path, starting from b, that has both incident edges leading in. Such a variable must exist because $b \notin pred_G^*(a)$. Because it is the first, there is a directed path to it from b. But b has no directed paths to elements of S. Therefore, neither t nor any of its successors are in S and t blocks the path via the second condition of Definition 4.8. □

Theorem 4.10

$$S^{\delta_1}(a, b, G) \wedge S^{\delta_2}(b, c, G) \wedge S^0(a, c, G) \Rightarrow S^{\delta_1 \otimes \delta_2}(a, c, red(b, G)),$$

where $\delta_i \in \{+, -, 0, ?\}$ and $\otimes$ denotes sign multiplication, described by Table 4.1.

Proof: I will prove the case $\delta_1 = \delta_2 = +$; the others are analogous. Choose a_1 and a_2 such that $a_1 \geq a_2$, and an x_0 in $X(pred(b) \cup pred(c) - \{a, b\})$ that is consistent with a_1 and a_2.[1] Let F_c denote the conditional CDF for c and $\underline{c}$ the minimal value of the variable. By the definition of cumulative probability we have

$$F_c(c_0|a_i x_0) = \int_{\underline{c}}^{c_0} \int f_{bc}(b_0 c_1 | a_i x_0) db_0 dc_1.$$

Changing the order of integration and decomposing the joint probability yields[2]

$$F_c(c_0|a_i x_0) = \int \int_{\underline{c}}^{c_0} f_c(c_1|a_i b_0 x_0) f_b(b_0|a_i x_0) dc_1 db_0. \tag{B.1}$$

Because a and c are conditionally independent given b and x, by the S^0 premise and Lemma 4.9, we can remove a_i from the f_c expression. Rewriting the density function as the derivative of a cumulative, we get

$$F_c(c_0|a_i x_0) = \int \int_{\underline{c}}^{c_0} f_c(c_1|b_0 x_0) dc_1 dF_b(b_0|a_i x_0). \tag{B.2}$$

---

[1] In all subsequent proofs, x is understood to range over assignments to relevant predecessor variables in a similar manner.

[2] If some values of b_0 are inconsistent with x_0, then distributions of c conditioned on b_0 and x_0 (and therefore the right-hand sides of equations (B.1), (B.2), and (B.3)) are not well-defined. This has no consequence, however, because the value of $f_b(b_0|a_i x_0)$ in such cases will always be zero.

The inner integral is simply the CDF for c given b_0.

$$F_c(c_0|a_ix_0) = \int F_c(c_0|b_0x_0)dF_b(b_0|a_ix_0). \tag{B.3}$$

Because b positively influences c, the pointwise FSD condition (4.3) implies that for any c_0, $F_c(c_0|b_0x_0)$ is a *decreasing* function of b_0. And $S^+(a,b)$ entails FSD of $F_b(b_0|a_1x_0)$ over $F_b(b_0|a_2x_0)$. Therefore, (4.4) applies with the inequality reversed (negating $F_c(c_0|bx_0)$ yields an increasing function), leading to the conclusion

$$\forall c_0 \quad F_c(c_0|a_1x_0) \le F_c(c_0|a_2x_0),$$

implying FSD. Because a_1, a_2, and x_0 were chosen arbitrarily, we have finally $S^+(a,c)$. □

Theorem 4.11

$$S^{\delta_1}(a,b,G) \wedge S^{\delta_2}(b,c,G) \wedge S^{\delta_3}(a,c,G) \Rightarrow S^{(\delta_1 \otimes \delta_2) \oplus \delta_3}(a,c,red(b,G)),$$

where $\oplus$ denotes sign addition, also described in Table 4.1.

Proof: Proceed as for the proof of Theorem 4.10 to equation (B.1). Because δ_3 is not generally zero, we cannot remove a_i in the next two steps.

$$F_c(c_0|a_ix_0) = \int F_c(c_0|a_ib_0x_0)dF_b(b_0|a_ix_0).$$

Define $\hat{F}_c$ as a variant where a_i is fixed to a_1 in the first term

$$\hat{F}_c(c_0|a_ix_0) = \int F_c(c_0|a_1b_0x_0)dF_b(b_0|a_ix_0).$$

Note that $\hat{F}_c(c_0|a_1x_0) = F_c(c_0|a_1x_0)$ and that

$$\delta_3 = +(-) \Rightarrow \forall c_0 \quad F_c(c_0|a_1b_0x_0) \le (\ge) F_c(c_0|a_2b_0x_0), \text{ therefore}$$

$$\forall c_0 \quad \hat{F}_c(c_0|a_2x_0) \le (\ge) F_c(c_0|a_2x_0). \tag{B.4}$$

When $\delta_3 = ?$ it is possible that the relation varies with c_0. Regardless of δ_3, $F_c(c_0|a_1b_0x_0)$ is a decreasing/increasing/non-monotonic function of b_0 as δ_2 is $+/-/?$. For concreteness, suppose $\delta_1 = \delta_2 = +$ (again, the other cases are analogous). Following the reasoning in the proof of Theorem 4.10 above, we get

$$\hat{F}_c(c_0|a_1x_0) = F_c(c_0|a_1x_0) \text{ FSD } \hat{F}_c(c_0|a_2x_0).$$

If $\delta_3 = +$ (more generally if δ_3 agrees with the polarity of the FSD relation), this result combines with (B.4) to imply FSD of the corresponding unhatted F_cs, thereby establishing the result. Without such agreement FSD may be violated, permitting us to conclude only $S^?(a,c,red(b,G))$. □

Theorem 4.12 *Let $G' = rev(a,b,G)$. G' inherits all the qualitative influences of G except:*

156

1. $dir(a, b, G')$ is undefined.

2. $dir(b, a, G') = dir(a, b, G)$.

3. $\forall w \in pred_{G'}(b)$,

$$dir(w, b, G') = [dir(w, a, G) \otimes dir(a, b, G)] \oplus dir(w, b, G).$$

4. $\forall w \in pred_{G'}(a) - \{b\}$,

$$dir(w, a, G') = \begin{cases} dir(w, a, G) & \textit{if } dir(w, b, G) = 0 \\ ? & \textit{otherwise.} \end{cases}$$

Proof: First, note that all variables outside $pred_G(a) \cup pred_G(b)$ retain the same set of d-separations. Second, let us verify each relation above:

1. There is no longer an influence from a to b.

2. To show that the influence on the reversed link remains unchanged it is convenient to work with the likelihood form of S^δ, equation (4.6). Applying Bayes's formula:

$$f_b(b_j|a_i x) = \frac{f_a(a_i|b_j x) f_b(b_j|x)}{f_a(a_i|x)}.$$

Choose four values $a_1 \geq a_2$ and $b_1 \geq b_2$.

$$\frac{f_b(b_1|a_i x)}{f_b(b_2|a_i x)} = \frac{f_a(a_i|b_1 x) f_b(b_1|x)}{f_a(a_i|b_2 x) f_b(b_2|x)} = g(b_1, b_2, x) \frac{f_a(a_i|b_1 x)}{f_a(a_i|b_2 x)}.$$

Using the monotone likelihood property, $dir(a, b, G) = +(-)$ implies

$$\frac{f_b(b_1|a_1 x)}{f_b(b_2|a_1 x)} \geq (\leq) \frac{f_b(b_1|a_2 x)}{f_b(b_2|a_2 x)}.$$

Rearranging we get

$$\frac{f_b(b_1|a_1 x)}{f_b(b_1|a_2 x)} \geq (\leq) \frac{f_b(b_2|a_1 x)}{f_b(b_2|a_2 x)},$$

the MLRP for b given a. As noted above (and proven by Milgrom [100]), this is necessary and sufficient for our posterior FSD condition to hold for any prior $F_a(a_0|x)$.

3. In G, the influence of w on b is relative to a predecessor set that includes a. In G' the influence is not so conditioned and is therefore equivalent to the influence on b obtained by splicing a out of the network. Applying Theorem 4.11 with the original influences yields the expression above.

4. Here the reversal transforms an unconditional relation to a conditional one. If $dir(w, b, G) = 0$, w and b are d-separated by $pred(b)$ in $dep(G)$ (by Lemma 4.9), therefore $f_w(w_0|abx) = f_w(w_0|ax)$ by conditional independence. In that case the MLRP obviously holds for the conditional density iff it holds for the marginal one. If w has nonzero influence on b in G, this independence does not hold. Because a and w may interact significantly in their influence on b we cannot say anything about their relation given b. For example, let the three variables be binary with a and w marginally independent (that is, $dir(w, a, G) = 0$), $\Pr(A) = \Pr(W) = .5$, $\Pr(B|\bar{A}\bar{W}) = .1$, $\Pr(B|\bar{A}W) = .2$, and $\Pr(B|AW) = .9$. Then $dir(w, a, G')$ can be $+$ or $-$ depending on whether $\Pr(B|A\bar{W})$ is less than or greater than .45. Either possibility is consistent with an initial G with $dir(a, b) = dir(w, b) = +$.

$\square$

Theorem 4.13 *Let $S^+(a, b)$ be defined by (4.10). Given the following conditions:*

1. *Theorem 4.10*

2. *For binary b, $a_1 \geq a_2$, and x,*

$$F_b(\cdot|a_1 x) \ R \ F_b(\cdot|a_2 x) \Leftrightarrow \Pr(B|a_1 x) \geq \Pr(B|a_2 x) \tag{B.5}$$

the weakest R is FSD.

Proof: First, note that FSD satisfies these conditions. Next, assume that R satisfies them but R does not entail FSD. We will start with an instantiation of Theorem 4.10 and derive a contradiction. Let a, b, and c be the only variables (so we can safely ignore x) with $S^+(a, b)$, $S^+(b, c)$, and no other direct links. For concreteness, let b range over the unit interval $[0, 1]$ and c be binary with $\Pr(C|ab) = \phi(b)$, for some $\phi : [0, 1] \to [0, 1]$ monotonic. The monotonicity of ϕ guarantees $S^+(b, c)$ and its independence from a validates $S^0(a, c)$ in the original network. By assumption, Theorem 4.10 applies, yielding the conclusion $S^+(a, c)$ and therefore $F_c(c_0|a_1) \ R \ F_c(c_0|a_2)$. Because c is binary, (B.5) must hold. Using $\Pr(C|a_i) = \int \Pr(C|a_i b_0) dF_b(b_0|a_i)$, the RHS of (B.5) becomes

$$\int_0^1 \phi(b_0) dF_b(b_0|a_1) \geq \int_0^1 \phi(b_0) dF_b(b_0|a_2). \tag{B.6}$$

Because ϕ may be any monotonic function, FSD is necessary for (B.6) and is therefore entailed by R. $\square$

Theorem 4.14 *Suppose $U^{\delta_2}(b, G)$ and $U^0(a, G)$. A necessary and sufficient condition for $U^{\delta_1 \otimes \delta_2}(a, red(b, G))$ is $S^{\delta_1}(a, b, G)$ as in Definition 4.4.*

Proof: The expected utility of a_i with any x is given by

$$u(a_i, x) = \int u(b_0, x) dF_b(b_0|a_i x). \tag{B.7}$$

Let us prove the case $\delta_1 = \delta_2 = +$. $U^+(a)$ is satisfied in the reduced network iff $u(a_i, x)$ is increasing in a_i. From (4.8) we know that $u(b_0, x)$ is monotonically increasing in b_0. In fact, it can be *any* monotonic function. Therefore, (B.7) is increasing in a_i under the same conditions as (4.4), which is exactly the S^+ condition (4.5) of Definition 4.4. □

Lemma 4.19 $Y^+(\{a, b\}, c)$ *(respectively Y^- and Y^0) holds iff the function*

$$e_\phi(a, b|x) = \int \phi(c_0) f_c(c_0|abx) dc_0 \tag{B.8}$$

is supermodular (submodular, modular) in a and b for all increasing functions ϕ and contexts x.

Proof: Choose arbitrary $a_1 \geq a_2$, $b_1 \geq b_2$, and x. By Definition 4.18, e_ϕ is supermodular iff

$$e_\phi(a_1, b_1|x) + e_\phi(a_2, b_2|x) \geq e_\phi(a_1, b_2|x) + e_\phi(a_2, b_1|x).$$

Rearranging,

$$e_\phi(a_1, b_1|x) - e_\phi(a_2, b_1|x) \geq e_\phi(a_1, b_2|x) - e_\phi(a_2, b_2|x).$$

Substituting the definition of e_ϕ (B.8) and combining the integrals,

$$\int \phi(c_0) \left[f_c(c_0|a_1 b_1 x) - f_c(c_0|a_2 b_1 x) \right] dc_0 \geq \int \phi(c_0) \left[f_c(c_0|a_1 b_2 x) - f_c(c_0|a_2 b_2 x) \right] dc_0. \tag{B.9}$$

A necessary and sufficient condition for (B.9) to hold for any increasing function ϕ is that the bracketed distribution differences be related by FSD. (Recall the equivalence between (4.3) and (4.4) in Section 4.3.2.) That is,

$$\forall c_0 \quad F_c(c_0|a_1 b_1 x) - F_c(c_0|a_2 b_1 x) \leq F_c(c_0|a_1 b_2 x) - F_c(c_0|a_2 b_2 x).$$

This is exactly the Y^+ condition of Definition 4.17. □

Theorem 4.21 *Synergies can be extended along qualitative influences by reduction according to the following.*

$$Y^{\delta_1}(\{a, b\}, c, G) \wedge S^{\delta_2}(c, d, G) \wedge S^0(a, d, G) \wedge S^0(b, d, G) \Rightarrow$$
$$Y^{\delta_1 \otimes \delta_2}(\{a, b\}, d, red(c, G)).$$

Proof: Let us assume that $\delta_1 = \delta_2 = +$; the other cases are analogous. We can describe the cumulative for d conditional on a and b by integrating over its counterpart for c.

$$F_d(d_0|abx) = \int_{\underline{d}}^{d_0} \int f_d(d_1|abc_0 x) f_c(c_0|abx) dc_0 dd_1 \tag{B.10}$$

$$= \int \int_{\underline{d}}^{d_0} f_d(d_1|c_0 x) dd_1 \, f_c(c_0|abx) dc_0 \tag{B.11}$$

$$= \int F_d(d_0|c_0 x) f_c(c_0|abx) dc_0. \tag{B.12}$$

In going from (B.10) to (B.11) I took advantage of the conditional independence between d and each of a and b given c implied by the S^0 conditions and Lemma 4.9. Because $S^+(c, d)$, $F_d(d_0|c_0)$ is a decreasing function of c_0 for any d_0. Therefore, equation (B.12) and Lemma 4.19 imply that $F_d(d_0|abx)$ is a submodular function of a and b for all d_0 (a function g is submodular iff $-g$ is supermodular). By the definition of submodularity,

$$\forall d_0 \quad F_d(d_0|a_1 b_1 x) - F_d(d_0|a_2 b_1 x) \leq F_d(d_0|a_1 b_2 x) - F_d(d_0|a_2 b_2 x), \tag{B.13}$$

which is the condition for $Y^+(\{a, b\}, d)$ of Definition 4.17. □

Theorem 4.22

$$Y^{\delta_1}(\{a, b\}, c, G) \wedge S^{\delta_2}(c, d, G) \wedge Y^{\delta_3}(\{a, c\}, d, G) \wedge Y^{\delta_4}(\{b, c\}, d, G)$$
$$\wedge S^{\delta_5}(a, c, G) \wedge S^{\delta_6}(b, c, G) \wedge Y^{\delta_7}(\{a, b\}, d, G) \Rightarrow$$
$$Y^{(\delta_1 \otimes \delta_2) \oplus (\delta_3 \otimes \delta_6) \oplus (\delta_4 \otimes \delta_5) \oplus \delta_7}(\{a, b\}, d, red(c, G)).$$

Proof: Start as in the proof of Theorem 4.21, but do not use conditional independence.

$$F_d(d_0|abx) = \int_{\underline{d}}^{d_0} \int f_d(d_1|abc_0 x) f_c(c_0|abx) dc_0 dd_1$$
$$= \int F_d(d_0|abc_0 x) dF_c(c_0|abx).$$

As in the proof of Theorem 4.11, define $\hat{F}_d$ to be the CDF with the conditioning variables fixed in the first term, to a_1 and b_1 in this case.

$$\hat{F}_d(d_0|abx) = \int F_d(d_0|a_1 b_1 c_0 x) dF_c(c_0|abx).$$

Regardless of a_1 and b_1, $F_d(d_0|a_1 b_1 c_0 x)$ has monotonicity properties determined solely by δ_2. Following the reasoning of the Theorem 4.21 proof, we have the following fact about $\hat{F}_d$ (a hatted version of (B.13)):

$$\forall d_0 \quad \hat{F}_d(d_0|a_1 b_1 x) - \hat{F}_d(d_0|a_2 b_1 x) \ R \ \hat{F}_d(d_0|a_1 b_2 x) - \hat{F}_d(d_0|a_2 b_2 x), \tag{B.14}$$

with R the relation $\leq$, $\geq$, $=$, or ? as $\delta_1 \otimes \delta_2$ is $+$, $-$, 0, or ?. Henceforth I will refer to functions satisfying conditions of the form (B.14) as *R-modular*. Let $\hat{F}'_d$ be intermediate between F_d and $\hat{F}_d$ where only b is fixed

$$\hat{F}'_d(d_0|abx) = \int F_d(d_0|ab_1 c_0 x) dF_c(c_0|abx).$$

Note that $\hat{F}'_d(d_0|a_1 b_i x) = \hat{F}_d(d_0|a_1 b_i x)$ for either b_i. Therefore $\hat{F}'_d$ is R-modular iff

$$\forall d_0 \quad \hat{F}_d(d_0|a_1 b_1 x) - \hat{F}'_d(d_0|a_2 b_1 x) \ R \ \hat{F}_d(d_0|a_1 b_2 x) - \hat{F}'_d(d_0|a_2 b_2 x). \tag{B.15}$$

Using (B.14) and a little rearrangement, a sufficient condition for (B.15) is

$$\forall d_0 \quad \Delta_1(d_0) \ R \ \Delta_2(d_0), \text{ where} \tag{B.16}$$

$$\Delta_i(d_0) \equiv \hat{F}_d(d_0|a_2b_ix) - \hat{F}'_d(d_0|a_2b_ix) \tag{B.17}$$

Expanding the definitions for $\hat{F}_d$ and $\hat{F}'_d$,

$$\Delta_i(d_0) = \int [F_d(d_0|a_1b_1c_0x) - F_d(d_0|a_2b_1c_0x)] \, dF_c(c_0|a_2b_ix). \tag{B.18}$$

The difference inside the integral of equation (B.18) is an increasing, decreasing, or constant function of c_0 as δ_3, the synergy of a and c, is $-$, $+$, or 0. The influence of b on c, δ_6, determines an FSD relation among the $F_c(c_0|ab_i)$. Therefore, condition (B.16) holds if $\delta_3 \otimes \delta_6$ agrees with R, which was determined by $\delta_1 \otimes \delta_2$.

Another application of this line of reasoning with the roles of a and b reversed leads to the conclusion that $\hat{F}''_d$, where

$$\hat{F}''_d(d_0|abx) = \int F_d(d_0|a_1bc_0x)dF_c(c_0|abx).$$

is R-modular if $\delta_4 \otimes \delta_5$ agrees with R. Thus, agreement among these pairwise products yields R-modularity of $\hat{F}_d$, $\hat{F}'_d$, and $\hat{F}''_d$.

Suppose that δ_7 also agrees with R. Then, from the Y^δ definition we have

$$\forall d_0 \quad F_d(d_0|a_1b_1c_0x) - F_d(d_0|a_2b_1c_0x) \quad R \quad F_d(d_0|a_1b_2c_0x) - F_d(d_0|a_2b_2c_0x),$$

which entails the following inequality when integrating over a positive function:

$$\forall d_0 \quad \int [F_d(d_0|a_1b_1c_0x) - F_d(d_0|a_2b_1c_0x)] \, dF_c(c_0|a_2b_2x)$$

$$R \quad \int [F_d(d_0|a_1b_2c_0x) - F_d(d_0|a_2b_2c_0x)] \, dF_c(c_0|a_2b_2x).$$

Equivalently,

$$\forall d_0 \quad \hat{F}_d(d_0|a_2b_2x) - \hat{F}'_d(d_0|a_2b_2x) \quad R \quad \hat{F}''_d(d_0|a_2b_2x) - F_d(d_0|a_2b_2x). \tag{B.19}$$

We can transform (B.19) to a relation on F_d alone by applying some R-modularity conditions already known and taking advantage of the equivalences among the hatted and primed Fs for particular values of a and b. Combining (B.19) with R-modularity of $\hat{F}''_d$,

$$\forall d_0 \quad F_d(d_0|a_1b_1x) - \hat{F}''_d(d_0|a_2b_1x) + \hat{F}_d(d_0|a_2b_2x) - \hat{F}'_d(d_0|a_2b_2x)$$

$$R \quad F_d(d_0|a_1b_2x) - F_d(d_0|a_2b_2x).$$

Applying R-modularity of $\hat{F}'_d$ yields

$$\forall d_0 \quad 2F_d(d_0|a_1b_1x) - F_d(d_0|a_2b_1x) - \hat{F}''_d(d_0|a_2b_1x) + \hat{F}_d(d_0|a_2b_2x)$$

$$R \quad F_d(d_0|a_1b_2x) - F_d(d_0|a_2b_2x) + \hat{F}'_d(d_0|a_1b_2x),$$

and finally, R-modularity of $\hat{F}$ leads to the result

$$\forall d_0 \quad F_d(d_0|a_1b_1x) - F_d(d_0|a_2b_1x) \quad R \quad F_d(d_0|a_1b_2x) - F_d(d_0|a_2b_2x).$$

Therefore, unanimity among the terms in the new synergy expression given by the theorem statement implies R-modularity of F_d, the condition of interest. Dissent by any term results in a synergy of $Y^?$, vacuously true. $\square$

Theorem 4.24 *Given* $S^{\delta_6}(b, c, G)$ *and* $S^0(a, c, G)$, $Y_U^{\delta_3}(\{a, c\}, G)$ *is both necessary and sufficient for* $Y_U^{\delta_3 \otimes \delta_6}(\{a, b\}, red(c, G))$.

Proof: By the expected utility property and the conditional independence of a and c we have

$$u(a, b, x) = \int u(a, c_0, x) dF_c(c_0 | bx).$$

Let Δ_i represent the utility difference upon varying a between a_1 and a_2 when $b = b_i$, that is, $\Delta_i = u(a_1, b_i, x) - u(a_2, b_i, x)$. Expanding,

$$\Delta_i = \int [u(a_1, c_0, x) - u(a_2, c_0, x)] \, dF_c(c_0 | b_i x)$$

Note that δ_6 determines an FSD condition on $F_c(c_0 | b_i x)$. A corresponding relation on the Δ_i is entailed iff the term in brackets is monotone in the same direction with respect to c_0. This is exactly the condition for $Y_U^{\delta_3}(\{a, c\})$. $\square$

Theorem 4.25

$$Y^{\delta_1}(\{a, b\}, c, G) \wedge S^{\delta_2}(c, d, G) \wedge Y^{\delta_3}(\{a, c\}, d, G) \wedge Y^{\delta_4}(\{b, c\}, d, G)$$
$$\wedge S^{\delta_5}(a, c, G) \wedge S^{\delta_6}(b, c, G) \wedge Y^{\delta_7}(\{a, b\}, d, G) \Rightarrow$$
$$Y^{(\delta_1 \otimes \delta_2) \oplus (\delta_3 \otimes \delta_6) \oplus (\delta_4 \otimes \delta_5) \oplus \delta_7}(\{a, b\}, d, rev(c, d, G)).$$

Proof: The post-reversal distribution for d is conditioned on all d's pre-reversal predecessors except c and therefore is the same as that obtained by reducing c from the network. The result is identical to the expression from Theorem 4.22. $\square$

C SUDO-Planner Knowledge Base

This appendix provides a complete description of SUDO-PLANNER's KB for the running example.

C.1 Event Taxonomy

Figure C.1 is a graphical view of the event taxonomy, which includes the action taxonomy fragment depicted in Figure 3.4. The taxonomy consists of NIKL concepts representing event types. All of SUDO-PLANNER's event variables are defined by combining these concepts with the NIKL roles depicted in Figure C.2. The specialization relations in these two taxonomies define the taxonomic dimension of the event variable KB described in Section 6.2.

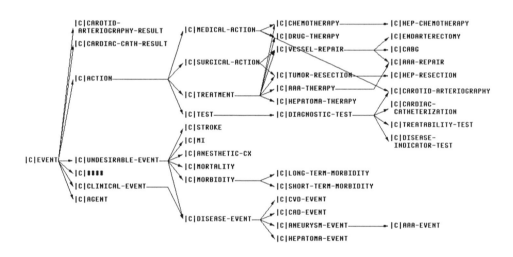

Figure C.1: SUDO-PLANNER's event taxonomy. The taxonomy also includes several event types not used in the running example.

C.2 Qualitative Relation Assertions

Table C.1 lists the qualitative influence (S^δ) assertions in SUDO-PLANNER's KB. A subset of these assertions appear in graphical format in the event variable KB fragment of Figure 6.3.

163

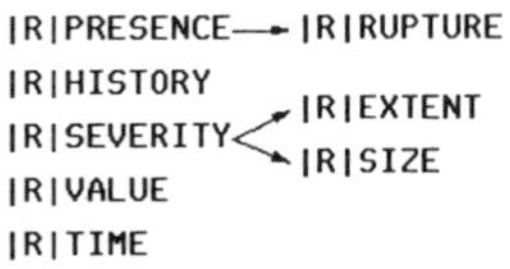

```
|R|PRESENCE——►|R|RUPTURE
|R|HISTORY
|R|SEVERITY◄——|R|EXTENT
            ◄——|R|SIZE
|R|VALUE
|R|TIME
```

Figure C.2: Roles used to define event variables in the running example.

Qualitative synergy (Y^δ) assertions are listed in Table C.2 and Markov influences (K^{δ_1,δ_2}) in Table C.3.

C.3 Observable Creators

The SUDO-PLANNER KB requires only two tests for this example (see Table 1.2):

$CO(\text{cardiac-catheterization(true)}, \text{extent}\langle\text{cardiac-cath-result}\rangle$

$CO(\text{carotid-arteriography(true)}, \text{extent}\langle\text{carotid-arteriography-result}\rangle$

presence⟨undesirable-event⟩	$\xrightarrow{-}$	value⟨agent⟩
time⟨undesirable-event⟩	$\xrightarrow{-}$	value⟨agent⟩
severity⟨morbidity⟩	$\xrightarrow{-}$	value⟨agent⟩
history⟨disease-event⟩	$\xrightarrow{+}$	severity⟨disease-event⟩
presence⟨treatment⟩	$\xrightarrow{?}$	value⟨agent⟩
presence⟨surgery⟩	$\xrightarrow{+}$	severity⟨short-term-morbidity⟩
presence⟨surgery⟩	$\xrightarrow{+}$	time⟨mortality⟩
presence⟨surgery⟩	$\xrightarrow{?}$	value⟨agent⟩
presence⟨vessel-repair⟩	$\xrightarrow{?}$	value⟨agent⟩
presence⟨medical-action⟩	$\xrightarrow{?}$	value⟨agent⟩
presence⟨anesthetic-cx⟩	$\xrightarrow{+}$	time⟨mortality⟩
presence⟨surgery⟩	$\xrightarrow{+}$	presence⟨anesthetic-cx⟩
rupture⟨aneurysm-event⟩	$\xrightarrow{+}$	time⟨mortality⟩
size⟨aneurysm-event⟩	$\xrightarrow{+}$	rupture⟨aneurysm-event⟩
size⟨AAA-event⟩	$\xrightarrow{+}$	rupture⟨AAA-event⟩
presence⟨AAA-repair⟩	$\xrightarrow{-}$	rupture⟨AAA-event⟩
history⟨CAD-event⟩	$\xrightarrow{+}$	extent⟨CAD-event⟩
presence⟨MI⟩	$\xrightarrow{+}$	time⟨mortality⟩
presence⟨stroke⟩	$\xrightarrow{+}$	time⟨mortality⟩
presence⟨stroke⟩	$\xrightarrow{+}$	severity⟨long-term-morbidity⟩
presence⟨vessel-repair⟩	$\xrightarrow{+}$	presence⟨MI⟩
presence⟨vessel-repair⟩	$\xrightarrow{+}$	presence⟨stroke⟩
presence⟨vessel-repair⟩	$\xrightarrow{+}$	time⟨mortality⟩
presence⟨AAA-repair⟩	$\xrightarrow{+}$	time⟨mortality⟩
extent⟨CAD-event⟩	$\xrightarrow{+}$	presence⟨MI⟩
extent⟨cardiac-cath-result⟩	$\xrightarrow{+}$	extent⟨CAD-event⟩
history⟨CVD-event⟩	$\xrightarrow{+}$	extent⟨CVD-event⟩
extent⟨CVD-event⟩	$\xrightarrow{+}$	presence⟨stroke⟩
extent⟨carotid-arteriography-result⟩	$\xrightarrow{+}$	extent⟨CVD-event⟩

Table C.1: Qualitative influences in the SUDO-PLANNER KB.

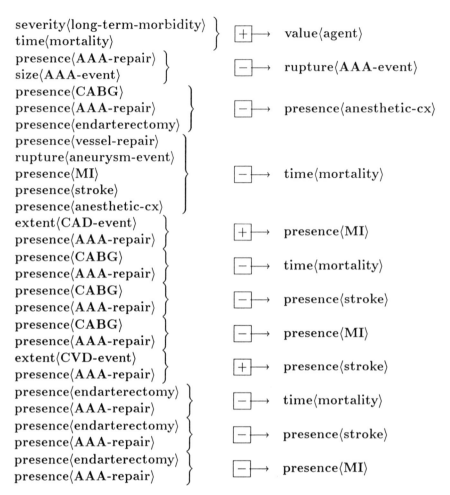

Table C.2: Qualitative synergies in the SUDO-PLANNER KB.

presence⟨CABG⟩ $\xrightarrow{-}$ extent⟨CAD-event⟩
presence⟨endarterectomy⟩ $\xrightarrow{-}$ extent⟨CVD-event⟩

Table C.3: Markov influences in the SUDO-PLANNER KB.

Bibliography

[1] James F. Allen. Towards a general theory of action and time. *Artificial Intelligence*, 23:123–154, 1984.

[2] Steen Andreassen, Marianne Woldbye, Bjørn Falck, et al. MUNIN: A causal probabilistic network for interpretation of electromyographic findings. In *Proceedings of the Tenth International Joint Conference on Artificial Intelligence*, pages 366–372, 1987.

[3] Fahiem Bacchus. A modest, but semantically well founded, inheritance reasoner. In *Proceedings of the Eleventh International Joint Conference on Artificial Intelligence*, pages 1104–1109, 1989.

[4] James O. Berger. *Statistical Decision Theory and Bayesian Analysis*. Springer-Verlag, second edition, 1985.

[5] Colin R. Blyth. On Simpson's paradox and the sure-thing principle. *Journal of the American Statistical Association*, 67:364–366, 1972.

[6] Colin R. Blyth. Some probability paradoxes in choice from among random alternatives. *Journal of the American Statistical Association*, 67:366–381, 1972.

[7] Daniel G. Bobrow, editor. *Qualitative Reasoning about Physical Systems*. MIT Press, 1985.

[8] Ronald J. Brachman. 'I lied about the trees,' or, Defaults and definitions in knowledge representation. *AI Magazine*, 6(3):80–93, 1985.

[9] Ronald J. Brachman, Richard E. Fikes, and Hector J. Levesque. Krypton: A functional approach to knowledge representation. *Computer*, 16(10):67–73, 1983.

[10] Ronald J. Brachman and Hector J. Levesque. The tractability of subsumption in frame-based description languages. In *Proceedings of the National Conference on Artificial Intelligence*, pages 34–37. AAAI, 1984.

[11] Ronald J. Brachman and James G. Schmolze. An overview of the KL-ONE knowledge representation system. *Cognitive Science*, 9:171–216, 1985.

[12] John S. Breese. Construction of belief and decision networks. Draft manuscript, Rockwell International Science Center, 1989.

[13] Jack Breese and Edison Tse. Integrating logical and probabilistic reasoning for decision making. In *Proceedings of the Workshop on Uncertainty in Artificial Intelligence*, pages 355–362, July 1987.

[14] B. Chandrasekaran and Sanjay Mittal. Deep versus compiled knowledge approaches to diagnostic problem-solving. In *Proceedings of the National Conference on Artificial Intelligence*, pages 349–354. AAAI, August 1982.

[15] David Chapman. Planning for conjunctive goals. *Artificial Intelligence*, 32:333–377, 1987.

[16] Eugene Charniak and Robert Goldman. A semantics for probabilistic quantifier-free first-order languages, with particular application to story understanding. In *Proceedings of the Eleventh International Joint Conference on Artificial Intelligence*, pages 1074–1079, 1989.

[17] Eugene Charniak and Drew McDermott. *Introduction to Artificial Intelligence*. Addison-Wesley, Reading, MA, 1985.

[18] Gregory Floyd Cooper. NESTOR: *A Computer-Based Medical Diagnostic Aid that Integrates Causal and Probabilistic Knowledge*. PhD thesis, Stanford University, November 1984.

[19] Gregory F. Cooper. The computational complexity of probabilistic inference using belief networks. *Artificial Intelligence*, to appear.

[20] Louis Anthony Cox, Jr. *Mathematical Foundations of Risk Measurement*. PhD thesis, Massachusetts Institute of Technology, May 1986.

[21] Ernest Davis. Order of magnitude reasoning in qualitative differential equations. Technical Report 312, New York University Computer Science Department, August 1987.

[22] Martin Davis and Reuben Hersh. Nonstandard analysis. *Scientific American*, 226(6):78–86, June 1972.

[23] Johan de Kleer. An assumption-based TMS. *Artificial Intelligence*, 28:127–162, 1986.

[24] Johan de Kleer. Problem solving with the ATMS. *Artificial Intelligence*, 28:197–224, 1986.

[25] Thomas Dean and Mark Boddy. Incremental causal reasoning. In *Proceedings of the National Conference on Artificial Intelligence*, pages 196–201. AAAI, 1987.

[26] Thomas Dean and Mark Boddy. An analysis of time-dependent planning. In *Proceedings of the National Conference on Artificial Intelligence*, pages 49–54. AAAI, 1988.

[27] Keith L. Downing. Diagnostic improvement through qualitative sensitivity analysis and aggregation. In *Proceedings of the National Conference on Artificial Intelligence*, pages 789–793. AAAI, 1987.

[28] Jon Doyle. A truth maintenance system. *Artificial Intelligence*, 12(2):231–272, 1979.

[29] Jon Doyle. A model for deliberation, action, and introspection. AI-TR 581, MIT Artificial Intelligence Laboratory, 545 Technology Square, Cambridge, MA, 02139, 1980.

[30] Jon Doyle. Artificial intelligence and rational self-government. Technical Report CS-88-124, Carnegie-Mellon University Computer Science Department, 1988.

[31] Jon Doyle. Constructive belief and rational representation. *Computational Intelligence*, 5:1–11, 1989.

[32] Jon Doyle and Michael P. Wellman. Impediments to universal preference-based default theories. In *First International Conference on Principles of Knowledge Representation and Reasoning*, pages 94–102, 1989.

[33] Van H. Dunn. Grand rounds, Beth Israel hospital. Unpublished decision analysis consult report, Division of Clinical Decision Making, Tufts-New England Medical Center, 1984.

[34] Richard Engelbrecht. A note on multivariate risk and separable utility functions. *Management Science*, 23:1143–1144, 1977. Note on Richard [125].

[35] Ronald Fagin, Joseph Y. Halpern, and Nimrod Megiddo. A logic for reasoning about probabilities. Research Report RJ 6190, IBM, April 1988.

[36] Jerome A. Feldman and Robert F. Sproull. Decision Theory and Artificial Intelligence II: The hungry monkey. *Cognitive Science*, 1:158–192, 1977.

[37] K. W. Fertig and J. S. Breese. Interval influence diagrams. In *Proceedings of the Workshop on Uncertainty in Artificial Intelligence*, pages 102–111, 1989.

[38] Richard E. Fikes and Nils J. Nilsson. STRIPS: A new approach to the application of theorem proving to problem solving. *Artificial Intelligence*, 2:189–208, 1971.

[39] Peter C. Fishburn. Analysis of decisions with incomplete knowledge of probabilities. *Operations Research*, 13:217–237, 1965.

[40] Peter C. Fishburn. Von Neumann-Morgenstern utility functions on two attributes. *Operations Research*, 22:35–45, 1974.

[41] Peter C. Fishburn and Raymond G. Vickson. Theoretical foundations of stochastic dominance. In Whitmore and Findlay [178].

[42] Kenneth D. Forbus. Qualitative process theory. *Artificial Intelligence*, 24:85–168, 1984.

[43] Kenneth D. Forbus. Interpreting measurements of physical systems. In *Proceedings of the National Conference on Artificial Intelligence*, pages 113–117. AAAI, 1986.

[44] Kenneth D. Forbus. QPE: Using assumption-based truth maintenance for qualitative simulation. *International Journal of AI in Engineering*, 1988.

[45] Mark S. Fox. *Constraint-Directed Search: A Case Study of Job-Shop Scheduling*. Pitman and Morgan Kaufmann, 1987.

[46] Peter Gärdenfors. Qualitative probability as an intensional logic. *Journal of Philosophical Logic*, 4:171–185, 1975.

[47] Michael P. Georgeff and Amy L. Lansky, editors. *Reasoning about Actions and Plans: Proceedings of the 1986 Workshop*. Morgan Kaufmann, 1986.

[48] I. J. Good. On the principle of total evidence. In *Good Thinking: The Foundations of Probability and Its Applications* [50]. Originally appeared in *British Journal of Philosophy of Science*, 17:319-321, 1967.

[49] I. J. Good. The Bayesian influence, or How to sweep subjectivism under the carpet. In *Good Thinking: The Foundations of Probability and Its Applications* [50]. Originally appeared in 1973.

[50] I. J. Good. *Good Thinking: The Foundations of Probability and Its Applications*. University of Minnesota Press, 1983.

[51] G. Anthony Gorry, Howard Silverman, and Stephen G. Pauker. Capturing clinical expertise: A computer program that considers clinical responses to digitalis. *American Journal of Medicine*, 64:452–460, 1978.

[52] Benjamin N. Grosof. Non-monotonicity in probabilistic reasoning. In Lemmer and Kanal [88], pages 237–249.

[53] Ira J. Haimowitz, Ramesh S. Patil, and Peter Szolovits. Representing medical knowledge in a terminological language is difficult. In *Symposium on Computer Applications in Medical Care*, pages 101–105, 1988.

[54] Joseph Y. Halpern and David A. McAllester. Likelihood, probability, and knowledge. In *Proceedings of the National Conference on Artificial Intelligence*, pages 137–141. AAAI, 1984.

[55] Joseph Y. Halpern and Michael O. Rabin. A logic to reason about likelihood. *Artificial Intelligence*, 32:379–405, 1987.

[56] Steve Hanks and Drew McDermott. Nonmonotonic logic and temporal projection. *Artificial Intelligence*, 33:379–412, 1987.

[57] Gordon B. Hazen. Partial information, dominance, and potential optimality in multiattribute utility theory. *Operations Research*, 34:296–310, 1986.

[58] David E. Heckerman and Eric J. Horvitz. The myth of modularity in rule-based systems for reasoning with uncertainty. In Lemmer and Kanal [88], pages 23–34.

[59] Max Henrion. Practical issues in constructing a Bayes' belief network. In *Proceedings of the Workshop on Uncertainty in Artificial Intelligence*, pages 132–139, July 1987.

[60] Max Henrion and Daniel R. Cooley. An experimental comparison of knowledge engineering for expert systems and for decision analysis. In *Proceedings of the National Conference on Artificial Intelligence*, pages 471–476. AAAI, 1987.

[61] Carl Hewitt. Offices are open systems. *ACM Transactions on Office Information Systems*, 4:271–287, 1986.

[62] Jerry R. Hobbs. Granularity. In *Proceedings of the Ninth International Joint Conference on Artificial Intelligence*, pages 432–435, 1985.

[63] J. P. Hollenberg. The decision tree builder: An expert system to simulate medical prognosis and management. *Medical Decision Making*, 4(4), 1984. Abstract from the Sixth Annual Meeting of the Society for Medical Decision Making.

[64] Samuel Holtzman. *Intelligent Decision Systems*. PhD thesis, Stanford University, March 1985.

[65] John E. Hopcroft and Richard M. Karp. An $n^{5/2}$ algorithm for maximum matchings in bipartite graphs. *SIAM Journal on Computing*, 2:225–231, 1973.

[66] John E. Hopcroft and Jeffrey D. Ullman. *Introduction to Automata Theory, Languages, and Computation*. Addison-Wesley, 1979.

[67] Eric J. Horvitz, John S. Breese, and Max Henrion. Decision theory in expert systems and artificial intelligence. *Journal of Approximate Reasoning*, 2:247–302, 1988.

[68] Ronald A. Howard and James E. Matheson. Influence diagrams. In *The Principles and Applications of Decision Analysis* [69], pages 719–762.

[69] Ronald A. Howard and James E. Matheson, editors. *The Principles and Applications of Decision Analysis*. Strategic Decisions Group, Menlo Park, CA, 1984.

[70] Patrick Humphreys and Wendy McFadden. Experiences with MAUD: Aiding decision structuring versus bootstrapping the decision maker. *Acta Psychologica*, 45:51–69, 1980.

[71] Paul Humphreys. Cutting the causal chain. *Pacific Philosophical Quarterly*, 61:305–314, 1980.

[72] Harry B. Hunt, III, Daniel J. Rosenkrantz, and Thomas G. Szymanski. On the equivalence, containment, and covering problems for the regular and context-free languages. *Journal of Computer and System Sciences*, 12:222–268, 1976.

[73] Toshihide Ibaraki. The power of dominance relations in branch-and-bound algorithms. *Journal of the ACM*, 24:264–279, 1977.

[74] Thomas S. Kaczmarek, Raymond Bates, and Gabriel Robins. Recent developments in NIKL. In *Proceedings of the National Conference on Artificial Intelligence*, pages 978–985. AAAI, 1986.

[75] Samuel Karlin and Herman Rubin. The theory of decision procedures for distributions with monotone likelihood ratio. *Annals of Mathematical Statistics*, 27:272–299, 1956.

[76] Ralph L. Keeney. Identifying and structuring values. Decision analysis series report, University of Southern California, Los Angeles, CA, December 1986.

[77] Ralph L. Keeney and Howard Raiffa. *Decisions with Multiple Objectives: Preferences and Value Tradeoffs*. John Wiley and Sons, New York, 1976.

[78] Jin H. Kim and Judea Pearl. A computational model for causal and diagnostic reasoning in inference systems. In *Proceedings of the Eighth International Joint Conference on Artificial Intelligence*, pages 190–193, 1983.

[79] B. O. Koopman. The axioms and algebra of intuitive probability. *Annals of Mathematics*, 42:269–292, 1940.

[80] David H. Krantz, R. Duncan Luce, Patrick Suppes, et al. *Foundations of Measurement*. Academic Press, New York, 1971.

[81] David M. Kreps and Evan L. Porteus. Temporal von Neumann-Morgenstern and induced preferences. *Journal of Economic Theory*, 20:81–109, 1979.

[82] Benjamin Kuipers. Qualitative simulation. *Artificial Intelligence*, 29:289–338, 1986.

[83] Benjamin Kuipers and Daniel Berleant. Using incomplete quantitative knowledge in qualitative reasoning. In *Proceedings of the National Conference on Artificial Intelligence*, pages 324–329. AAAI, 1988.

[84] Benjamin Kuipers and Jerome P. Kassirer. Causal reasoning in medicine: Analysis of a protocol. *Cognitive Science*, 8:363–385, 1984.

[85] Curtis P. Langlotz, Lawrence M. Fagan, Samson W. Tu, et al. A therapy planning architecture that combines decision theory and artificial intelligence techniques. *Computers and Biomedical Research*, 20:279–303, 1987.

[86] S. L. Lauritzen and D. J. Spiegelhalter. Local computations with probabilities on graphical structures and their application to expert systems. *Journal of the Royal Statistical Society*, B50:157–224, 1988.

[87] E. L. Lehmann. Some concepts of dependence. *Annals of Mathematical Statistics*, 37:1137–1153, 1966.

[88] John F. Lemmer and Laveen N. Kanal, editors. *Uncertainty in Artificial Intelligence 2*. North-Holland, 1988.

[89] Doug Lenat, Mayank Prakash, and Mary Shepherd. CYC: Using common sense knowledge to overcome brittleness and knowledge acquisition bottlenecks. *AI Magazine*, 6(4):65–85, 1986.

[90] Hector J. Levesque. Making believers out of computers. *Aritificial Intelligence*, 30:81–108, 1986.

[91] Vladimir Lifschitz. On the semantics of STRIPS. In Georgeff and Lansky [47], pages 1–9.

[92] W. J. Long, S. Naimi, M. G. Criscitiello, et al. Using a physiological model for prediction of therapy effects in heart disease. In *Proc. of the Computers in Cardiology Conf.* IEEE, October 1986.

[93] W. J. Long, S. Naimi, M. G. Criscitiello, et al. An aid to physiological reasoning in the management of cardiovascular disease. In *Proceedings of the Computers in Cardiology Conference*, pages 3–6. IEEE, September 1984.

[94] William J. Long and Thomas A. Russ. A control structure for time dependent reasoning. In *Proceedings of the Eighth International Joint Conference on Artificial Intelligence*, pages 230–232, 1983.

[95] David A. McAllester. An outlook on truth maintenance. AIM 551, MIT Artificial Intelligence Laboratory, 545 Technology Square, Cambridge, MA, 02139, 1980.

[96] David A. McAllester. ONTIC: A knowledge representation system for mathematics. AI-TR 979, MIT Artificial Intelligence Laboratory, 545 Technology Square, Cambridge, MA, 02139, 1987.

[97] J. McCarthy and P. J. Hayes. Some philosophical problems from the standpoint of artificial intelligence. In B. Meltzer and D. Michie, editors, *Machine Intelligence 4*, pages 463–502. Edinburgh University Press, 1969.

[98] Drew McDermott. Planning and acting. *Cognitive Science*, 2:71–109, 1978.

[99] Nestor Michelena and Alice Agogino. Deterministic monotonic influence diagrams. Working Paper 89-1101-0, Berkeley Expert Systems Technology Laboratory, November 1989.

[100] Paul R. Milgrom. Good news and bad news: Representation theorems and applications. *Bell Journal of Economics*, 12:380–391, 1981.

[101] Perry L. Miller. *Expert Critiquing Systems: Practice-Based Medical Consultation by Computer*. Springer-Verlag, 1986.

[102] Robert C. Moore. A formal theory of knowledge and action. In Jerry R. Hobbs and Robert C. Moore, editors, *Formal Theories of the Commonsense World*, pages 319–358. Ablex, Norwood, NJ, 1985.

[103] J. Mostow and K. Voigt. Explicit integration of goals in heuristic algorithm design. In *Proceedings of the Tenth International Joint Conference on Artificial Intelligence*, pages 1090–1096, 1987.

[104] D. S. Nau. Hierarchical abstraction for process planning. In D. Sriram and R. A. Adley, editors, *Knowledge Based Expert Systems in Engineering: Planning and Design*, pages 129–141. Computational Mechanics Publications, 1987.

[105] Bernhard Nebel. Computational complexity of terminological reasoning in BACK. *Artificial Intelligence*, 34:371–383, 1988.

[106] Eric Neufeld. Defaults and probabilities; extensions and coherence. In *First International Conference on Principles of Knowledge Representation and Reasoning*, pages 312–323, 1989.

[107] Eric Neufeld and J. D. Horton. Conditioning on disjunctive knowledge: Defaults and probabilities. In *Proceedings of the Workshop on Uncertainty in Artificial Intelligence*, pages 272–278, 1989.

[108] Allen Newell. The knowledge level. *Artificial Intelligence*, 18(1):87–127, 1982.

[109] Ramesh S. Patil. Causal representation of patient illness for electrolyte and acid-base diagnosis. TR 267, MIT Laboratory for Computer Science, 545 Technology Square, Cambridge, MA, 02139, October 1981.

[110] Ramesh S. Patil and Oksana Senyk. Efficient structuring of composite causal hypotheses in medical diagnosis. In *Symposium on Computer Applications in Medical Care*, pages 23–29. IEEE, November 1987.

[111] Ramesh S. Patil, Peter Szolovits, and William B. Schwartz. Causal understanding of patient illness in medical diagnosis. In *Proceedings of the Seventh International Joint Conference on Artificial Intelligence*, pages 893–899, 1981.

[112] Judea Pearl. Fusion, propagation, and structuring in belief networks. *Artificial Intelligence*, 29:241–288, 1986.

[113] Judea Pearl. Embracing causality in default reasoning. *Artificial Intelligence*, 35:259–271, 1988.

[114] Judea Pearl. *Probabilistic Reasoning in Intelligent Systems: Networks of Plausible Inference*. Morgan Kaufmann, 1988.

[115] Judea Pearl. Probabilistic semantics for nonmonotonic reasoning: A survey. In *First International Conference on Principles of Knowledge Representation and Reasoning*, pages 505–516, 1989.

[116] Judea Pearl, Dan Geiger, and Thomas Verma. Conditional independence and its representations. *Kybernetika*, 25:33–44, 1989.

[117] Judea Pearl and Thomas Verma. The logic of representing dependencies by directed graphs. In *Proceedings of the National Conference on Artificial Intelligence*, pages 374–379. AAAI, 1987.

[118] Edwin P. D. Pednault. Preliminary report on a theory of plan synthesis. Technical Note 358, SRI Artificial Intelligence Center, August 1985.

[119] Edwin P. D. Pednault. Extending conventional planning techniques to handle actions with context-dependent effects. In *Proceedings of the National Conference on Artificial Intelligence*, pages 55–59. AAAI, 1988.

[120] Harry E. Pople, Jr. Heuristic methods for imposing structure on ill-structured problems: The structuring of medical diagnostics. In Peter Szolovits, editor, *Artificial Intelligence in Medicine*, volume 51 of *AAAS Selected Symposium Series*, pages 119–190. Westview Press, Boulder, Colorado, 1982.

[121] John W. Pratt, Howard Raiffa, and Robert Schlaifer. The foundations of decision under uncertainty: An elementary exposition. *Journal of the American Statistical Association*, 59:353–375, 1964.

[122] Howard Raiffa. *Decision Analysis: Introductory Lectures on Choices Under Uncertainty*. Addison-Wesley, Reading, MA, 1968.

[123] Olivier Raiman. Order of magnitude reasoning. In *Proceedings of the National Conference on Artificial Intelligence*, pages 100–104. AAAI, 1986.

[124] Glenn D. Rennels. *A Computational Model of Reasoning from the Clinical Literature*, volume 32 of *Lecture Notes in Medical Informatics*. Springer-Verlag, 1987.

[125] Scott F. Richard. Multivariate risk aversion, utility independence and separable utility functions. *Management Science*, 22:12–21, 1975.

[126] Chuck Rieger and Milt Grinberg. The declarative representation and procedural simulation of causality in physical mechanisms. In *Proceedings of the Fifth International Joint Conference on Artificial Intelligence*, pages 250–256, 1977.

[127] Stanley J. Rosenschein and Leslie Pack Kaelbling. The synthesis of digital machines with provable epistemic properties. In Joseph Y. Halpern, editor, *Theoretical Aspects of Reasoning About Knowledge: Proceedings of the 1986 Conference*, pages 83–98. Morgan Kaufmann, 1986.

[128] Sheldon M. Ross. *Introduction to Stochastic Dynamic Programming*. Academic Press, 1983.

[129] Cynthia J. Rutherford, Byron Davies, Arnold I. Barnett, et al. A computer system for decision analysis in Hodgkins Disease. TR 271, MIT Laboratory for Computer Science, 545 Technology Square, Cambridge, MA, 02139, 1981.

[130] Earl D. Sacerdoti. Planning in a hierarchy of abstraction spaces. *Artificial Intelligence*, 5:115–135, 1974.

[131] Earl D. Sacerdoti. *A Structure for Plans and Behavior*. American Elsevier, 1977.

[132] Elisha P. Sacks. Hierarchical reasoning about inequalities. In *Proceedings of the National Conference on Artificial Intelligence*, pages 649–654. AAAI, 1987.

[133] Erik Sandewall. Nonmonotonic inference rules for multiple inheritance with exceptions. *Proceedings of the IEEE*, 74(10):1345–1353, 1986.

[134] Leonard J. Savage. *The Foundations of Statistics*. Dover Publications, New York, second edition, 1972.

[135] James G. Schmolze and Thomas A. Lipkis. Classification in the KL-ONE knowledge representation system. In *Proceedings of the Eighth International Joint Conference on Artificial Intelligence*, pages 330–332, 1983.

[136] Ross D. Shachter. Evaluating influence diagrams. *Operations Research*, 34:871–882, 1986.

[137] Ross D. Shachter. Probabilistic inference and influence diagrams. *Operations Research*, 36:589–604, 1988.

[138] Ross D. Shachter and David E. Heckerman. Thinking backward for knowledge acquisition. *AI Magazine*, 8(3):55–61, 1987.

[139] Glenn Shafer. *A Mathematical Theory of Evidence*. Princeton University Press, 1976.

[140] Glenn Shafer. Constructive probability. *Synthese*, 48:1–60, 1981.

[141] Glenn Shafer. Savage revisited. *Statistical Science*, 1:463–501, 1986.

[142] Glenn Shafer and Amos Tversky. Languages and designs for probability judgment. *Cognitive Science*, 9:309–339, 1985.

[143] Yoav Shoham. What is the frame problem? In Georgeff and Lansky [47], pages 83–98.

[144] Yoav Shoham. Nonmonotonic logics: Meaning and utility. In *Proceedings of the Tenth International Joint Conference on Artificial Intelligence*, pages 388–393, 1987.

[145] Herbert A. Simon. Spurious correlation: A causal interpretation. *Journal of the American Statistical Association*, 49:467–479, 1954.

[146] Herbert A. Simon. *The Sciences of the Artificial*. MIT Press, second edition, 1981.

[147] Brian Cantwell Smith. Limits of correctness in computers. Technical Report CSLI-85-36, Center for the Study of Language and Information, October 1985.

[148] David J. Spiegelhalter. Probabilistic reasoning in predictive expert systems. In Laveen N. Kanal and John F. Lemmer, editors, *Uncertainty in Artificial Intelligence*, pages 47–67. North-Holland, 1986.

[149] David J. Spiegelhalter and Robin P. Knill-Jones. Statistical and knowledge-based approaches to clinical decision-support systems, with an application in gastroenterology. *Journal of the Royal Statistical Society*, 147:35–77, 1984.

[150] Richard M. Stallman and Gerald J. Sussman. Forward reasoning and dependency-directed backtracking in a system for computer-aided circuit analysis. *Artificial Intelligence*, 9(2):135–196, 1977.

[151] Mark Stefik. Planning with constraints (MOLGEN: Part 1). *Artificial Intelligence*, 16:111–140, 1981.

[152] Mark Stefik. Planning and meta-planning (MOLGEN: Part 2). *Artificial Intelligence*, 16:141–170, 1981.

[153] Devika Subramanian and Michael R. Genesereth. The relevance of irrelevance. In *Proceedings of the Tenth International Joint Conference on Artificial Intelligence*, pages 416–422, 1987.

[154] Patrick Suppes. *A Probabilistic Theory of Causality*. North-Holland Publishing Co., Amsterdam, 1970.

[155] William R. Swartout. XPLAIN: A system for creating and explaining expert consulting programs. *Artificial Intelligence*, 21:285–325, 1983.

[156] William Swartout and Robert Neches. The shifting terminological space: An impediment to evolvability. In *Proceedings of the National Conference on Artificial Intelligence*, pages 936–941. AAAI, 1986.

[157] Peter Szolovits, Ramesh S. Patil, and William B. Schwartz. Artificial intelligence in medical diagnosis. *Annals of Internal Medicine*, 108:80–87, 1988.

[158] Peter Szolovits and Stephen G. Pauker. Categorical and probabilistic reasoning in medical diagnosis. *Artificial Intelligence*, 11:115–144, 1978.

[159] Josh Tenenberg. Planning with abstraction. In *Proceedings of the National Conference on Artificial Intelligence*, pages 76–80. AAAI, 1986.

[160] Josh D. Tenenberg. Inheritance in automated planning. In *First International Conference on Principles of Knowledge Representation and Reasoning*, pages 475–485, 1989.

[161] Donald M. Topkis. Minimizing a submodular function on a lattice. *Operations Research*, 26:305–321, 1978.

[162] David S. Touretzky. *The Mathematics of Inheritance Systems.* Pitman and Morgan Kaufmann, 1986.

[163] David S. Touretzky, John F. Horty, and Richmond H. Thomason. A clash of intuitions: The current state of nonmonotonic multiple inheritance systems. In *Proceedings of the Tenth International Joint Conference on Artificial Intelligence*, pages 476–482, 1987.

[164] A. Tversky. On the elicitation of preferences: Descriptive and prescriptive considerations. In David E. Bell, Ralph L. Keeney, and Howard Raiffa, editors, *Conflicting Objectives in Decisions*. John Wiley and Sons, 1977.

[165] Marc B. Vilain. The restricted language architecture of a hybrid representation system. In *Proceedings of the Ninth International Joint Conference on Artificial Intelligence*, pages 547–551, 1985.

[166] Detlof von Winterfeldt. Structuring decision problems for decision analysis. *Acta Psychologica*, 45:71–93, 1980.

[167] Richard Waldinger. Achieving several goals simultaneously. In E. Elcock and D. Michie, editors, *Machine Intelligence 8*, pages 94–136. Edinburgh University Press, 1977.

[168] Sholom M. Weiss, Casimir A. Kulikowski, Saul Amarel, et al. A model-based method for computer-aided medical decision making. *Artificial Intelligence*, 11:145–172, 1978.

[169] Daniel S. Weld. Exaggeration. In *Proceedings of the National Conference on Artificial Intelligence*, pages 291–295. AAAI, 1988.

[170] Daniel S. Weld. Theories of comparative analysis. AI-TR 1035, MIT Artificial Intelligence Laboratory, 545 Technology Square, Cambridge, MA, 02139, May 1988.

[171] Michael Paul Wellman. Reasoning about preference models. TR 340, MIT Laboratory for Computer Science, 545 Technology Square, Cambridge, MA, 02139, May 1985.

[172] Michael P. Wellman. Representing health outcomes for automated decision formulation. In R. Salamon, B. Blum, and M. Jørgensen, editors, *MEDINFO 86: Proceedings of the Fifth Conference on Medical Informatics*, pages 789–793, Washington, October 1986. North-Holland.

[173] Michael P. Wellman. Dominance and subsumption in constraint-posting planning. In *Proceedings of the Tenth International Joint Conference on Artificial Intelligence*, pages 884–890, 1987.

[174] Michael P. Wellman. Review of Perry L. Miller, *Expert Critiquing Systems*. *Artificial Intelligence*, 35:273–276, 1988.

[175] Michael P. Wellman. Graphical inference in qualitative probabilistic networks. *Networks*, to appear.

[176] Michael P. Wellman, Mark H. Eckman, Craig Fleming, et al. Automated critiquing of medical decision trees. *Medical Decision Making*, 9:272–284, 1989.

[177] Michael P. Wellman and David E. Heckerman. The role of calculi in uncertain reasoning. In *Proceedings of the Workshop on Uncertainty in Artificial Intelligence*, pages 321–331, July 1987.

[178] G. A. Whitmore and M. C. Findlay, editors. *Stochastic Dominance: An Approach to Decision Making Under Risk*. D. C. Heath and Company, Lexington, MA, 1978.

[179] Robert Wilensky. Meta-planning: Representing and using knowledge about planning in problem solving and natural language understanding. *Cognitive Science*, 5(3):197–233, 1981.

[180] Brian C. Williams. MINIMA: A symbolic approach to qualitative algebraic reasoning. In *Proceedings of the National Conference on Artificial Intelligence*, pages 264–269. AAAI, 1988.

[181] William A. Woods. What's in a link: Foundations for semantic networks. In Bobrow and Collins, editors, *Representation and Understanding*, pages 35–82. Academic Press, New York, 1975.

[182] Yang Xiang, Michael P. Beddoes, and David Poole. Can uncertainty management be realized in a finite totally ordered probability algebra? In *Proceedings of the Workshop on Uncertainty in Artificial Intelligence*, pages 385–393, 1989.

[183] Ramin Zabih. Dependency-directed backtracking in non-deterministic Scheme. Master's thesis, Massachusetts Institute of Technology, Cambridge, MA, January 1987.

[184] Ramin Zabih, David McAllester, and David Chapman. Non-deterministic Lisp with dependency-directed backtracking. In *Proceedings of the National Conference on Artificial Intelligence*, pages 59–64. AAAI, 1987.

Name Index